BIG

CITIZENSHIP

BIG

CITIZENSHIP

*How Pragmatic
Idealism Can Bring
Out the Best in America*

ALAN
KHAZEI

PUBLICAFFAIRS

New York

Library of Congress Control Number: 2010927910

First PublicAffairs edition 2010
ISBN: **978-1-58648-786-7**

Published by PublicAffairs
A Member of the Perseus Books Group
www.publicaffairs.com

PublicAffairs books are available at special discounts for bulk purchases in the U.S. by corporations, institutions, and other organizations. For more information, please contact the Special Markets Department at the Perseus Books Group, 2300 Chestnut Street, Suite 200, Philadelphia, PA, 19103, or call (800) 810-4145, ext. 5000, or e-mail special.markets@perseusbooks.com.

10 9 8 7 6 5 4 3 2 1

*For Vanessa, Mirabelle, and Reese,
the lights of my life.*

Table of Contents

INTRODUCTION

THE HIGHEST OFFICE: CITIZEN

Sitting in the cramped hotel room of the Omni Parker House in Boston, Massachusetts, I typed speedily on my laptop as the hour approached 8:00 pm, when the polls across the state would close. Images flashed through my mind: the seniors in Lowell and small business owners in Quincy; the patrons at the classic Orchid Diner in New Bedford; walking Main Street in Hyannis and going door-to-door in Worcester; the veterans in Pittsfield, the student volunteers at Smith, and Sunday churchgoers across Boston; the many people who were hurting in the terrible economy; and the entrepreneurs and innovators who were showing new ways to attack old problems, from clean energy breakthroughs to education reform.

I have been an active citizen and voter, but this election was different for me. My name was on the ballot. I was quickly editing my remarks to share with hundreds of people who had gathered for our election-night party. Old friends from all times of my life and new ones I had made along the campaign trail.

The clock struck 8:00 pm and within minutes the newscasts reported the early results. As expected, the front-runner from the beginning of the race, the state attorney general, was far ahead, a well-regarded Congressman was in second, I was third, and a successful businessperson was fourth. I had come up short, but I was at peace. I had started just twelve short weeks earlier, an obscure candidate with 400 supporters, on Boston Common. With the help of a spirited campaign, we finished with 90,000 votes in the Massachusetts special election to fill the senate seat vacated by Ted Kennedy. And we had run the race our way by emphasizing grassroots, citizen-led politics and fighting the influence of special interests. With the help of my outstanding policy team, many noted that I added importantly to the debate and I achieved some unexpected endorsements. And we brought many new people and voices into the political process for the first time. Despite the results, the campaign was a hugely positive experience. And I was encouraged that, within a short window of time, our campaign's message and ideas started to resonate and break through in the final weeks. I realized the insights I had gained from almost twenty-five years in the service and social entrepreneurship movements, about how to rally people and all sectors to make progress, were applicable to the larger challenges facing my state and our country.

Campaigning across Massachusetts as a first time candidate in the Democratic Senate Primary, I had a profoundly moving, learning experience. That is one of the real privileges of being a candidate for national office. It is like having a passport or permission slip to talk to anyone and everyone about everything and anything. Whether it is meeting people from all walks of life, in schools, diners, and community centers at seven am or midnight, or connecting with practitioners and experts on major issues such as the economy, education, energy, health care, the wars, and more, you receive an unparalleled education and insight into what people are thinking and feeling. They speak freely of their hopes, dreams, and anxieties for themselves, their children, families and friends.

I know there has been a lot of talk about how angry voters are. But we cannot simply give in to that anger. I heard, for sure, a lot of anxiety over the economy and the rising cost of health care, especially for small business owners. People shared frustration with the dominance of special interests in Washington. Worried parents felt they couldn't get a high quality public education for their children and wouldn't be able to afford college. And there was significant concern about rising youth violence in our urban areas and the need for more opportunities for young people. Numerous others voiced disagreement with escalating the war in Afghanistan. Many voters across the state had lost their jobs, homes, or retirement savings. The pain and suffering was palpable.

But in addition to this anxiety, I also felt an undaunted spirit and quiet determination, a desire and willingness of people to roll up their sleeves, come together and tackle our state's and our country's problems. People were ready to regroup and rebuild, to find lasting and meaningful solutions and try new approaches, and to seize the opportunities of transformational times. And people wanted from their political leaders and candidates direct, honest, and straight talk about the challenges we face and what we can do about them. They wanted to recapture the spirit of common purpose that has always brought out the best of America in challenging times. But whether people are angry or anxious, we need to move beyond the recriminations and the finger pointing. Anger may or may not make us feel better, but it won't solve our problems.

I had decided to run for the Senate after spending nearly twenty five years as a civic entrepreneur, taking the entrepreneurial spirit and innovative approaches often found in the private sector, to address social problems—starting from the ground up as the cofounder and CEO of City Year. As a civic entrepreneur, I work to put ideas into action as a way to improve civic life and participation and effect policy change.[1] I also work to engage citizens and unite all three sectors—non-profit, private, and government—in new partnerships to promote innovative solutions. Throughout my career I have been involved in numerous efforts to make social progress. The key to each of these endeavors has been the willingness of people to unite in common purpose beyond their own self-interest. From that experience, I believe we need a fundamentally new approach to our politics and to how we solve problems, one that articulates a new public philosophy, a new way both to seize the opportunities and address the challenges of the uniquely demanding times we live in.

Immediately after President Obama's election, and in response to the greatest economic crisis since the Great Depression, leaders in Congress looked backwards for inspiration. Most Democrats argued for a return to Franklin Delano Roosevelt and talked of enacting some kind of new New Deal in which the federal government would be the driving force to rescue us from the economic crisis. Republicans reached back for Reaganism—tax cuts and smaller government. One side took refuge in ideas that were seventy-five years old, the other in ideas that were thirty years old. They are both out of date. They depend on a stale and discredited argument: that you must either be for big government or against it; government is either the solution to all problems or the cause of them.

The severity of the economic and social challenges of our times does not allow us the luxury of casually casting aside the possibility that government can help people. Nor can Democrats assume that government alone can solve problems. We need everyone to pitch in. The private sector has developed delivery mechanisms that should make government blush. Great innovation comes from many new, small, and medium sized businesses. Much breakthrough thinking and action for social progress is coming not from government or academia, but from the myriad not-for-profit organizations that are a rapidly growing feature of our national and international landscape. This mixture did not exist seventy-five or thirty years ago. Our times are our times; they are in our hands. So why should we look to Reagan or Roosevelt to guide us? We have to step up for ourselves.

President Lincoln's words spoken at a time of even greater crisis are an excellent inspiration for us today, because they contain a timeless principle and not a time-specific political ideology. He said: "The dogmas of the quiet past are inadequate to the stormy present. Our occasion is piled high with difficulty and we must rise to the occasion. As our case is new, we must think anew and act anew. We must disenthrall ourselves, and then we shall save our country."

We do need to disenthrall ourselves and develop a new politics, a new agenda, an improved role for government, and a public philosophy that supports us as we work together to solve problems. We need to do what we as Americans have always done, from the very founding of our country, at times of great crisis: turn to ourselves, get everyone engaged in addressing our challenges, and embrace the innovative solutions and approaches that will make our future even better than our past. The answer isn't to return to the past. So where instead should we look?

This book is not exactly a career memoir nor an autobiography. It's a story—and it contains many stories culled from many different people—of an idea. The idea is a perennial one in American life: that our greatest natural resource as a country is the diversity, talent, and commitment of the American people. Each generation of Americans has the opportunity to discover this fact and explore its boundless potential. The constant theme, however, is that America regularly calls upon its people to assume what Harry Truman called, on leaving the White House, the highest office in the land: that of citizen. The demands of citizenship, and the rewards, have never been greater. Our times call for "Big Citizens," individuals prepared not to seek what their country owes them, or what they can get from it, but how they can contribute to making it stronger. I have believed in this since, in a college dorm, I began to sketch out with my friend, Michael Brown, the idea of an organization that would allow young people, from every kind of background, to serve their communities in tackling some of the most entrenched and neglected problems.

Now, that idea needs to serve the nation.

What our national politics has lost in the partisan gridlock is the sense of our common purpose. When we neglect our shared purpose, we neglect an essential aspect of America, and in the end, the country loses touch with itself and its principles: we risk losing our soul. It becomes too easy not to embrace our shared responsibilities or to believe there's no value in learning from others. The evidence of every great leap forward should tell us this does not make any sense: the more widely we draw our inspiration, and the more broadly we encourage participation, the greater our chance of transformative success. We cannot solve a damaged economy individually any more than we can create a safe environment individually. We would be alarmed if we were singly responsible for our country's security in the face of hostile threats; we need to have that same sense of common cause in tackling our challenges at home.

America is a vast country that invites big contributions. This book looks at ways in which we can all contribute, inspired by an ideal of service to our communities and our nation, and attempts to show how that commitment might just fix Washington's broken political system.

▼▲▼

Big Citizenship first and foremost means contributing to a cause larger than your own self-interest. It calls on each and every one of us to get involved in politics, to perform community service, to join with other citizens in larger movements for change, and to take personal responsibility. A philosophy of Big Citizenship also means having an economy that works for everyone and reclaims America's historic place as an opportunity society. We cannot afford to waste the talents or contributions of any single person. It also demands that we embrace entrepreneurs and innovators in both the private and public sectors to develop the new solutions and ideas to address pressing problems. It means that while rejecting both the big government and no government approaches of the past, we define a new role for government, one that sets standards and the rules of the game to ensure a transparent and level playing field, monitors and reports on performance, provides incentives and rewards results especially for innovation, and uses proven market mechanisms like competition and choice, while not relying on exclusively market solutions. Our problems and challenges are so great and so systemic we need all hands on deck and all three sectors—Public, Private, and Non-Profit—to work together in new partnerships. Most solutions will come from leveraging the unique talents, resources, and abilities of each sector working together.

Finally, a new philosophy of Big Citizenship and Common Purpose must be introduced to recapture the spirit that we are all in this together. We will rise or fall based on how we fare as a community and as a country. We must reassert the spirit of our founding fathers and mothers who "mutually pledged their lives, fortunes, and sacred honor."

The spirit of the Greatest Generation, united in common bonds to survive the Depression and defeat Hitler and the Nazis, might seem to have passed into history, but that's not so. Times have changed and our wars are fought by a dedicated professional all-volunteer military and not soldiers drafted from across the nation. But the spirit of the servicemen and women in uniform is just as great as ever, discernible on every military base across the globe. Nor is that fervent spirit limited to the military.

▼▲▼

In the summer of 2009, I was asked to speak to the annual conference of the Military Child Education Coalition (MCEC). It is an extraordinary organization founded by a small group of military spouses in 1998, over a kitchen table discussion about the special needs, challenges, and opportunities that military children face. Military children generally move between six to nine times during their K–12 years. MCEC recognizes that when a family member serves, the whole family serves. The organization identifies the challenges facing the highly mobile military child, increases awareness of these challenges in military and educational communities, and initiates and implements programs to meet the challenges. MCEC's goal is to level the educational playing field for military children wherever they are located around the world, and to serve as a model for all highly mobile children.

Before I gave the speech, I contacted Colonel John Tien and his wife, Tracy, whom I have been proud to know as friends for more than sixteen years. I wanted their perspective on MCEC and the unique situation facing military families, especially during a time of war. John is an extraordinary human being, a true American hero, the son of Chinese immigrants to America. Because of his belief in this country and the opportunities it provided him, he enrolled at West Point. John graduated number one in his class, went on to serve as a White House Fellow and a Rhodes Scholar. He served in Operation Desert Storm in 1990–'91, and John has also completed three tours in Iraq. Like many in our armed forces, he has literally put his life on the line for our country. He now serves as the Senior Director for Afghanistan policy on the National Security Council in the White House. He and his family represent the very best of America. Tracy is also an amazing person. She is a wonderful mother to their two teenage girls, Amanda and Becky, and a great public servant in her own right as a teacher and military spouse of a high ranking officer. In response to my asking for her perspective, Tracy sent me an email that both profoundly moved and inspired me:

> When I talk to people about the difference between civilian life and military life, I usually talk about how in "real life" (what my girls call non-military life), if you run a company, you do not live next door to all of your employees, you don't go to the same doctor (who is also a neighbor) that they do, you don't have your employees' spouses seeing you discipline your children in the grocery store that you all shop at, your employees don't see you or your spouse at the pool or gross in your workout clothes, your children don't go to school with their children who then tell their parents all the good or bad things that your child said or did in school that day. In the military, there is no privacy.
>
> Military life is indeed a fishbowl, but the incredible tight sense of community usually makes up for it.
>
> I feel that the girls and I serve and sacrifice for our country, too. During the deployment, I felt that my job was to support the families of the battalion, so the soldiers in our battalion could concentrate on fighting the fight and coming back safely to us. We did many things to keep life going—by "we" I mean the all-volunteer force of battalion

spouses who were willing to take on a leadership role during the deployment. If that meant babysitting some kids overnight while their mom had emergency surgery, we did it. If that meant calling all the women to let them know that there had been an accident, but all of our guys were safe, we did it. We trained spouses how to help other spouses if their husbands were killed or injured, and we took training to recognize signs of possible suicide. We attended all the memorial services. There were just so many things that we as a team did.

The girls were troopers also. Amanda took a babysitting course taught by the Red Cross. I would then use her and some of her friends to babysit some of the younger kids during meetings so that the moms could attend. Both Becky and Amanda helped me prepare for meetings by stapling papers, putting together information packets, wrapping door prizes for me. They supported me, so that I could support others.

During a deployment, maintaining the connection within the family unit is crucial. It is hard to know what to share and what not to share with the other spouse—why worry your spouse when they can't do anything about it? It was hard for me not to feel guilty that I was relatively safe while John was continually in harm's way and for John not to feel guilty that he wasn't contributing to the parenting of our daughters. We talked when we could, sent daily emails, sent weekly packages and letters, but it really takes a lot of commitment on everyone's part to keep doing that for over a year; without it, however, the family unit just breaks apart.

To survive a deployment—and I mean for the families, not for the soldier—the military community is crucial. You need your neighbors and your friends to talk to and to listen to. Professionally, we neighbors would bounce ideas off of each other and share opportunities. For example, as a teacher, I would usually organize and run seminars for my spouses on stress management, dealing with angry children, managing personal funds, etc. Another neighbor was not so good with people, but was great with a computer and spreadsheets and she would share all of these forms and flyers so we didn't have to recreate the wheel. Another neighbor, a former cheerleader, had an abundant amount of energy and loved to socialize and seemed to know the name of every person she came across; she came up with great ideas for fun social activities for the spouses and their children and we would all piggyback on those. So we all shared our skills to make things best for the community. We probably all had dinner together at least once a week, shared birthdays, Thanksgiving, and Christmas together. For one of the memorial services for a soldier who was killed, one of the neighbors just could not emotionally bear to attend another service, but she volunteered to collect everyone's kids after school and watch them and then have dinner waiting for us when we got home. There is no way that I could have made it through 15 months of John away without my neighbors, my battle buddies.

Probably the lowest point of the deployment for me was when, a week before school started after summer vacation, I had to tell our youngest daughter that her best friend's father had been killed and that the friend might not be returning to school. Somehow I had to convince Becky that even though her friend had lost her daddy and that John was at the same place the friend's dad had been, John was fine and would continue to be fine. How do you tell an 11-year-old that?

The girls have never had an opportunity not to be involved with service. They were born into it—literally, since they were born in army hospitals. Their father is in the army, their mother a teacher. They have learned about citizenship and what it means to serve others and their country their whole lives. Even on an army base, when you go to see a movie, they play the national anthem before the pre-views. During the deployment, we read the book about "Molly," one of the American Girl Dolls that was set during WWII. In the story, Molly's dad is an army doctor overseas, but Molly keeps busy knitting socks for soldiers, collecting cans, planting victory gardens, etc. As we read it together, the girls asked me why it is so different now (in 2006), why only army kids feel the war and are doing things, why does-n't everyone know there is a war? I didn't really have a good answer for them.

I think now they both realize that there are ways outside of the military to serve others. Becky is always volunteer-ing herself (and John) to help our local environment by clearing weeds from parks, planting new trees, picking up trash along the riverbank. Amanda likes to volunteer at homeless shelters; this year, she also worked with a club that sponsors girls in other countries so that they can at-tend secondary school. Amanda plans to do City Year after college and Becky told me she wants to get a degree in math from MIT and then do Teach for America. Both have big personal hopes and dreams, but both continue to think of ways to incorporate service into their lives.

Traci's description of her life as part of a military family con-tains a vision of an America where people support each other, look after each other, and have a deep commitment to service, Big Cit-izenship, and to the best of our ideals. I have seen this America not only in the military but over and over through my work in the service and social entrepreneurship movements. And we all rec-ognize this America in the way the country responds in times of crisis or natural disaster—after 9/11, and after the disasters of Hurricanes Katrina and Rita. We saw it after the terrible Indian Ocean Tsunami of 2004, when Americans opened their hearts and their wallets once again, and reached out literally half a world away to help those in need. It was evident in the reaction to the Haitian earthquake of 2010. The first response of the Big Citizen is not simply to take care of ourselves, but always to reach out to a neighbor in need. We rally around. We support each other. We gather together around our common purpose. Traci Tien's America demonstrates that when community is strong anything is possible. All obstacles can be overcome. All challenges can be met. Traci Tien's America is the America we love. It need not be limited to military bases; in fact, it's vital that it isn't.

I felt that same sense of community at Judy Cockerton's Treehouse Foundation in Easthampton. Judy was running two successful children's toy stores in Brookline, Massachusetts called No Kidding! One day, reading the newspaper, she was struck by an article about a five month old foster baby who had been kidnapped from the crib. Then and there, she decided to become a foster parent. But she didn't stop there. She studied the foster care system and realized it was flawed: foster children who "age out" of the system at eighteen are much more likely to drop out of school, be unemployed, struggle in poverty, and become homeless.

So Judy sold her stores, moved to Easthampton and established the Treehouse Foundation, which is a residential and intergenerational community that offers a comprehensive approach to meet the needs of foster children. As part of Treehouse, Judy provides affordable housing for foster families who adopt, and also for "elders" who want to be surrogate grandparents. It is a win-win for everyone. What makes it all work is an entrepreneurial approach and the willingness of citizens to serve others. Judy soon recognized that the foster care system relied too heavily on an "all-or-nothing" approach. Essentially people could either choose to be foster or adoptive parents, or not be involved. She realized that others would want to help, but may not be able to make such a tremendous commitment. So Treehouse has a variety of ways people can support it, from volunteering in the afterschool program or community garden, to serving as a mentor for a child, to joining community activities and holiday celebrations, to making a donation. Treehouse, a not-for-profit organization, is a creative public–private partnership. She has partnered with a private real estate company, Beacon Communities, LLC, to develop and manage her property, and with Berkshire Children and Families to provide ongoing programming. Treehouse is funded through a combination of state and federal tax credits and grants and private philanthropy.

In addition to Treehouse, Judy has founded two other non-profits. Sibling Connections helps to maintain contact among siblings who have moved into separate homes. And through Imagine That!, Judy is working to replicate her model and advocate for a change in government policies to make the foster care system more effective. Asked in an interview what motivated her, Judy, who has an optimistic and can do spirit backed by steely determination, responded:

"What struck me was the disconnect between the general public—you, me, everyone—and the 800,000 children in foster care. It was like they were invisible, they became members of a stigmatized club, with no intention or desire to be members of this club. I started Treehouse in 2002 because I wanted every child in the Foster Care system to be treated with respect and dignity. When I have a quiet moment, I ask, what else can I do to support children and how can I get more people involved? Getting the country to turn around and embrace children, that's the real challenge. I'm pouring my heart and soul into making that happen. *And I believe we can succeed. I believe Treehouse can make that happen. I do believe that.*"

When you visit Treehouse, you believe, too. You see elders who have found a new sense of purpose and belonging; new adoptive parents who have found a supportive community; and children who have recaptured a sense of joy, hope, and possibility.

▼▲▼

Throughout my nearly twenty-five years as a civic entrepreneur, I have witnessed over and over the power of belief backed up by a hard-nosed, entrepreneurial pragmatic idealism. I have been privileged to be part of many efforts for progress. What usually begins as the seemingly impossible turns out to be a reality, with the common thread for success being Big Citizens working together in pursuit of Common Purpose. And more often than not, especially at the beginning, these Big Citizens are not household names. They are not the elected officials or prominent leaders. They are regular, good hearted people blessed with a loving heart and an open mind. Anyone can be a Big Citizen and join with others in common purpose. You just need to listen to that voice inside that says: "I, too, want to be part of making my neighborhood, my school, my community, my country, my world, a better place for all of us."

If you have been a Big Citizen, this book is for you. And if you desire to be a Big Citizen, this book is also for you. At times of great crisis, we often want to find that one great leader to bring us to a better day, but what we need to recognize is that throughout our history, it has been the willingness of regular people looking in the mirror and committing to causes larger than themselves that has been the key to making progress. At the end of the day, it is up to all of us.

I have learned it is an extremely rewarding experience to join with others in common cause to pursue a dream to make a difference and see it become a reality. It leaves one with a profound sense of gratitude. So, this book is one citizen's attempt to capture the experience and lessons learned from Big Citizens who dedicate their time and energy to the great, ongoing cause that is uniquely America.

1

STARTING CLOSE TO HOME

Most people's first sense of community is their home, and if you are lucky—and I was—home can be full of Big Citizens.

I was born in Pittsburgh, and lived with my grandparents in Kittanning, a small industrial town in Western Pennsylvania for much of my first two years. Grandma and Grandpa were helping out while my Dad—Amir, an immigrant from Iran—finished his medical residency, and Mom—Carmeline, a nurse—worked to make ends meet. As first- and second-generation immigrants, my parents offered me a unique appreciation for America's gifts, and the inimitable legacy of our country's history and democracy. My passion for justice first and foremost comes from them—two people, who have given me the most powerful thing parents can give: unconditional love and role models of hard work and high standards.

My mother's family is Italian. My grandpa, John Picardi, left Naples, Italy, when he was a teenager. Like legions before him and countless more ever since, he looked to America to start a new life, and once he arrived he was the happiest man on the planet. His deep contentment came not from material things. He was happy because he knew inside what was most important to him—family, friends, the love of his wife, Antina, his children, being able to hunt and fish, sharing good stories and conversations over a three-hour home-cooked Italian meal, and a devout faith in "the good Lord."

My mother also embodies this spirit of generosity and the belief that love and family are the most important things in life. "You know, I never saw a U-haul behind a hearse. You can't take it with you!" she often says, laughing and poking her finger into the air for emphasis. My mother is the classic Italian—she will fall in love with you over the phone. And after experiencing her warmth, you will fall in love with her, too. Always seeing the good in people, Mom taught by example and showed me that every person has a gift to give. She surrounded me and my three siblings with endless affection. One of my strongest memories from childhood was my mother yelling each day as I left for school and boarded the bus, "I love you, Alan!!!!" Now the last thing any second grader wants is for your friends to hear your Mom screaming she loves you. But I learned from her the power of unconditional love.

My grandma Antina's parents, Augusto and Anita Mantini, whom I was blessed to know as a child, emigrated from Italy just after the turn of the century, and made their way to Pennsylvania where Great Grandpa got a job working in the coalmines. We often heard stories of how he worked to unionize the coalminers and fought for better working conditions. John L. Lewis, the founder of the coalminer's union, was revered in their house. Great Grandpa was not a big man, not much taller than five feet, but he was strong as an ox with a barrel chest, hands that grasped yours with an iron grip, and big, bushy brows framing the perpetual twinkle in his eyes. Great Grandma spoke little English, and communicated to us with smiles and hugs. She was the center of the house and known as Bossa, because on all things related to family, she was the final word.

In Kittanning, my grandparents ran a corner store and survived the Depression despite giving goods away to friends in need. Grandpa fought in World War II, and although he only received the benefit of an eighth-grade education, he was one of the wisest men I have ever known, because he knew, understood, and loved people. He was a man of many aphorisms: "Don't plant onions and expect to grow roses." "You attract more bees with honey than with vinegar." When once told he was a very lucky man to be married to my grandmother, he responded after a slight pause, "Well you know, the good go to the good."

My grandmother was the hardest-working woman I have ever known, perhaps because she started working at family chores when she was only five. She was the eldest of six children, and as a young girl she would rise at the crack of dawn and retrieve the coal to heat the house. Waking up early became a habit, and every Sunday, she began at five in the morning to make her pasta from scratch for a Sunday feast for any family or friends who wanted to come by.

Grandpa and Grandma lived at 1427 Johnston Avenue in a small but comfortable house with a sitting room, modest kitchen, a bathroom with a tub but no shower, and three bedrooms upstairs. To a young child, the basement seemed like a treasure trove full of canned goods, hanging laundry, kids' toys, a freezer stuffed with goodies, barrels of homemade wine, and Uncle Johnny's barbells, dumbbells, and punching bag. It was the first home I ever knew, and to this day, it is my favorite house. It may have been modest in its size and decor, but it was huge in terms of love. You just got a good feeling when you walked in. It was full of laughter, an endless supply of great homemade Italian food, and colorful stories that came one after the other. Family and neighborhood friends would come and go, have a glass of homemade wine or a bowl of soup, and share anecdotes about the day.

My grandparents also had a perpetual houseguest—Don Berline. "Berline," as he was affectionately known, was a big burly man, with a balding pate, gnarled and roughhewn hands from strenuous manual work, and teeth that showed clear signs of neglect. He was as strong as a bear but mentally challenged. Grandpa discovered Berline abandoned by his family and living alone in a small cabin in the woods, and welcomed him into his home and he became part of our family. He didn't sleep at my grandparents' house, but he was there every night for dinner and he had his own chair in the sitting room. My grandparents didn't have a lot, but my grandfather realized Berline needed a family. And Berline made for a good sidekick to my grandfather, who supplemented his income with odd jobs and some inspired local projects. Grandpa provided the pick-up truck, Berline did the heavy lifting.

Every night, my great uncle Red—Angelo Mantini—would come by the house to visit his sister, my grandmother. He lived a fifteen- to twenty-minute drive away in Ford City. Sure, he could have simply called his sister, but the phone just wasn't good enough for him: he needed to check in on her and her family. He wanted to make that personal connection every day, a tradition he continued into his eighties. Uncle Red was a boxer, a real champion, and his face would turn red in the ring from the fighting—hence the nickname that he acquired from his army buddies. He was also a decorated war hero in World War II.

I lived with my grandparents because my parents worked long hours in the hospital. My grandparents also looked after my sister Darla, born twenty months after me, but by the time my second sister Mia and my brother Lance were born, our family had moved to Boston so my father could pursue cancer research at the Lahey Clinic. Five years later, when I was seven, we moved to the town of Bedford, New Hampshire, and that's where I grew up.

In small town New Hampshire, people tend to be independent-minded and freedom-loving, as well as diehard Boston sports fans. New Hampshire still employs the democratic institution of the town meeting, which introduced to me the idea of participatory, citizen democracy when I was around ten years old. I remember my dad taking me to town meetings, which were held in the cafeteria of my grade school, McKelvie, in the early evenings. Initially, the last thing I wanted to be doing was going to school at night, but my dad insisted I come along with him to see and learn how regular citizens in Bedford worked through local issues. We didn't have a mayor; we had selectmen, who helped to govern the town with input from the town residents. The town produced a booklet of all of the issues that were going to be discussed, including the budget. My dad gave me this booklet and asked me to study it so that I could follow the meeting. I was an earnest student and did my best, but couldn't fully understand it all. I do remember a big debate as to whether Bedford should build its own high school. (This issue came up year after year and was always voted down, until finally, just three years ago, Bedford opened its own high school.) While some discussions were over my head, I was impressed that the cafeteria was full with several hundred people turning out and everyone was actively participating and cared strongly about their views.

It was in New Hampshire that I learned from my family, friends, and teachers many of the important lessons that shaped my life and my work. In Bedford, with my two sisters and brother and many neighborhood friends, I enjoyed a childhood similar to that of millions of others in small-town America. I was a cub scout and earned merit badges, played sports year-round, and participated in neighborhood activities after school. Ripping through dirt trails on my red Honda S-L 70 mini-bike was a favorite after-school hobby. We rode our bicycles everywhere and bought penny candy at Ray's country store, where Charlotte, who worked behind the counter, always had a warm smile and kind word for the kids.

While I was growing up, my father would frequently extol the virtues of America to me, with a passion that only a recently arrived immigrant can convey. He would tell me (and still does): "Son, America is the single greatest country in the world because of its constitution, declaration of independence, and ideals grounded in freedom, democracy, and justice." While he loved being in Europe—he had studied in Switzerland—he never felt fully accepted there as a foreigner. In America, he would remind me, everyone's family had come from another country, except for the Native Americans. He would tell me, "Don't ever let anyone call you a foreigner in this country. And remember, you can be anything you want to be in America, as long as you work hard, get a good education, are honest, and believe in yourself and this country."

But my father understood that America was not perfect. While he had been in medical school at the University of Lausanne, his family in Tehran watched the CIA, British government, and the Shah crush a growing democracy movement in Iran and overthrow the elected government of Mohammad Mossadegh in 1953, for whom my great uncle worked. My father's belief in America's unique potential was unshakeable, but he knew that it rested on the country's ideals. When America abandoned those ideals, the country would sooner or later suffer for it: America's support for Baptista in Cuba, Somoza in Nicaragua, Marcos in the Philippines, and Pinochet in Chile showed policymakers straying from our country's ideals; our role in Vietnam, and not supporting Mandela in South Africa, were other examples when policymakers strayed from our country's principles in favor of short-term benefits. My father put what the CIA did in Iran into this larger historical context. He taught me to love America enough not only to appreciate it, but also to want to make it better and to help it to live up to its powerful ideals. That, he would insist, is what true patriotism is all about.

My father's wisdom and guidance didn't stop at love for country—he also taught me the power of professional excellence. He practiced medicine the old-fashioned way. He was completely devoted to the hospital and his patients, and would make rounds visiting his patients seven days a week and remain on call during nights and weekends. There was a universal health care policy in Dr. Khazei's office: No one had to have proof of insurance to be treated, they just needed to be sick. My dad believed that if people could afford to pay him they would. Over thirty years, while practicing medicine at the Catholic Medical Center in Manchester, NH, he treated more than 20,000 patients and saved countless lives. He also held numerous volunteer leadership positions at the hospital, with the New Hampshire Medical Society and the American Cancer Society, trying to make his contribution to improving the practice of medicine in his hospital, state, and adopted country.

Mom continued to work as a nurse at a youth development center, as a traveling nurse and as a school nurse. She was also the primary caretaker for us four kids. She made sure we got to sports practices, CCD classes, and CYO at the local Catholic Church, Cub Scouts, and Brownies and more. With two young children of my own now, in a two parent working household, trying to balance everything, I marvel at what my mom managed with four kids—at one point with three of us in diapers—while working as a nurse. She just shrugs it off, saying: "You kids were easy and I loved you so much. It wasn't hard for me."

Like many immigrant families, my parents had an extraordinary commitment to providing all their children with the best educational opportunities in America. A main reason they chose Bedford when we moved to New Hampshire was because of its excellent public school system. I attended the McKelvie public school from second through eighth grade, and was blessed with incredibly dedicated and talented teachers, who I still remember vividly today: Mrs. O'Brien, my third-grade teacher, taught us the dangers of smoking and pollution, and to care for the environment. Mrs. Edmunds, who was Welsh, led me to fall in love in love with the magical world of J.R.R. Tolkien's *The Hobbit* and *The Lord of the Rings*. Mr. Pero had a unique approach to help every student become comfortable with public speaking by giving us a choice of writing increasingly long papers or doing short oral presentations in front of the class. Mr. Lombard took it upon himself to develop and offer an Algebra class for eighth-grade students who excelled at math. Mr. Landry, our science teacher, led a four-day camping trip for the entire eighth grade as a way for us to directly experience science in nature.

Back then, Bedford didn't have a high school. So when one of my father's colleagues told him he was visiting a college preparatory school named St. Paul's in Concord, because he, like my father, had a son in eighth grade, my dad accepted his invitation to come along. St. Paul's is an extraordinary place—beautiful, cloistered, and dedicated to both strong ideals and first-rate education—and my dad was smitten. He returned home, debriefed Mom and me, and the three of us were soon on our way to see what he was so excited about.

I could hardly believe my eyes. Nearly 2000 acres of perfectly manicured, tree-lined streets, brick laid paths and rolling green hills. Several ponds, including one big enough to hold something called "crew" races and another for playing hockey on "black ice" in the winter, added to the school's charm. The buildings were a mix of old and new architecture, which reflected the school's more than 120 years of existence.

To get a sense of St. Paul's, think of Harry Potter's Hogwarts boarding school, but without the wizardry and witchcraft. That said, for me, on that first visit, it certainly did seem like a magical place.

I had never been to a college, but this is what I imagined a campus might be. Located in Concord, NH, St. Paul's was only thirty minutes from my hometown, but it was a world away for me and my family.

I received an excellent education at St Paul's from tremendously dedicated teachers, and made lifelong friends there. One of the great opportunities we enjoyed was the speakers program. The school would regularly host outstanding artists, musicians, political and community leaders, and even Presidential candidates, since New Hampshire was the first primary state. One such speaker proved to be pivotal to my education and the trajectory of my professional life. Mayor Harvey Sloane of Lexington, Kentucky visited and made the case for universal voluntary national service. He argued that America should have a rite of passage whereby all young adults would be challenged and given the opportunity to spend a year in full-time service with a diverse group of their peers. Participants could choose military or civilian service. Those who chose civilian service could work in schools, care for the elderly, preserve the environment, and more—but everyone would be urged to serve in some way. Sloane argued myriad benefits would result—better citizens, a more united country, deep impact on pressing problems like education, the environment, racism, and a sense that we were all in this together.

I loved this idea. Then and there I became a big believer in the concept of national service; it combined the deep patriotism and potential to close that gap between America's ideals and its reality that Dad espoused, while also giving every person a chance to explore their potential and exercise their own goodness that Mom had taught me. National service also grabbed me as a systemic solution to many challenges. I believed then, and still believe today, that if everyone chose to do a year of service with diverse peers it would improve our country and our world for the better, more than any other single program or initiative. I have found when people spend a year in full-time service—working with others whose backgrounds are different—they get what I like to call their "justice nerves" turned on. When you come face-to-face with injustice—under-resourced schools, homeless people, blighted neighborhoods, or a ravaged environment—you want to do something about it. You can't walk away. And once justice nerves are turned on, they rarely turn off.

▼▲▼

National service, of course, is not a uniquely American idea—it has its roots in the Greek city states and Aristotelian notions of democracy, and the citizen soldiers who founded America's democracy. The first formal articulation of the power of national service was by William James, who, in his famous essay, *The Moral Equivalent of War*, published in 1910, said:

> Individuals, daily more numerous, now feel this civic passion. It is only a question of blowing on the spark until the whole population gets incandescent...If now...there were, instead of military conscription, a conscription of the whole youthful population to form for a certain number of years a part of the army enlisted against Nature, the injustice would tend to be evened out...would our gilded youths be drafted off, accord-

ing to their choice, to get the childishness knocked out of them, and to come back into society with healthier sympathies and soberer ideas. They would have paid their blood-tax, done their own part in the immemorial human warfare against nature; they would tread the earth more proudly, the women would value them more highly, they would be better fathers and teachers of the following generation.

President Franklin D. Roosevelt's Civilian Conservation Corps, President John F. Kennedy's inaugural address and his creation of the Peace Corps, and President Lyndon B. Johnson's establishment of VISTA were all policy formulations of national service as a way to directly involve citizens in our democracy. And yet, since the creation of VISTA in 1965, nothing had been done at the federal level on national service.

While I was captivated by the promise of national service in high school, in the same way others might fall in love with ancient history or baseball or filmmaking, I didn't cut my education short to pursue the dream. Instead, I enrolled at Harvard University in the fall of 1979—the fulfillment of the American dream in the eyes of both my parents. During my first visit to Harvard, when I was exploring colleges, there was a large protest for divestment from companies doing business in South Africa. More than 1,000 students had boycotted classes for the day and gathered in Harvard Yard to urge Harvard to change its policies. That vivid campus activism and idealism helped to convince me Harvard was where I wanted to be.

Of the many brilliant and gifted friends I made at Harvard, one became central to my idealistic adventures and has remained so to this day.

Michael Brown, my roommate, was a basketball point guard, a local, and an extremely cool guy. He was about 5' 8" but seemed taller as he carried himself with an easy confidence. Michael knew where we could score beer and find great parties on campus—not always an easy task at Harvard. We shared a passion for the heroes and icons of the 1960s: Jack and Bobby Kennedy and Martin Luther King; Star Trek and its idealistic vision for the future—its diverse crew and the Prime Directive of non-interference[2] that Captain Kirk somehow always seemed to find a wrinkle around when the situation required it. We were hopeless romantics, too; Humphrey Bogart as Rick in Casablanca was a role model we both aspired to but never came close to emulating. And we both held a deep desire to try to make a difference and change the world.

Michael immediately struck me as brilliant. His incisive mind always put a thought-provoking perspective on everything. From the day I met him, I loved the way he looked at the world. Michael's critical-thinking skills had been honed by his dad, a lawyer and Talmudic scholar who would conduct conversations about justice and morality over Friday family Shabbat dinners. But even bigger than his brain is Michael's heart. He is intensely loyal and loving to the people he cares about and will do anything for them.

Like many college students, Michael and I and other close friends would occasionally stay up late into the night discussing why in the richest country in the world we had some of the deepest poverty, division, and hopelessness? We wanted to do something to make a difference. Michael and I were particularly inspired by Robert Coles's class, the Literature of Social Reflection, which dealt with deep moral questions and challenges. Professor Coles was and is one of the preeminent psychologists and moral teachers of our time. He had marched with Robert Kennedy and Cesar Chavez and participated in the civil rights movement. His is a passionate voice on behalf of children, the poor, the dispossessed, and the left out.

Professor Coles's enthusiastic and heartfelt lectures challenged us to be moral beings that would use the extraordinary opportunity of a Harvard education to fight for justice and make a difference in the world. He had us read and discuss a lifetime's library of great books like James Agee and Walker Evans' *Let Us Now Praise Famous Men*, Walker Percy's *The Moviegoer*, and Ralph Ellison's *Invisible Man*. These books challenged us to think critically about our world and how different people lived and were treated. Through Coles's class and conversations with fellow students, we came to believe the gap in America between our ideals and reality came down to three main causes:

People are not exposed directly enough to the diversity of life in America, especially the lives of the poor, dispossessed, and disconnected. It's not good enough to see it on TV, hear about it on the radio, or even read about it in books. TV, in fact, has a numbing experience on most people, almost making them immune to others' suffering. People need a direct and sustained experience with others who are different in order to have their natural compassion and sense of justice turned on.

Many Americans don't realize that one person can make a difference in tackling what JFK called "The vast array of the world's ills." We came of age when young people were branded the "me generation." We rejected that label strongly. The problem was not that young people in the late 1970s and early 1980s were selfish, it was that no one like JFK had challenged us or shown us how to be a "we" generation.

We aren't fully cognizant that we are all in this together. Rather, we look to some infamous "they" to address and solve our problems. Instead of understanding we all have a role to play, we have come to believe that the solution lies with some big institution like "big government," "big labor," "big business." People need to embrace, at the end of the day, that we *are* they. Ultimately, the solution lies with us.

Like many college students then and today, we were young, idealistic and blessed with great opportunity. And we felt the desire to participate and give something back to our community.

As a way to move beyond late night reveries and academic textbooks, Michael and I decided to spend the summer after our freshman year traveling across America to get a firsthand feel for the country. We thought it would be a blast to do a summer-long road trip visiting college friends and having the freedom to explore some of America's better known landmarks and destination cities. We had a rough route planned based on where we could find a free place to stay, but also kept ourselves open to where the road might take us. We joined with two of my best friends from high school, Tim Zimmermann, my high school roommate, and Brett Love. Tim had a 1979 Honda Accord hatchback. Back then, it was a sub-compact two-door car, with no air conditioning, and it barely fit four big guys. Some of our stuff shared what little leg room we had; most was stacked on the roof.

We had a memorable summer, driving through the South, across the enormity and searing heat of Texas, up the picturesque coast of California to Vancouver, back through the Great Plains of the West, and traversing the mid-west to the east coast. Working off small budgets, we unashamedly milked our network of college friends to scrounge places to crash and ended up surrendering to hotels for only two nights out of a nine-week trip—one night in New Orleans and one night in Las Vegas. We camped in the Grand Canyon and Yellowstone Park, and endeavored to soak up as much of America as we could.

We discovered how enormous America is—and it is one helluva long drive to cross it! We reveled in its diversity. Parts of the trip we planned out; most often we just got lucky. I remember pulling into Cheyenne, Wyoming when they happened to be celebrating Cheyenne Days—which was like journeying back to the Old West. We were fortunate to be hosted by Pat Fleming, a friend from college, who was a local football star and had the town in his pocket. Pat took us to rodeos, cowboy bars, and the biggest country fair we had ever seen. It felt like we were stepping back in time, and we had a blast. While each region of the country—and indeed, each state and city—had its own character and unique aspects to its culture, people were united by a common sense of the special nature of being an American. And they were universally friendly and intrigued by four college guys traveling the country, inspired by the Simon and Garfunkel ballad—"I've gone to look for America. . .".

▼▲▼

During the summer of our junior year, 1981, we took a different journey of discovery, trading the vast spaces of America at large for the internal workings of the nation's capital. There, ideas could be acted upon. Michael had secured an internship working for Congressman Tom Downey the previous summer. He had such a great time on Capitol Hill he decided to take a year off and work with a then relatively unknown but interesting rising star, a three-term congressman named Leon Panetta.[3] Congressman Panetta hired Michael as a legislative assistant and assigned him to a bill to set up a National Commission to study the idea of national service and propose options to implement a program.

Following Michael's example, I applied for and received an internship with Congressman Norm D'Amours, who represented New Hampshire's First District, including my hometown of Bedford. Congressman D'Amours had served in the military and was a believer in bringing back the draft. I thought comprehensive voluntary national service with civilian and military options was a better idea. So I asked Congressman D'Amours if I could prepare a report for him on national service as an alternative to the draft, and he agreed. Little did I know that summer would set me on a path for the next twenty-five years.

Michael's first task in moving Congressman Panetta's commission for national service bill, HR2500, was to organize a hearing on the issue. Another Harvard roommate, Michael Alter, interned for Massachusetts Senator Paul Tsongas, co-sponsor of Panetta's bill in the Senate, so we figured we had the thing wired. We were young, idealistic, and believed that at the ripe old age of twenty-one, we had Capitol Hill in our pocket.

We joined forces using the full resources available to young people on Capitol Hill (which are significant) to deeply investigate the various proposals for national service and to meet the individuals who were pushing the idea in various forms. As we dove into the ideas and philosophy behind national service, we became even more convinced that something was missing from America's democracy: a shared citizenship experience—a rite of passage—that could serve as a civic platform for turning on the "justice nerves" of young Americans, so they learn a sense of democratic responsibility and feel empowered in the world. This shared experience in active-duty citizenship needed to meet pressing societal needs. It could also engage the general public, and generate new social capital, public ideas, civic will, and social entrepreneurs. The question in our mind was: "How can America systematically awaken its citizens to take an active, positive, and effective public role in building our democracy?"

We had seen firsthand that America, the richest of nations, could not generate the ideas, resources, will, or imagination to solve some of its most pressing problems: poverty, homelessness, failing schools, racial and ethnic strife, and more. Establishing a rite of passage for young Americans to spend a year or two in full-time service to our country was a way to generate the citizen power and citizen will to tackle these entrenched problems.

We quickly became captivated by the vision, promise, and potential of national service on a nationwide scale, imagining that every September, along with the millions of young people marching off to college, at least one million were entering a year of full-time service—in our nation's public schools, after-school programs, senior citizen centers, homeless shelters, public parks, playgrounds, and more.

Instead of only 7,500 Peace Corps volunteers annually, America might enlist more than 100,000 Americans every year as "citizen ambassadors" to fight injustice and poverty all over the world, showing the true American spirit of service and idealism while exposing Americans to the wondrous diversity of people from every continent.

Like other devotees to the idea of comprehensive voluntary national service, we saw it as a systemic solution to many of our nation's pressing problems. Steve Waldman in his book about the development of AmeriCorps, *The Bill*, likens national service to a Swiss Army knife, because of its multiple effectiveness.[4] First, national service could tap the energy and idealism of youth to meet critical national and community needs. For example, through their millions of hours of domestic service, national service participants could ensure that every child could read by the third grade, transform thousands of vacant lots into community gardens and playgrounds, and run thousands of after school programs to provide children a safe, educational, and values-based out-of-school experience.

Second, national service would serve as a "civic rite of passage" for all Americans, instilling an ethic of civic responsibility and community in each generation as they came of age. Rather than thinking and acting just about themselves, national service in either the military or the civilian sector would teach and train each generation of Americans to be active duty citizens. As a result, every generation would have a chance to become a Greatest Generation.

Third, national service would help complete America's mission written into our Constitution—"to form a more perfect union." It would bind the country together, hand-in-hand with military service, around the idea of service to the nation. It could help heal America's racial and class divides by uniting people from diverse backgrounds for a cause larger than themselves. The civil rights movement of the 1960s changed the laws of America, but it did not entirely change people's hearts and minds. That best happens through shared service experiences, working together for the common good, and voluntary comprehensive national service is perhaps the best way to complete the civil rights movement in our country; a country that by 2050 will have no majority race.

Fourth, national service would serve as a civic innovation machine, with youthful idealists shaking up non-profit and governmental bureaucracies. Inspired by their service experience, some national service participants would become social entrepreneurs, bringing new ideas and energy into public problem solving. There is nothing more American than entrepreneurship, whether it is on the private sector side, like Steve Jobs co-founding Apple, or on the civic side, like Wendy Kopp, who started Teach for America because she saw that the country had a deficit of urban and rural teachers in low-income districts, and a surplus of idealistic college graduates who could be inspired to teach.

Fifth, and finally, by tying a year or more of service to life-changing benefits—college education, home ownership, support to be an entrepreneur by starting a small business or non-profit, and retirement security—national service can, in tandem with military service, provide young Americans from all backgrounds with an array of ways to access the American Dream through service with opportunity going hand-in-hand with responsibility.

Motivated by the limitless promise and potential of national service, we poured into our work on Capitol Hill that summer. By the end of my internship, I had written a twenty-three-page report for Congressman D'Amours, recommending a new comprehensive voluntary national service program with both civilian and military options as an alternative to the draft. He dutifully read it, and agreed to co-sponsor Panetta's legislation. By the end of the summer, Michael had managed to organize a hearing on Panetta's bill, at which Senator Tsongas testified along with a veritable "who's who" of the national service movement either appearing in person or submitting written testimony. We learned that all hearings produced a "hearing book" so we tried to identify as many people as possible to submit written testimony so that the hearing book would become a definitive text on ideas and arguments for national service.

The hearing seemed like a triumph for us, but Panetta's legislation never moved after that. It was an early lesson in the realities of politics at the Federal level. Under the Reagan Administration, there was little appetite for new federal initiatives, even for the relatively small expense of a commission to study the idea of national service. Fortunately, there were others around to breathe life into our ideals after the summer's brief collision with Washington realpolitik.

Jamie Raskin, a college friend, organized a private meeting for about twenty Harvard summer interns, with Ralph Nader, whom I had heard speak, brilliantly and inspiringly, in front of a crowd of 1,000. Nader challenged us:

"You all are at the peak of your idealism right now because you are young, have the luxury to be in college and just learn, have great friends and peers all around you with time on your hands, have tremendous energy and are not encumbered by worldly possessions or responsibilities. It is in your twenties when you need to take risks. Pursue your dreams. Don't take the conventional route. Because if you don't act on your idealism in your twenties, you won't do it later in life. As you get older, you may get married and have children, you will have mortgages and car payments and other responsibilities. You won't be as free to just pursue your ideals and your idealism. So take the risks now."

Nader then told us the story of how he took on General Motors, at the time, the largest and far and away most powerful company on the planet, on the issue of car safety. And he shared how they hired a private detective and tried to dig up "dirt" on him so as to be able to discredit him personally and thus blunt his criticism and attacks.

And then he gave us his second big piece of advice:

"In whatever you do, maintain your integrity and stick to what you believe in. If you do things that compromise your integrity or your personal reputation, it will harm your ability to fight for justice and what you are passionate about."

I never forgot Nader's advice, and would need to draw on it often in the months and years ahead.

My Harvard undergraduate thesis was on the rise of neo-liberalism and the role of ideas in politics. The neo-liberals, first dubbed as such by Randall Rothenberg in a piece for the New Republic in 1982, never reached the cohesion or status of the neo-conservatives. Rather, they were a loose collection of political leaders, journalists, and academics who largely came of age during the 1960s. Sometimes they were referred to as the "Atari Democrats" because of their belief in the power of technology to drive economic growth. Many were inspired by the words and deeds of John Kennedy and looked to him as a political role model. People dubbed neo-liberals at that time included Senators Gary Hart, Paul Tsongas, and Bill Bradley among others. They also included academics Lester Thurow and Robert Reich, and journalists James Fallows, Morton Kondracke, and Charlie Peters—whose *Washington Monthly Magazine* was a showcase of neo-liberal thinking. The neo-liberals shared a commitment to developing a new progressive agenda for the country that was post-New Deal, post-Great Society and also an alternative to Ronald Reagan. The neo-liberals also shared a passion for ideas as a driving force in politics, as opposed to relying on the constituency groups that dominated the Democratic Party. Among the ideas the neo-liberals embraced was voluntary comprehensive national service as a way to recapture a sense of civic duty and replace government bureaucracy with citizen activism.

My thesis topic gave me a chance to get to know some of these newer, younger thinkers and actors—either in person or through their writings. And it led naturally to my working on Senator Gary Hart's 1984 outsider run for president.

Hart was a strong believer in national service, and from the extensive research I had done on him for my thesis, I discovered I agreed with many of his ideas for the country.

My thesis advisor, a wonderful young professor named Shep Melnick, who was also from New Hampshire, offered to introduce me to the New Hampshire primary campaign manager, a young, extremely talented woman named Jeanne Shaheen.[5]

I liked Shaheen's pragmatic idealism right away, her focus on a grassroots campaign, and willingness to hire a young person like me and give him real responsibility. She liked the fact that I was energetic and cheap—I could live at home with my folks.

Three weeks after I signed up, *Newsweek* predicted Gary Hart would be the first candidate to drop out of the race due to a lack of money and support. I made sure my parents didn't see the article. Of course, Hart didn't drop out right away. We went on to win the New Hampshire primary in a stunning upset no one had predicted. And even though Hart ultimately and narrowly lost the nomination to Vice President Walter Mondale, the campaign was a powerful experience for me.

The New Hampshire Hart campaign was driven by a very small group of thoughtful, committed citizens. One of the things that made it so special was that everyone was involved with the campaign for the right reasons—no one was there because they expected a job in the White House. They believed in the candidate'and in the cause of reforming the Democratic Party and defining a new agenda for the country. The New Hampshire Hart campaign taught me that a small group of committed people who shared a dream and a goal, and were willing to work hard enough, could make a huge difference, even when the odds seemed almost impossible. The Hart campaign also reinforced in me the power young people have to change the world. Absolutely essential to Hart's winning the New Hampshire primary were the thousands of young people who trooped up to New Hampshire, enabling us to canvass the state twice.

The experience taught me how to be an effective grassroots organizer and entrepreneurial thinker. As a field director, I was responsible for all campaign activities in part of southern New Hampshire—Nashua and eleven surrounding smaller cities and towns. I performed voter outreach, arranged candidate events, organized grassroots voter activities such as door-to-door canvassing drives, hosted surrogates including Lee Hart and Congressman Tim Wirth, among others, for events, and more. And I had very little resources to draw upon as the campaign had a very limited budget.

Jeanne Shaheen once told me that Hart would be available for a house party in Nashua in early August with a goal of getting at least seventy-five people there. She instructed me to find a host for the party, someone prominent enough to attract a good crowd. I asked her what the budget was for food, invitations, stamps, and the like, and she said, "Zero, we have no money for that kind of stuff. You have Gary—get the rest donated."

That was pretty much how the rest of the campaign went until the primary. There was great instructional value in this, as I would eventually learn. Every need was an opportunity to get someone involved and more committed to the campaign. I had to learn how to ask people to donate things and how to scramble for resources, a necessary skill every successful civic entrepreneur eventually develops.

Most important, I made many lifelong friends on the Hart campaign, several of whom, including Eric Schwarz and Billy Shore, would play critical roles in helping to launch, develop, and grow City Year, and in Eli Segal's case, found and lead Ameri-Corps. All of them would continue to work to make a real difference in our country.

After the Hart campaign, I returned to Harvard to attend law school, and Michael Brown moved to New York City to work for the City Volunteer Corps (CVC), a model national service program New York Mayor Koch started because the federal government wasn't doing anything on the idea of national service. It was during that year that Michael and I first started talking about trying to start a similar program in Boston.

Interestingly, we came full circle in our thinking on how national service should happen in America. We saw that national service wasn't moving much in Washington, D.C., and indeed, many people, even those who liked the idea, questioned whether it could ever work. We realized that if national service was going to happen, it likely wouldn't start at the federal level with a federal program, but rather it had to come from the grassroots. It would need some local models to demonstrate the ideas, principles and values of national service—to show how it could work in practice—before it would become national policy.

Michael and I used the time in law school in part to prepare to launch City Year. We did this primarily in three ways. First, we studied all of the existing programs we could in the country. We learned that Honda, the Japanese car company, buys one model of every single car made every year and studies each of them for their best innovations and designs, and then incorporates the best things they learn into their new car designs. We decided to take the same approach in designing City Year. And the wonderful thing about the national service movement is that it was full of civic minded people who were more than happy to share experiences and lessons learned with two young idealistic law students who wanted to join their cause.

In addition to learning from CVC, we also studied many other innovative, local programs, including the San Francisco Conservation Corps, where we welcomed the tutelage of the extraordinary Robert Burkhardt; the East Bay Conservation Corps, which was founded by the indefatigable Joanna Lennon; the California Conservation Corps which proudly—and accurately—came up with the motto: "Hard work, low pay, miserable conditions," and the Los Angeles Conservation Corps led by Martha Diepenbrock and Bruce Saito. We also talked to Peace Corps alumni and Coro alumni[6]; we became good friends with Roger Landrum and Frank Slobig, the co-founders and co-directors of Youth Service America, the nation's leading policy and advocacy organization for national service, as well as Don Eberly, founder of the National Service Secretariet, who had dedicated his life to the cause of national service. We attended the annual National Association of Service and Conservation

Corps (now the Corps Network) conference and met numerous wonderful people who shared their experience and offered to help us. Our goal was to learn as much as possible from leaders and practitioners in the field so that we might become experts ourselves. We knew that when it came time to ask people to support us financially and to help us launch City Year, we needed to be absolutely sure of our program and why it would be a breakthrough approach. Expertise would be the key to our sales pitch and to getting the model right.

The second thing we did to prepare to found City Year was to explore some of the intellectual underpinnings of national service while we were in law school. At Harvard Law, we were exposed to a new interpretation of the founding of America known as "civic republicanism." Civic Republicans, such as theorists Gordon Wood and Bernard Bailyn and law school professors Cass Sunstein, Frank Michelman, Richard Parker and others, argued that our nation's founders were not interested in simply establishing a democracy that would facilitate competing interest groups in a political "marketplace." Rather, they were striving for something greater—a republic that would encourage civic virtue in its citizens who would, through deliberation and civic engagement, seek the common good and common interest. Thomas Jefferson, who was in France as ambassador when the Constitution was being written and adopted, reviewed it and sent back his comments highlighting an area of serious concern. He argued that the Constitutional Convention had designed a system of government that rested on the citizens as the base that legitimated government power and authority, and yet it had nothing in the constitutional framework that enabled and encouraged citizens to act as citizens—it was all representative.

Jefferson proposed two ideas in response. First, that the town meeting, which had been popularized in New England, be written right into the constitutional system as the first locus of government whereby citizens could come together, make local decisions and deliberate about the great issues of the day and pass their deliberated recommendations on to their elected representatives.

Second, every twenty years or so, there should be another Constitutional Convention, whereby each generation would have to completely review the Constitution and decide what to keep, what to get rid of, and what to change. Jefferson thought that the "dead hand" of one generation shouldn't rule over future generations. Jefferson, an avid student of history, knew that America would continue to change and grow, and that what the founding generation designed for the Constitution, and the compromises they struck, may not necessarily apply as time moved on. And as a strong believer in small "d" democracy, Jefferson felt that each generation of Americans should have to go through that same constitutional process of reviewing and deciding what was most important to them.

Neither of Jefferson's ideas was adopted. During law school, we came to see national service as another idea that could meet Jefferson's concerns—the validity of which was even more evident in 1980s America. It confirmed in our minds the notion that national service could become "the missing link" in American democracy. (I got so excited about this theory, that I wrote my third year law school paper—like a law school thesis—under the guidance of visiting Professor Cass Sunstein on national service as a civic republican institution.)

Finally, we took advantage of our time in law school to put together the initial plan for City Year and what it would take to make it happen. We even secured a meeting with the President of Harvard, Derek Bok, who gave us strong encouragement to make our dream a reality. As my third year of law school progressed, I had to face a decision. Michael and I had received a strong response from a variety of people to the notion of trying to start City Year. Some of my friends were accepting corporate law offers, others were joining legal aid organizations or getting ready to start judicial clerkships. City Year was a great dream but I also had to figure out how to pay my expenses if I chose to try to get it going. My dad advised that I should accept one of the excellent corporate law offers, gain some great experience and make some money to pay off my student loans, and then after a few years, when I was established, get City Year started. My mom, characteristically, advised that I should do what would make me the most happy, and that if I really believed in City Year, I should pursue that. My parents, who had made enormous sacrifices to educate me and my siblings, all of whom were still in college at the time, were not in a position to help me financially. Ultimately, they both said they would support whatever decision I made.

As the deadline for accepting or rejecting the corporate law offers approached, I thought hard about what I should do. Through the time Michael and I had put in working on and studying the idea of national service and developing the plan for City Year, I was convinced the idea of national service was an idea whose time had come. I also believed that a model like City Year could play a significant role in helping to bring it about and influencing how it was designed. I figured that someone would be willing to put up some initial money to help get City Year off of the ground and had two promising prospects right at Harvard Law School: the Harvard Fellowship in Public Interest Law and a new Loan Forgiveness program the school had just started. So, I turned down my corporate law offers and dove into preparing my applications for the Public Interest fellowship and loan forgiveness programs.

The Harvard Fellowship in Public Interest Law was a special

program started by Harvard Law Students whereby graduating students going into private law practice would donate a small percentage of their first year salary (usually about one percent) to provide fellowships of between $10,000 to $15,000 to their peers who wanted to pursue social justice work right out of law school. I saw this fellowship as my key opportunity as it would at least give me enough money to live on once I graduated. It would also validate my decision to use my legal education to try to start City Year and something I could point to as I approached other potential funders. With Michael's help, I put together an eighty-page application, including a full business plan for City Year, letters of recommendation, and a number of appendices to back it up. I made it to the final round interviews, and was very hopeful that I would be selected, but it wasn't meant to be. A group of my peers who made up the committee concluded that what I wanted to do didn't fit their criteria, and they turned me down.

I then applied for a new student loan forgiveness program that Harvard Law School had just launched for graduates who were doing public interest work. I thought for sure I would be selected for this program, especially because I had no source of financial support to pursue City Year and more than met the income guidelines. I pointed to my third year paper on national service, and other work I had done that informed the development of City Year while in law school. I also said that trying to develop national service was very much in keeping with legal ideals. I even pointed out that trying to convince people to support City Year was like one neverending oral argument and writing grant proposals was like writing legal briefs, but to no avail. They also concluded I didn't fit the purpose of the program.

These two rejections coming right on top of each other were a huge disappointment, especially because they came from students and administrators at Harvard Law School. In the back of my

mind, I just believed I would get accepted for both of these programs and would be able to start City Year. If I couldn't convince
folks at Harvard to support me, how would I cope with total
strangers? I didn't really have any back-up plan and would be
graduating in a matter of weeks. I learned right away and faced
the stark reality that while I thought City Year was a wonderful
idea, it was not going to be an easy road to get support for it.

2

BE PREPARED TO GIVE
UP YOUR SHIRT

Despite all our strategizing and preplanning, the event that cata-
pulted City Year from a tiny, largely unknown Boston experiment
to a nationally recognized brand was, essentially, an inspired fluke.
The lesson of the story: you never know who is going to be in a
position to help you, so be open to everyone; and the best ambassadors for any program are not its founders and theorists, but
the people who sign up for it and make it their own.

The unexpected growth opportunity presented itself three
years after Michael Brown and I founded City Year. We were
standing inside our headquarters, a cavernous hall of a converted
warehouse, on a frigid December day in the old waterfront district of Boston. By this time, City Year had grown to 100 corps
members in Boston and served 2,500 children throughout the
city. Michael and I developed City Year to be a model program
that showcased the power of service to change lives and communities, and unite citizens from every walk of life. But it would
only be a model that was adopted elsewhere if we could attract
leaders to visit it and be inspired. Otherwise, we would labor on
being largely ignored. For that reason, we always welcomed vis-

itors, as a way to leverage our work and have a larger impact beyond the direct service City Year completed. Now, on this chilly December day, we were about to get a visit from a long-shot presidential candidate: a young governor from Arkansas named Bill Clinton, who at that time barely registered around three percent national name recognition in the polls. Clinton had heard that City Year might be a model for national service, an idea he believed passionately in, so his campaign had called and asked if he could come visit.

City Year headquarters always had a scrappy, start-up feel, with lots of donated, mismatched furniture, exposed wooden beams and pipes, a beautiful hardwood floor, and a large open space for full community meetings. The offices around this open space were partitioned cubicles. What they lacked in privacy they made up for by encouraging lots of teamwork and collaboration, and a free flow of ideas. As a staff, we had spent several weekends scraping old paint off the walls and ceilings, "prepping" it for professional union workers who donated their time to transform an old abandoned warehouse space into a funky, functioning, youth corps command center. We had built most of the tables ourselves from old doors nailed to sawhorses. The walls were covered with whiteboards and a blizzard of paper and to-do lists. Overlooking it all were pictures of our heroes—John F. Kennedy, Robert F. Kennedy, Martin Luther King, Gandhi, and more.

We loved the atmosphere, and the fact that we wasted no money on frills and décor. But our mean-and-lean look wasn't exactly the perfect backdrop for a visit from a presidential candidate. Our staff had whipped through the offices, trying to transform the controlled chaos of our workspace into something slightly more presentable. It had all come together well enough and we had assembled a great audience for Governor Clinton, including Boston Mayor Ray Flynn, Mitt Romney, CEO of Bain and Company and a strong City Year champion, Hubie Jones, a civic leader and Dean of the Boston University School of Social Work, all of whom waited patiently with seven corps members from seven different socio-economic, ethnic, and educational backgrounds.

The governor was running late, and as soon as Clinton's van pulled up, he jumped out and immediately grabbed my out-stretched hand with his right hand as he threw his left around my shoulder. I was enveloped in the famous "Clinton grip," and felt the power of his charm. He was larger than I had imagined. His hands were huge and his arm length enveloping. Rather than using his size to intimidate, he pulled me to him in an inviting way, fixed his gaze directly at me as if I was the only person there, and immediately put me at ease. I said: "Hello Governor Clinton, I'm Alan Khazei, City Year Co-Founder. We are so honored to have you here and deeply appreciate your taking the time from your busy campaign schedule to visit with us today. We have the mayor, some special guests and some City Year corps members waiting for you inside, so if you could just follow me up these stairs we will get started right away."

Clinton responded as if we were old friends. "Alan, I've heard so many wonderful things about your City Year program," he said with that soft drawl. "I'm honored and excited to be here and know that I'm going to learn a lot from you all. Thank you for having me today. I've been so looking forward to this visit." But he had no intention of following my suggestion that we might start right away.

Many of our staff members, excited to meet this dynamic new presidential candidate, had gathered at the top of the stairs to say hello and shake his hand. Clinton, of course, was more than happy to pause and oblige. I was starting to panic. The mayor, Hubie, and Mitt Romney had already been waiting for some time. It was one of the biggest days in City Year's young life, and critical to the vision that Michael and I had been working so hard to bring to life, but all I could think was that the event might be about to break up before Clinton even got to the main hall.

Clinton, who would later be described by journalist Joe Klein as "The Natural" for his extraordinary political gifts, would not be hurried. He not only proceeded to shake every single City Year staffer's hand, he looked them in the eye and asked them a question. He made sure to make a personal connection with each and every one of them, and for the first time I saw up close the Clinton magic at work. I didn't have time to admire it, though. When he finally had completed his bid to convert everyone before him, I grabbed his arm and said, "Governor, we are going this way." I desperately tugged him toward the room where the mayor and others were waiting. But even a half-mugging wasn't enough to divert Clinton from what he does best: working potential voters one by one until everyone surrenders. Before I could get him into the reception area, he spotted out of the corner of his eye a couple of City Year staff he had somehow missed in his procession through the headquarters. He broke free from my grip, briskly turned away, and strolled over to them. "Hi, I'm Governor Clinton, I'm so excited to be here at City Year today," he announced, once again reaching his big hands out to touch and shake the hand of everyone before him. "What are your names? What do you do with City Year? I'm honored to meet you. Thank you for your work and service."

I had no choice but to abandon the schedule and let the man move through the room at his pace. If the mayor, Romney, Jones, or anyone else had to leave before the event even got started, there was nothing I could do. The planned ninety-minute event was clearly going to run overtime.

Luckily, there were only so many hands to shake. Clinton finally allowed me to steer him to the large open space in our headquarters where folks were waiting. He bounded over to the table we had set up and introduced himself to all the assembled dignitaries and corps members, pumped their hands, and said again with utter sincerity how glad he was to be with us. He had met Hubie just once before at a conference on social policy at Boston University a few years earlier, and gave him a big bear hug. "Hubie," he boomed, "I'm so glad that you are here. I didn't know you were coming." It was the first, but not at all the last, time I would witness his steel trap memory for names and faces.

Everyone was relaxed and smiling, and we settled down to business on folding metal chairs for what came to be one of our most effective tools for engaging public officials: a roundtable discussion with the City Year corps members. As we often did when we had visitors, we decided that the most powerful spokespeople for City Year would be our young corps members who had committed a year of their lives to service. Neither Michael nor I sat at the table; we were happy to let the program speak for itself.

Clinton removed his blue blazer, hung it on the back of his chair, and rolled up his sleeves. He opened with some very brief remarks, stating he was a strong believer in the idea of national service, was proud of our work, and that he was here mostly to listen and learn. He then pulled out a pad and pen so he could take notes as people talked.

Mayor Flynn, who had supported City Year from the very beginning (and would later become Clinton's ambassador to the Vatican), spoke about City Year's partnership with the city and our strong work in the public schools. Hubie Jones spoke about City Year's approach to making change from the grassroots up, and that a key part of our model was partnering with community based organizations and uniting young people from all backgrounds in a shared mission of service as we developed them into

51

leaders. Mitt Romney, who as part of his Mormon faith had spent two years in service, explained City Year's strong corporate partnership program with companies like his, Bain, and others providing not just financial support, but employee volunteer time as well, in a win-win situation for both City Year and the companies. As a leading Republican businessperson, we especially appreciated his presence that day. We wanted to send the message that we were a non-partisan organization, even when we hosted a Democratic Presidential candidate.

Despite these strong testimonials from leading Bostonians, it was the corps members themselves who made the most compelling case for City Year and service. Individually, they spoke about being a first-generation Dominican family, or about what it was like to come from streets that were dangerous and without rules, and how City Year was a way to transcend the violence. Many speakers talked about how, in spite of having so many issues in common with other members of the City Year corps, there had been no connections or efforts to work together until City Year had begun to establish them. Each shared stories about the difference they were making through their service projects and how they were one by one changing lives and communities.

Stephen Spaloss, in particular, riveted Clinton's attention. He told Clinton about growing up as a tough African-American kid who was branded a "dolt" early in school by his teacher and turned to life in the streets. Eventually, his antics landed him in front of a judge, who assigned him a "City Year," rather than jail, to straighten him out. Spaloss confessed he had barely heard of City Year, and then explained to Clinton that his first service project focused on developing and presenting a violence-prevention curriculum to inner city middle school children. Spaloss admitted how uncomfortable that made him feel, how hard it was to confront his own violent behavior. But it had also made him realize that he could turn his past into an asset because of his firsthand experience that violence was a dangerous trap that children had to work to avoid.

Stephen also explained to the rapt Clinton how he had become best friends with someone that, were it not for City Year, he never would have met. Creighton Reed was a graduate of Phillips Exeter Preparatory Academy and on his way to Harvard. He came from a world of privilege and opportunity entirely alien to Stephen. Before Stephen got to know Creighton, he had assumed that all "preppies" were stuck up and didn't care at all about what went on in the city or its neighborhoods. But Creighton was funny, passionate, and full of concern for what was happening in those parts of Boston City Year was working in. His very presence in the corps forced Stephen to rethink all his stereotypes about people. Now he was closer to Creighton than he was to most of his old gang. And Creighton had learned just as much from Stephen.

The two friends shared an apartment with three other City Year corps members in Somerville. They called themselves the "fearsome fivesome frat." Stephen told a story to illustrate how he came to rethink his preconceptions in relation to his friendship with Creighton:

> "Creighton was a big guy—6'2" and could bench-press 350 pounds. He was always eating—his favorite snack was to dip raw spaghetti in honey. One night, I got really sick. I had a really high fever, and Creighton heard me stumbling around in the hallway and came out to see what was going on. He took one look at me and put me to bed with a wet cloth on my head. I remember waking up a few hours later to a dark room, and there was Creighton, sitting on the floor next to the bed, dipping raw spaghetti into honey. I asked him what he was doing there and he said he was just making sure I was okay. I

was 21 years old when I went to do City Year and I had a perspective that was formed by my previous experiences, but it was things like that that broke down my preconceptions. I could no longer say: 'I think an Exeter kid is this' or 'I think a Harvard kid is that.' Because I knew Creighton, and he was so much more than that."

Clinton was visibly moved.

At the time of the roundtable, Stephen was in his second year at City Year as a senior corps member, and he remembers feeling antsy that day as the roundtable began. He had participated in other roundtables and although he understood the importance of sharing City Year's work with visitors, that morning he wanted to be working with kids in Chelsea, not sitting at City Year headquarters. As the corps members began to tell their stories, however, and as Clinton soon showed himself to be a very active listener, Stephen began to feel engaged and excited. He had begun to learn to "read people" through his experiences with City Year, and what he saw of Clinton, was someone who was deeply interested in hearing what he had to say. As Stephen tells it:

> "Most of my experiences in these roundtables, if I told people too much deep stuff about me, they would flinch and be uncomfortable. Clinton was different. I remember him saying: 'tell me everything.' And I said: 'Really? Everything?' And he said yes. So I told him more about myself than I had told anyone in a roundtable. You know how sometimes you carry things around until you can finally let them go? I had been carrying a lot of things. Bad feelings about how I hadn't done enough to stop friends' suicides. A lot of violence I'd been part of. With Clinton, it was so easy to talk: He wasn't judging me. I didn't understand politics at the time, but if you had asked me if he was going to win the presidency I would have said yes, because he got me believing in politics by giving me a

sense of what politics could do. It wasn't because I had met
him, it was because he listened so deeply. I had a sense of how
grassroots change and politics might connect."

When the session drew to a close almost two hours later, Clinton stood up and told the assembled crowd: "I have always believed in the idea of national service. You all have made it real
for me today. I promise you that if I become President, I will
make this a national program. It has the potential to transform
America."

Stephen was so moved by this response, and the way that Clinton seemed to really get what City Year was all about, he suddenly took off his City Year sweatshirt and handed it to Clinton.
"Thank you so much for coming," he said, choking up a little. "I
want you to have my sweatshirt and I hope that you don't forget
about us."

"Don't worry, I never will," Clinton responded. And then he
wrapped Stephen in a big bear hug.

After Clinton was whisked away, I strode over to Stephen.
"Okay, you gave away your official uniform sweatshirt," I said
with mock severity, "What are you going to do now? You know
you have to be in full uniform every day." Stephen was caught
totally off-guard. "Uh, uh, I didn't know, I just felt it was the right
thing to do," he stammered. I let him sweat for a second and then
replied "Don't worry, I'm sure we can manage to find another
one for you. That was just awesome."

Almost exactly one year later, the day before Thanksgiving, I
was sitting in my apartment packing up to get ready to head
home to New Hampshire to see my folks. The television was on
in the background and CNN was showing footage of now Pres-
ident-elect Clinton finishing up a jog. I saw a flash of white let-

tering on a black sweatshirt and did a double-take. Clinton was wearing Stephen Spaloss's City Year sweatshirt. He had kept that sweatshirt somewhere safe throughout the grueling primary and then general election campaign. And now that he had won, and was going to be president of the United States, he was sending a beautiful little message about what he cared about.

As I listened, transfixed, a sweating Clinton explained to the reporters gathered around him that establishing a national service program would be one of his top four priorities as president. Instantly, my phone rang. I didn't even say hello and ask who it was. I knew it was Michael Brown. "Are you watching this?!? This is incredible," he blurted. "Yeah, it's awesome!" I responded. "Let's get off the phone and make sure we catch every word." Click. Click.

In the following weeks, President Clinton would wear Stephen's City Year sweatshirt over and over. It got to the point that I became more interested in Clinton's jogging schedule than his news conferences. Our phone started ringing off the hook with inquiries from the news media, supporters, and new champions. Al From, Founding Chairman of the Democratic Leadership Council and head of Clinton's transition effort, called to say he was bringing a high-powered group, led by Senator Sam Nunn and Congressman Dave McCurdy, to visit City Year and learn from what we were doing. I was even more excited when I got a confidential call from an old friend, Eli Segal, whom I had first met during Gary Hart's 1984 presidential campaign, telling me that he wanted to spend a couple of days at City Year right away, because the new president had just asked him to lead the effort to create his national service program (as Eli would soon show, President Clinton could not have picked a better person to ensure that his vision would become reality).

It was a transformative leap, unimaginable from our beginnings barely more than four years earlier and impossible without two spontaneously generous acts: that Governor Clinton gave City Year his time and focus, and that Stephen Spaloss gave the governor his sweatshirt.

▼▲▼

City Year, a newly minted 501C3 not-for-profit, began its first program on a beautiful sun-filled morning on Saturday July 2, 1988. Gathered with Michael Brown and me were fifty young people ages seventeen to twenty-one, excitedly and nervously waiting to board the boat to Thompson's Island, part of the Boston Harbor Islands National Park. They represented a panoply of diversity from the street corners and neighborhoods of Greater Boston: African-American, Asian, Caucasian, and Latino, inner-city and suburban, low-, middle-, and upper-income, Ivy Leaguers and gang-connected youth. They were coming together for a summer of service in exchange for $100 a weekend and a college scholarship of $500 if they successfully graduated the program. They had been recruited by a magical woman, Kristen Atwood, who mixed the spontaneity, delight, and magic of Mary Poppins, with the iron determination and will of Margaret Thatcher in equal measure. Kristen left no stone unturned to find an extremely diverse and compelling founding group for City Year's summer pilot program. From roller skating at Chez Vous, a popular rink in Boston's inner city, to connecting to ministers, priests, and rabbis, to reaching out to high school guidance counselors and leading youth workers, promising them one spot in the corps if they would refer at least three to five great young people, Kristen was the key to recruiting that first group of City Year summer program corps members.

As I looked at the inaugural City Year corps members, I suggested to Michael that I use the Moccasins prayer, and the "Ripples" quote from Robert Kennedy's speech in South Africa as a way to explain to them what City Year was about. The Moccasins prayer says: "Great spirit, grant that I shall not criticize my brother or sister until I have walked a mile in his or her moccasins."

"Ripples" refers to Robert Kennedy's assertion that: "It is from numberless diverse acts of courage and belief that human history is thus shaped. Each time a man stands up for an ideal, or acts to improve the lot of others, or strikes out against injustice, he sends forth a tiny ripple of hope, and crossing each other from a million different centers of energy and daring, those ripples build a current which can sweep down the mightiest walls of oppression and resistance."[7]

I wanted to communicate the importance of appreciating diversity and empathy, and to challenge the corps members to take the time to get to know one another, and to try and understand their fellow corps members, as well as the people they would be serving and working with, before judging them, no matter what their background. I also emphasized that City Year would give them a chance to walk a mile in the moccasins of many people they would be serving with or working with, people they would otherwise never have a chance to know, and that they should seize that opportunity.

I explained to the corps the RFK quote meant their principle job was to try to send ripples, no matter how small, as together those ripples would build a mighty current that ultimately would change the world. To this day, every meeting at City Year begins with people sharing their "ripples"—stories of courage, belief, and inspiration. To these quotes, we have added a set of short inspirational stories and aphorisms from other heroes and role models, including Margaret Mead, Gandhi, and Nelson Mandela, and together they have become our Founding Stories which help to explain the values City Year is built on and which guide our work.

The first City Year service mission included assisting handicapped children at Camp Joy (by organizing the first ever Special Olympics for them), working for the neighborhood kids in Roxbury (by reclaiming and re-opening the Mt. Street Pleasant Tot Lot), brightening the lives of the homeless men staying at the Pine Street Inn (by landscaping their grounds and rebuilding their gardens), and organizing summer camp activities for needy children. We also did painting and rehab work at the Elizabeth Stone House, which provided transitional housing for women who were victims of domestic violence. And we conducted home repair work for senior citizens living in East Boston so that they could stay living independently in their homes. We also worked with a Roxbury-based community development organization to reclaim vacant lots, construct a fence for safety, and conduct day trips for neighborhood children. And we served at the Mass Hospital School where we worked directly with handicapped children through reading, mentoring, and engaging them in physical activities.

In addition, the mission was for all City Year corps members to serve as role models who would supplant the image of the "me" generation with the example of a "we" generation. (Just a year earlier the prevailing ethos of the times seemed to have been captured by the film *Wall Street* in which the character Gordon Gecko memorably snarled, "Greed is good.") Through their idealism and service, they could show that they and their young peers were not the selfish, self-centered, and self-absorbed caricatures often portrayed in the popular media. Instead, they were a dedicated generation, ready and willing to try to change the world if challenged and given the chance. Our objective, I concluded, was not just to have a successful summer pilot program, so that we could open a full-year City Year program a year later, but to contribute to a new movement for national service with the goal of creating a voluntary and universal program in which millions could participate. It would begin with, and depend on, fifty young people in Boston.

After studying other programs, and consulting with Charlie Rose, the foremost expert on young people in Boston, who led Mayor Flynn's youth work and was a founding City Year board member, and other youth experts including Stanley Pollack, we had decided to launch the first City Year pilot with a four-day retreat that was a combination of boot camp and summer camp. Activities included workshops on diversity, the history of national service, understanding the city of Boston, teamwork, and the issues we would be tackling that summer through our service. We also had the corps go through a ropes course and a set of trust building exercises. Overall, it was a powerful, meaningful, and productive launch, perhaps best summed up by something none of us had planned.

In that founding corps, we had two hearing impaired young people, Winda Maldonado and Jack Lyons. Kristen, who knew sign language, was determined to make the founding City Year corps as inclusive as possible.

Everyone embraced the idea of having Jack and Winda in the summer corps, but suddenly Jack ran across to Kristen and me, very agitated. He signed to Kristen that he had lost his ring in the field where we had been doing the activities. It had been given to him by his father, and it was his most precious possession. He was completely distraught.

The three of us started searching for the ring, and soon, without anyone asking, all fifty corps members and ten staff had joined the effort, but no one could find the ring. Then someone suggested that everyone should get on our hands and knees, side by side and slowly crawl across the field. About three quarters of the way down the field, a twenty-year-old staff member, Mitch Berman, jumped up and yelled that he had found a ring. He threw his arm in the air and pretended to throw the ring sky-high. Everyone laughed, and Jack came running over to Mitch and hugged him. It had taken the entire corps and staff working together to find that ring. Everyone got the message right away that City Year was about teamwork and persistence. I turned to Kristen and said, "City Year is surely blessed." I had a very strong feeling from that moment that the organization was going to work.

It was a sweet feeling after a long period of uncertainty. Just thirteen months earlier I had graduated from Harvard Law School wondering how I would pay my bills after being turned down for the public service fellowship. At the time, I was living at Currier House as the pre-law tutor, courtesy of a program in which the undergraduate houses at Harvard gave graduate students free room and board in exchange for advising the undergrads living in the dorm. Currier was where I had lived as an undergraduate, and I had moved back there during my third year of law school to help pay for school.

There was an understandable catch, though. Once you completed your advanced degree and graduated, you were supposed to leave because you no longer had an official Harvard affiliation. While there, I had become good friends with Holly Davidson and Greg Nagy, the co-masters of Currier House. Holly had even sat in on a couple of our original planning meetings for City Year, many of which we held at Currier. She was extremely enthusiastic about what I wanted to do after law school. So, facing the prospect of soon being out on the street, I went to see her.

I explained my predicament and asked Holly if there was any way I could stay on at Currier House, as I needed a place to live while working to get City Year started. Holly didn't miss a beat. "Well, the official rules say no," she said. "But, Greg and I are the masters of Currier House, at least that's what Harvard tells us, so let me look into it and let's meet again soon."

My mother has often reminded me that when God closes a door, he opens a window. Sure enough, less than a week later Holly called and said, "Let's get together. I have an update for you." She told me she and Greg had decided to create a new position called Public Service Tutor. The Public Service Tutor would advise the students on careers in public service, and Holly wanted to know if I wanted to apply for it. I crawled through that open window as quickly as I could.

In this way, Holly Davidson and Greg Nagy became the first supporters of City Year. Having secured a place to live at Harvard, I then approached the government department about continuing on as a teaching fellow for the "Introduction to Government" and "American Presidency" classes. I had taught both of those while in law school. Again, I was welcomed, and the government department was happy to keep me on. So, in addition to room and board, I would be earning some money to cover my expenses. All in all, I made about $10,000 that first year out of law school. Not anywhere near the Wall Street salaries I had been offered, but I was "following my bliss," as Joseph Campbell counsels in *The Power of Myth* and was excited for the future.

Once settled at Harvard, I focused on recruiting the initial team to work with me and Michael Brown. Neil Silverston, who was graduating from Harvard Business School, was thoughtful, bright, and I soon discovered that he had a very strong justice nerve. He was anxious to use his Harvard Business School degree to make a difference. He liked the concept for City Year right away, and also liked the idea of joining me and Michael in becoming a "civic entrepreneur." His family had a real estate business and he said if he did City Year, he could do that part-time in order to pay his bills. Neil had worked at Bain and Company, a premier management consulting firm based in Boston, between college and business school.

At the same time, I was continuing a conversation about City Year with a good friend Jennie Eplett. Jennie is an extraordinary person. She just exudes positive energy and a passion for changing the world. She is a natural recruiter of people and has a completely infectious enthusiasm for whatever project she is putting her great talent toward. I had met her on Gary Hart's campaign and we became fast friends while she was dating Sean Reilly, a good friend from college, with whom Michael and I shared an apartment during my second year of law school. After graduating from Wellesley, Jennie had joined the two-year management training program at E.F. Hutton. I knew she would be finishing up that program at the same time I was graduating from law school, so I started talking to her about City Year right from the beginning. Over many conversations Jennie shared that Wall Street wasn't really her passion and that she planned to leave E.F. Hutton after the two-year stint was up. So I wrote her a long handwritten letter explaining that I was going to try to start City Year right after law school and that I couldn't think of anyone better to help get it off the ground. I asked her to please think hard about joining me as soon as she could.

I was thrilled when Jennie called and said "I'm in!" To top it off, she had saved some money from her two years on Wall Street and said initially she could work as a volunteer. In addition to doing all of the general work to get City Year started, Jennie agreed to lead the fundraising effort.

The four of us, Neil, Jennie, Michael, and I all shared a desire to change the world and felt that together we would be unstoppable. Having this team was essential to getting City Year off the ground. After City Year was up and running and had been operating for a few years, when people asked me or Michael for advice on how to be a civic entrepreneur, we would always say, "Find a partner that makes everything easier and more fun and then focus on building a strong team. Everything flows from that." It is still our number one rule.

We got to work refining the business plan for City Year, and trying to raise $200,000 to cover the budget for that first pilot summer program. We had decided to start with a summer pilot program, rather than a full-year program, because raising the million dollars necessary for a full-year of City Year, when we had absolutely no track record, was probably impossible. But raising $200,000 for a brand-new program, while a stretch, seemed do-able—or, at least, we hoped it was. It was essential to us that we have a very diverse group of young people in the corps because one of the main ideas we wanted to demonstrate was that national service could unite people from all backgrounds and help to complete the civil rights movement. And we thought it would be much easier to achieve that diversity, at least initially, with a summer program. Also, we knew that many successful businesses—and we wanted to apply proven business principles to our approach whenever we could—often pilot their ideas. We needed to do the same thing, and a summer program would give us a chance to test out our model and our approach. It would also give us something tangible to point to—assuming it worked—when trying to raise a million dollars for the full-year program.

We met with anyone and everyone: from people who could help develop service projects, to others who could help with recruiting participants, to others who could help us navigate Boston politics and neighborhoods, to potential board members, to anyone who could help us raise the money we needed. Michael got his father's law firm, Sherin and Lodgen, to donate their services to get us incorporated and to file our tax exempt status; without that we wouldn't be able to operate.

We were fired up and full of hope and dreams. But we simply hadn't realized how hard it would be to raise even our "pilot" sum of $200,000. We were young, extremely idealistic, passionate about the idea of national service and City Year, and we assumed people naturally would be willing to give us the money to get it launched. We asked every person we met with for advice and help on fundraising, and after each meeting, Neil would say, "Well, I think we are thirty handshakes away from getting some money." Eventually, it was down to twenty handshakes, then fifteen. We all believed that if we just met with enough people, eventually someone would support City Year financially.

That philosophy eventually proved true, but it was hard to keep the faith when we didn't raise any money at all during the first six months. In December, Neil finally reported that The Analytical Sciences Corporation (TASC) was going to make a donation of $1,000 to get City Year going. It was one half of one percent of what we needed. But it was a start.

We may not have raised a lot of money, but during this fallow time we did get some good advice. One meeting was with Bob Farmer, who had led the fundraising for the 1988 Dukakis for President campaign, at that time the most successful presidential campaign fundraising effort ever. We eventually connected with Paul Rosenberg, who had worked with him on the Dukakis campaign and agreed to do fundraising training with our team.

Paul said there were three basic rules to fundraising. First, people give to people. Yes, your idea is important and your plans are important, but they need to connect with you, the person asking them for the money. Second, urgency is critical. You need to give people a sense that you needed the money yesterday, Paul counseled. There are a lot of great causes out there, and people will always wait to fund you, thinking something more worthy may come along. Unless, Paul emphasized, they have the sense that you really need the money right away, and that the entire project might otherwise not happen. Third, Paul encouraged us to be specific about exactly what the money would be used for. People want to know what their money is going to fund so they know how it is making a difference.

Twenty years later, when people come to ask me for fundraising advice, I always start with these three basic rules.

Our big break finally came through a good friend of mine and Michael's from law school, Nancy Kelley, who introduced us to Winthrop (Win) Knowlton at the Center for Business and Government at the Kennedy School at Harvard.

Win was terrific. He took a great interest in what we were doing. He said he was a passionate believer in national service and also admired how we were using our educations. Right away, he offered to help. He asked what we needed. We responded we needed an office and we needed to raise $200,000 to fund our pilot program. He immediately offered us a spare office on Church Street in Harvard Square for free. We jumped at it—I was getting tired of working out of my dorm room, and we felt that once we had an office, City Year would become more real. I will never forget the excitement we felt of getting our first proper office, and donated at that. It was about 12' by 12' and could barely fit four small desks and chairs, but we loved it. We quickly moved in and hung posters of our heroes, Bobby Kennedy and Martin Luther King, on the walls.

Win also said he thought he could help us with fundraising. By then, we had developed a good strategy for our fundraising pitch, which directly addressed fundraising rule number three, "specificity." Taking a page from the 1984 Olympics in Los Angeles, we had decided to pitch companies on sponsoring a full City Year team of ten corps members for $25,000 per team. The 1984 Olympics, led by Peter Ueberroth, was the first Olympics to sell corporate sponsorships, because most previous Olympics had lost money. It was extremely successful; the games made a profit. Seeing that, we thought if companies would sponsor teams of young athletes, maybe they would sponsor teams of young people in service.

Our core theory for City Year was that it was all about promoting strong citizenship. We were asking young people to be Big Citizens by dedicating their energy full-time to community service for just a small stipend. We were asking non-profits and government agencies to be Big Citizens by taking on young people—who did not have a lot of skills or previous work experience—and having them do meaningful work in partnership with their organizations. And we wanted to show that the private sector could also be Big Citizens by not just providing money, but by also getting involved with the program. So, when approaching companies to sponsor a team, we asked them to provide mentors for our corps members and to have their employees join us for a day of service. As Paul had recommended, this would give companies a very tangible sense of what their sponsorship money was actually doing in the community.

We set the $25,000 sponsorship level for each team because that would cover the cost of the team leader, as well as the stipends and scholarships for the ten corps members. It would also cover the costs of their uniforms and some supplies. And, we figured if we could get each team sponsored that would raise $125,000 in total, more than half of our target. (Another fundraising rule we learned over time was to try to raise half of the money you need with a few big gifts, and then you can piece together the other half with numerous smaller gifts of various levels.)

Win Knowlton opened the doors to us at The Equitable Insurance Company, but they declined to sponsor a team, saying the top grant they could give us was for $20,000. So we quickly shifted gears and presented them with a proposal to be our training sponsor. Next, Win arranged for us to see Ira Jackson and Judith Kidd at Bank of Boston. We joined them for a private lunch in a beautiful, wood-paneled private dining room that just screamed, "This bank is over 200 years old and has a proud tradition." Ira and Judith were open to new ideas, though. They got the concept behind City Year right away. I think we reminded them of themselves when they were our age. They were intrigued by our corporate team sponsor concept.

Being bankers, though, they understandably wanted to make sure we could pull off our ambitious plans. Ira Jackson, in particular, grilled us, asking detailed questions about our plans for recruitment and for service projects. He pointedly stated, "You all say you are about diversity, but you are a bunch of white folks from Ivy League schools. How are you going to pull this off?" Ira also didn't like the name City Year, as he didn't think it communicated what we were trying to accomplish. But he finished the meeting by saying, "Get us a proposal right away, but I have a set of benchmarks I will need you to meet before we can commit to funding your effort." Then, he laid out key progress he wanted to see us make in the area of recruitment, service project development, diversity on our staff team, and more. He and Judith didn't just send us on our way, however, they offered to make introductions and open doors so that we could have the best chance of meeting the benchmarks they considered essential to our success.

Soon after the Bank of Boston meeting, Neil met Kristen Atwood. Kristen had read our four-page description of City Year (somehow received via the Brown University placement office), and had decided she just had to be part of this new endeavor. Neil told us he thought Kristen was exactly the person we needed to lead the recruitment effort for our corps. Still, Michael and my initial reaction was we hadn't raised any real money yet so we couldn't afford to bring her in. Neil, believing she would blow us away, said "Just meet her, and then let's discuss it."

Neil was right. Kristen went to South Africa as a college student in the early 1980s and arranged to be smuggled into Soweto, where white people were not allowed, because she needed to see what was happening firsthand. Once she shared this story, we were smitten. We told her we hadn't raised any money yet, but had a proposal pending with the Bank of Boston and would likely hear back about six to eight weeks later. We promised her she would be the first person on the payroll as soon as we got the grant. Kristen said immediately that she was willing to start right away and work as a volunteer until we had raised some money. We offered her the job of recruitment director, and took the risk of bringing on our very first employee before we had raised any money to pay her.

And as soon as Kristen started recruiting the corps, we photocopied their applications and began collating them into groups of ten to create whole teams on paper. We brought them along to potential funders and said: "These young people are ready to serve. Read their comments about their desire to make a difference. Please fund them and allow them to serve." We would leave these applications behind and it proved powerfully effective. Anyone who read them left impressed by the idealism and commitment expressed by our first applicants.

Along with Kristen, who joined us in February of 1988, we

began to recruit other volunteers to round out our team. Jennie, who is a natural pied piper, soon brought on Sean's sister, Anna Reilly, to help put together our training program. Anna, who has an infectious and bountiful laugh, and boundless energy like Tigger from Winnie-the-Pooh, had experience with the National Outdoor Leadership School (NOLS) program and was ideal for the training director role. Jennie also recruited her good friend, Deb Taft, an organizational expert, to help with fundraising and organizational development. Until the start of the summer program, when we could afford to finally pay them, both Anna and Deb worked solely as volunteers, often putting in anywhere from twenty to forty hours a week. Michael reached out to Lisa Ulrich, who had worked with him on service projects at the City Volunteer Corps. Lisa, who was at the Kennedy School, invited us to her apartment in Cambridge so we could make our pitch. That was typical of Lisa. We were asking her to join our effort, and she offered to make us dinner. By the end of the dinner, she agreed to join up and we had our volunteer Director for Service Projects. Lisa, in turn, recruited a fellow Kennedy School student, Anthony Reese, to join our effort as a Team Leader for the summer program. The ripples were already spreading.

At the same time, we had been working on assembling a Board of Directors. We were thrilled and honored when Matina Horner, the president of Radcliffe, agreed to be our first chair. Former Senator Paul Tsongas also agreed to join the board, and did both media and fundraising outreach for us. Senator Tsongas was a particular hero and role model for us. As well as crafting the Senate companion to Leon Panetta's House bill, he was a Peace Corp alumnus, and agreed to join us partly because, "The Peace Corps changed my life and I'm a strong believer in national service and you remind me of me when I was your age." We told Tsongas we were having trouble raising money. We had dutifully applied to all of the major foundations, both national and local, and had accumulated a pile of short, nice, and (mostly) form letters rejecting our applications. And we hadn't had much success breaking into the Boston corporate world, either. Tsongas knew what to do. "You need some media coverage," he said, "so people know who you are and what you are doing when you go in to make your pitch." He called Kirk Scharfenberg at the *Boston Globe* and pitched him on doing a story about City Year. He also reached out to friends like Newell Flather, a fellow Peace Corps alum, who was advising a number of philanthropists and foundations on their charitable giving. And his twin sister, Thaleia Schlesinger, helped us secure bigger free office space right across from Boston Common, the perfect location.

▼▲▼

In the middle of February 1988, we were invited to attend a national service strategic leadership conference at Brown University organized by Youth Service America. I presented City Year to the Conference including our modest goal that "we wanted to change the world." As soon as I stopped speaking, a tall, distinguished-looking gentleman bounded up to the stage, stuck out his hand and said: "I'm Harris Wofford. I just love your vision for City Year and I will do whatever I can to help you."

"I know exactly who you are," I responded. "I've read your book *Of Kennedys and Kings* and the Potomac Institute 'Study on National Service' you chaired. You are a hero!" That, as Rick says at the end of *Casablanca*, was the beginning of a truly beautiful friendship. Wofford would go on to become a United States Senator from Pennsylvania and a key architect of the legislation that created AmeriCorps. He also became the CEO of the Corporation for National and Community Service and helped to save the program when it was under partisan attack. He became one of my closest friends and mentors, presided over my wedding, and is an ongoing and great blessing in my life.

The Brown conference proved a turning point for us. Kristen started working full-time that week, and applications to the pilot program started coming in. Soon after, The *Boston Globe* ran a nice feature story on City Year, thanks to Paul Tsongas's help, and others started to call us to say they wanted to support us. Patty Foley, Senator Kerry's Massachusetts State Director called out of the blue and said she loved our idea, wanted to help, and wanted to know what we needed. We said, computers. Within a week, a friend of hers who worked for Apple came to see us and arranged for us to get several donated Macintoshes. Patty also told Senator Kerry about our idea and he said he wanted to visit the program as soon as we got our first group of young people serving. He became a lead champion for City Year from the very beginning.

About that time, we got a call from an entrepreneur, Sherman somebody—I honestly cannot remember his last name. He said he had read the *Boston Globe* article and wanted to take us to lunch. We were excited: he had money and he promised lunch! Sherman came by our one-room office on Church Street. He told us how he had started several successful companies, and wanted to know if he could help us. The first thing he asked was how many people we had working full-time on City Year. At that point, we had five full-time, and about three to four more putting in substantial volunteer hours. He said, "Good, it takes five or six people to start anything." And then he added, with emphasis, "At this point, you don't need or want clear job descriptions or people working just on their own one piece of the organization. It needs to be all hands on deck." After a perfectly enjoyable lunch, we never heard from Sherman again. But I never forgot that piece of advice he gave us—and I've passed it on often when anyone asks about starting an organization.

The Equitable called us toward the end of February to say that the board of their foundation had indeed voted a $20,000 grant for City Year. We were finally raising real money. In the beginning of March, Bank of Boston voted a $25,000 grant to sponsor a City Year team. They were the first company to do so. In the middle of March, the General Cinema Corporation, led by the father and son team of Richard and Robert Smith, called to say they had approved a $50,000 grant for City Year's summer program and would be our second team sponsor. They knew that our overall budget was $200,000 and they wanted to give us a big enough grant to make sure we could succeed in raising it all. Newell Flather, Paul Tsongas's friend, a Peace Corps alum and a wonderful believer in service and in young people, was instrumental in helping us to secure that grant. With the support of General Cinema, we now had raised about half of the money we needed, had some good momentum and believed that we would get the other half from somewhere. We started to accept our first group of corps members and it all became very real.

During this time, we were also having discussions with Bain and Company, the management consulting firm that Neil had worked at between college and business school. Soon after joining the City Year effort, Neil brought us over to meet with Mark Nunnelly, his mentor at Bain. Mark wasn't much older than us, and he wasn't even a partner at Bain and Company. But he understood what we were trying to do, believed in it, and said he would do whatever he could to help us. It was a key connection. Mark would go on to become one of the most accomplished partners at Bain and Company, and one of the founding partners of Bain Capital, the extremely successful, private equity firm that was a Bain spin-off. He made it a personal cause for Bain and Company to become one of the founding sponsors of City Year.

At that time, Bain hadn't done any charitable giving at all, except to ask employees to contribute to the annual United Way campaign. So it seemed like a long shot. But Mark was determined, and he told us that while it would take time to get Bain invested, we should stay at it. He eventually secured for us a meeting with the founder, Bill Bain himself, who personally signed off on Bain becoming the third team sponsor for City Year's pilot program with a $25,000 grant. (Bain has sponsored a City Year team every single year since. They have also supported our programs in Chicago and New York, where they have offices. Bain, through David Bechoffer's leadership, has also contributed millions of dollars in pro bono case teams to help City Year with a myriad of strategic issues.)

Three team sponsors secured, two to go. A group of young consultants who had started something called the Volunteer Consulting Group offered to do a fundraising benefit dance for City Year. That raised about $15,000, so we decided to have a Citizens Team, which would be a team sponsored by individual donations. It fit nicely with our theme that City Year was about promoting Big Citizenship. Still, we were about ten thousand dollars short. One evening we got everyone who was associated with our City Year start-up effort by that time; in addition to our small staff, we had a core, active volunteer staff of about eight, and another ten or so regular volunteers. We all pulled out our Rolodexes and added handwritten notes to a fundraising letter we had drafted to everyone we knew. We asked for a contribution of any amount to the founding of the City Year Citizens Team, and added the *Boston Globe* article, a trick I had learned on the Hart campaign: always try to include a good piece of media with any mailing as a way to get people excited and give you credibility. We sent out hundreds of letters, and in the weeks following, checks and encouraging notes from our friends arrived every day (making the mail run a highlight). In all, we managed to raise another $12,000 dollars, more than enough to fund the rest of the Citizens Team. This whole effort was very empowering for the entire volunteer team that was pulling City Year together, as it took all of us reaching out to our friends, most of whom were in their twenties like us and not that wealthy, to raise the money we needed.

Although we had four of the five teams sponsored, there was no real prospect for a fifth team sponsor. After coming up short with several other potential supporters, we decided to go back to the Equitable Company, which had given us our first big donation of $20,000, and ask them if they would contribute $5000 more and be our fifth team sponsor. They said they were impressed with the progress we had made and agreed to do so.

While we were working on raising the money we needed, we continued to recruit corps members, set up service project partnerships, develop a relationship with Mayor Ray Flynn and other important civic and political leaders in the Boston area, and recruit and select the rest of the founding staff we needed for the summer program.

The Thompson's Island training program was the reward for all the hard work and dedication every one of our staff and volunteers poured into turning City Year from a dream into a reality. When it was over, we all returned to Boston for our official opening day kick-off celebration. We chose to do it at the Mt. Pleasant Street Tot Lot, one of our main service projects for the summer. A wonderful local woman named Mildred Daniels had devoted herself to keeping the tot lot open and running. But she had done it entirely on a volunteer basis, and over the years it had fallen into disrepair. The swing set and other play equipment were rusted out, and the grounds were a riot of brush and weeds. City Year committed to reclaiming the tot lot and working with Mildred to restore the moribund summer camp program. The Equitable Team, led ably by Stephanie Wu, took on this project.

We wanted to make sure people in greater Boston knew about this new experimental model for national service. We hoped to show how a diverse model of national service, one built from the grassroots up, could be effective. We would learn over the years that success required an ongoing effort to engage the media as a way to build public awareness for the ideas and policies that you are trying to promote. Michael did a masterful job securing every single local TV station—all five of them—to cover our official opening day kick-off. We also got editorials in both the *Boston Globe* and *Boston Herald*, good news stories and opinion pieces in both papers over the course of the summer and great coverage in many neighborhood-based papers. Day-by-day the citizens of Boston read and heard that there was an innovative and inspiring program for youth service—a new "urban Peace Corps" taking off in their community.

At the end of August, we returned to the Mt. Pleasant Street Tot Lot for our graduation. Everyone marveled at the transformation that had taken place as the Equitable Team had completely reclaimed the tot lot. There was a carpet of new grass, the swing set and play equipment were renovated and rust-free, and the team had painted beautiful murals on the brick walls that framed the lot. Volunteer artist Anne Haney, another old friend, had designed the murals with input from the neighborhood children, and the result was spectacular. The tot lot was full of laughter from happy children who had participated in the summer camp program that we helped Mildred restore. And the wholesale transformation of that one little urban corner was the perfect metaphor for the transformation we all felt had occurred over that summer.

At the graduation, we handed out certificates of achievement to the founding corps, with their families and friends all watching. We shared inspirational stories and thanked our service and corporate partners. It had been a wonderful summer. We all worked extremely hard, seven days a week. We had never done anything like this before and we were generally laying the tracks as the train pulled out of the station. But we had a wonderful spirit of camaraderie, idealism, and community, and the corps members' enthusiasm and commitment, and the dedication of our service partners, and support from our corporate partners and numerous volunteers had made it all possible.

As I looked out for a last time at that founding corps, I thought to myself, "Wow, national service really does work." During the short span of a summer, with just fifty corps members, we had transformed places like the Mt. Pleasant Street Tot Lot, the Pine Street Inn, and Elizabeth Stone House. We had directly touched the lives of the children we worked with at the Dorchester House, and had organized the first-ever Special Olympics program at Camp Joy. We had enabled senior citizens in East Boston to stay living in their own homes. We had inspired and empowered our corps members, helping them realize how each and every one of them could make a difference in the world. And we had delivered tangible results to our sponsors and corporate partners, many of who got directly involved in our work as mentors and volunteers.

Most important, City Year had come into being because literally hundreds of people had supported the idea. They had come from all walks of life to make a little dream of service a big reality. Their example confirmed that a spirit of public service, a desire of people to come together and work together to make a difference, was truly abundant if you could just find it. It was a powerful force that could be tapped into and mobilized to bring about meaningful change. I also realized that the dream—the full dream of what comprehensive national service could do for our country—was both mind-blowing in its potential and completely possible. The only question in my mind was whether we, as individuals and as an organization, were up to the task of contributing to making it all happen. But I drew great comfort in knowing that the hopes and aspirations we had invested in the idea that national service could unite citizens from every background, lead to real and positive change in communities, and send ripples of idealism and inspiration across our nation, were not at all misplaced.

There was only one cloud. While we had succeeded in raising the $200,000 we needed to fund our summer pilot program, we had been so busy running the program we had not put any time into additional fundraising. When the summer pilot ended, we had enough money in the bank to last for only about another month.

3

BOOTS ON THE GROUND

A full-time program for fifty new corps members, set to open in September 1989, and track the academic year through June 1990, would need one million dollars. We gave ourselves a year to find it, but we had learned that sponsor dollars, even for the best of programs, can be elusive. Beyond the fundraising, we had to identify meaningful service projects and staff an organization that could pull it all off. Neil Silverston and I stayed on full-time, and Kristen Atwood returned to her role as recruitment director. But the other team leaders went off to other jobs. Jennie Eplett had been accepted to Harvard Business School and was preparing to enter that September. Michael Brown was starting a judicial clerkship with the Chief Judge of the 1st Circuit Court of Appeals (and future Supreme Court Justice), Stephen Breyer.

Michael would do his clerkship during the day and then City Year in the evenings and on the weekends, burning the candle from both ends. Then, about midway through the year, he made the courageous decision to leave the clerkship and return to work on City Year full-time. He explained to Judge Breyer that while there were other talented law graduates who could fulfill his duties as a clerk, he had a passion for City Year and realized that's where he could make the biggest difference. I deeply appreciated this very hard decision by Michael, as he was indispensable to getting City Year launched as a full-time program. Judge Breyer, to his credit, was extremely understanding and supportive.

We stayed lean and mean. Everyone had agreed to work for the same salary, $18,000 a year. That would keep our costs low and also send a message to prospective funders that we had our own "skin" in the game. Our monthly "burn rate" or budget, was fairly low, at around $15,000 a month, when we added in administrative costs that included travel, materials and supplies, and computer equipment. But we still had very little money in the bank and were facing the prospect of having to forgo paychecks with the great triumph of the summer program barely behind us.

We needed money and we needed it fast. But fundraising takes time. There are a lot of worthy causes, and raising funds revolves around building deep relationships with people, which by definition is challenging for a start-up. We had conducted a successful summer program but we were young and had little track record. Many were skeptical about a full-year program being able to work; a summer program seemed a much more manageable undertaking. The worry we would soon be out of business was omnipresent. Then, about a week after the summer program ended, I got a phone call from Ira Jackson. He said the contributions committee of Bank of Boston had just met and had voted an additional $50,000 grant to City Year to enable us to start planning for our full-year program. I couldn't believe this news. I almost dropped the phone. We hadn't even had time to write a new grant proposal. We had barely even thanked everyone who had made the summer program possible.

It was a lifeline we gratefully grabbed, and it kept us going for the next three months. This was just one of many times over the coming years when a "guardian angel" would appear at a critical time to help us through a challenging moment.

Bain and Company did a pro bono evaluation and review of our summer program, and came to the conclusion that a full-year City Year program while not guaranteed to succeed, held promise. We used that as the beginning of our business plan for the next phase of the organization.

The full-year program would allow us finally to realize the intention captured in the name we had chosen: City Year. We were saying to young adults, aged seventeen to twenty-four, that just as they might do a college freshman, sophomore, junior and senior year, we wanted to challenge them and give them the opportunity to do a "City Year"—a year in which the City would be their classroom and public schools, after-school programs, homeless shelters, senior citizen centers, food banks, and more, would be their textbooks; a year when they could learn firsthand the power and importance of uniting with others for the common good.

City Year corps members serve full-time for an academic year from August through June on a team of eight to twelve people. They come from all backgrounds—African-American, Asian, Caucasian and Latino, women and men, upper-income and lower-income, urban and suburban, former gang members and prep school graduates, different faiths, and all regions of the country.

In its early years, City Year did a variety of both human and physical service projects, as we wanted to demonstrate the multiple needs that national service could address. Over time we discovered that our biggest impact was having our corps members work with younger children, especially in the area of education. Now, City Year's primary service focus is called "In School and On Track," in which corps members work to address the high school dropout crisis by serving high-need schools with low-income populations with a focus on improving attendance, behavior, and coursework, especially in math and English. Corps members also contribute to a positive school climate and help to run after school and extended-day programs. And they organize programs for middle and high school students to do service learning after school and on weekends through the Young Heroes and City Heroes programs.

Our corps members continue to do some physical service work such as renovating schools and educational facilities and converting vacant lots into parks and playgrounds. We have also developed Care Force, a division of City Year, to engage companies and other groups who want to do one-day, high impact, physical service projects.

In exchange for their 1,700 hours of service (it varies depending on the location in the country), the corps members receive a weekly stipend around minimum wage and upon graduation an AmeriCorps scholarship of $5,350 toward higher education or job training.

Corps members serve on their projects from Monday through Thursday and then reunite as a corps on Fridays for Leadership Development Days, which provide training and leadership development opportunities.

City Year's vision statement is that one day the most commonly asked question of an eighteen-year-old all over the world should be, "Where are you going to do your service year?"

Our original plan had been to have City Year run from July to July, but in exit interviews the corps members from the summer pilot program suggested that timetable was flawed. They told us people their age were generally in school from September through June. Since we would only be paying corps members a modest stipend that was less than minimum wage, with a post-service award that they could use for college or job training after they finished their City Year, they suggested young people would need their summers to get higher paying jobs that would allow them to afford to participate in City Year as well as pay their other bills. This was exactly the sort of feedback we had been hoping for when we designed the summer pilot, and it made all the sense in the world. We changed our program from a twelve-month program to a ten-month program, a crucial decision that made City Year a much more attractive option for many members

In order to raise the million dollars we needed, we decided to increase our Team Sponsorship cost to $100,000 for the year, or $50,000 for half the year. With five fully sponsored teams of ten corps members each, we would raise $500,000—half the money we needed. We figured we could piece together the other $500,000 through a variety of smaller grants and sponsorship opportunities. Our hope was to go back to the four companies that had launched City Year as Team Sponsors—Bank of Boston, Bain and Company, General Cinema, and The Equitable—and have each of them agree to be founding team sponsors of the full year City Year program for $100,000 each. We soon discovered that was a huge ask, and a big stretch. We went to Bank of Boston first, since they had been the first team sponsor and had invested in our planning. They responded: "We love you guys and totally believe in City Year, but we can't be first again. If you can get someone else to commit the $100,000, then we will come in second."

When we approached General Cinema, they gave us a similar answer and said if we could get two other sponsors at $100,000 they would consider being the third. Bain and company said they were interested, but couldn't commit and that we should keep them updated on our progress. We heard something similar from The Equitable.

It was like piecing a puzzle together. If we could only get the first few pieces in place, the rest would follow. We did succeed in getting a $100,000 grant, $50,000 a year for two years, from the Cox Foundation for our leadership training program, and another $100,000 grant over two years from the Reilly Foundation. By December, we were a long way short of a million dollars. No team had a sponsor. Things were not looking good.

It was then that we received a visit from an official from the US Department of Education, who said we had a very interesting program. The offical told us about a new grant program within the Department of Education, focused on developing job training skills, and he could almost guarantee us at least $100,000, and potentially much more. We were very torn by this tempting suggestion. We had committed to launching City Year entirely with private funds. Part of our developing "brand" was that City Year was the "privately sponsored Urban Peace Corps." We wanted to demonstrate that the private sector could be tapped for significant funding for national service programs, and that we would not have to rely on government funding to get launched. In addition, while City Year corps members developed valuable job skills, our program was primarily focused on service and citizenship, not job training, and we did not want to be taken off course in response to government funding requirements.

The City Volunteer Corps experience in New York had proved it was extremely hard to go from being a publicly funded program to a public–private partnership. Once private sector leaders learned there was significant public money already committed, they tended to say, "Well, you don't need our money then." We also wanted the flexibility to be entrepreneurial and design City Year based on the model and principles we believed were essential for a national service experiment, and to be able to learn quickly from our experience and make adjustments. Government funding inevitably came with more strings attached, and numerous program requirements.

After the proposal from the Department of Education, we had a long staff discussion as to what to do. We had been trying for almost four months and had had little success in raising money for the full-year program. Even a great champion like Ira Jackson from Bank of Boston was counseling that maybe we needed to think about doing another summer program and take more time to develop the full-year program.

After extended discussion, we decided that it impacted our model too much to accept government funding at that time. It was an excruciating choice, but leading with private sector support was one of the core principles of our vision for City Year and national service, and we weren't ready to abandon it yet, no matter how dire our financial circumstances. Our founding sponsors had not said "no." They had said "maybe, if." It was only December. We still had time to find the first pieces of the puzzle.

Against this backdrop of financial stress, we continued recruiting the corps, developing the service project partnerships, reaching out to civic leaders, and designing the leadership training program for our corps. Michael had always pointed out that City Year came down to three things: money, projects, and kids. We needed to stay focused on all three, even if one—money—was preoccupying us. So our team kept working. Indeed, we were newly inspired when we read the applications and interviewed the young people from all backgrounds who were excited to do a City Year. The service project possibilities were developing strongly as well with many non profits, community organizations, and schools excited to host a City Year team. Our problem was money.

The noted organizational expert, Jim Collins, emphasizes that everything starts with First Who, meaning that you must start by focusing on recruiting the right people and putting them in the right roles or "seats on the bus" as the key to success for any organization[8], and we definitely found that to be true. We needed help urgently, so we recruited Lonni Tanner, a summer camp friend of Michael's, to come join us as development director. Lonni had been working for Peat Marwick doing PR in New York and somehow we convinced her to move back to Boston, take a massive pay cut, and join our idealistic little adventure. Lonni is a tour de force.

She speaks a million words a minute, wears designer clothing, and is an absolute genius at getting people to make in-kind donations and do pro bono work. We made immediate and great progress on that front. She was able to get us an 8,000-square-foot abandoned warehouse as our new office space and then got all of the renovation work donated by local unions as well. She convinced Peat Marwick to take us on pro bono to do our financial audit and more. She got all of our uniform parts donated from leading companies including the Gap, Patagonia, and Timberland.

The Timberland relationship would turn out to be transformative for City Year. We sent a heartfelt letter to Jeff Swartz, the COO of Timberland, telling him all about City Year, that we were going to be doing some hard physical service work and needed very strong, sturdy, waterproof boots, and asking if they could please donate 50 pairs for our founding full year corps. We were delighted when we got a letter back saying, "sure, your organization sounds terrific, we are happy to help, please send the sizes." A year later, when we needed 75 pairs for our expanded corps, Timberland stepped up again. They seemed so naturally supportive that Lonni and I went to thank Jeff Swartz in person at Timberland's Stratham, New Hampshire headquarters. We hoped we could build a longer term relationship with Timberland and get them to become a Team Sponsor because we were growing. It was a bit of a long shot, because Timberland was based in New Hampshire and our work was centered in Boston, but we had learned that the best people to approach for new asks were the ones already supporting you. (Today, thanks to their partnership with City Year, in their corporate headquarters Timberland displays the City Year and service project photos in its lobby at every turn.)

After listening patiently to our passionate pitch, Jeff Swartz responded in kind: "My grandfather created the classic, waterproof, rugged Timberland Boot. My father built the Timberland Brand.

As the third generation to lead this company, I believe we need to make sure we are a company of Belief. That we stand not just for great products, but also for making a difference in the world. It seems that by partnering with City Year we can express our beliefs. Boot, Brand, Belief. That is the future of Timberland."

I loved Jeff Swartz on the spot. He was my generation and had a powerful vision for his company and a palpable desire to use the strengths of the private sector to make a difference in the world. It seemed like there could be a terrific fit between Timberland and City Year. We would generally almost never make a direct request in a first meeting, but Jeff was very special. He lived in Newton, MA, so he had a commitment to the Boston area and I figured we should ask Jeff and Ken Freitas, Chief Marketing Officer of Timberland, if they would be willing to continue providing the boots for a growing corps and staff, and also sponsor a team for half the year for $50,000. And as a sweetener I added that we would gladly come up to New Hampshire to organize a service project for Timberland employees with their team so their workforce could experience City Year and service directly.

Instead of stalling or asking for time or a more formal proposal, Jeff immediately said: "That all sounds terrific. We'd love to do it all and also talk about other ways we can work together."

I was blown away. We almost never landed a big commitment in a first meeting. We thanked Jeff and Ken profusely and thought we should leave while we were ahead.

Timberland would go on to become a leading Corporate Sponsor of City Year. To date, it has donated more than twenty-seven million dollars in cash and in-kind resources to the organization. The Timberland Red Jacket and classic yellow boots would become the signature of the City Year organization at work in communities across America and even in South Africa. They would put service into the DNA of the company, doing regular corporate service days and becoming the first company to offer a new employee benefit—forty hours of paid time off a year to do community service work.

Jeff would soon join our Board of Directors and serve as Chair for almost ten years, helping to lead the organization from a local program based in Boston to a national organization operating across America. Through those years we became dear friends. I learned from Jeff constantly about leading and managing a growing, entrepreneurial organization, and I have often reflected on what one simple letter asking for fifty pairs of boots led to.

Lonni Tanner also cold called every single venture capitalist in Boston trying to get us a meeting, thinking that since they backed entrepreneurs, maybe they would back civic entrepreneurs, people who had the same passion to take risks for a breakthrough idea, but this time in the civic space as opposed to business world. Only one, Steve Woodsum, agreed to a meeting, but that was well worth it. In that meeting, Steve agreed to have his firm Summit Partners sponsor a team for half the year. He, too, joined our board, would also serve as chair, and he has been an outstanding leader and champion for City Year ever since. Through Bob Fraser, the then managing partner of Goodwin, Proctor and Hoar, one of the top three law firms in Boston, and his good friend, Ned Helms, who was the head of the Boston Bar Association, we raised more than $50,000 from a group of law firms to sponsor a Boston Lawyers Team.

Progress was steady, but by mid-February, we still hadn't secured a single $100,000 full-year sponsor and had only raised about $300,000 toward our million dollar goal. And we were running out of time. Then, Jennie Eplett called to say she had been interviewing for jobs, and that a New York–based venture capital firm, General Atlantic Partners, was looking at starting a new foundation and was intrigued by City Year. The managing partner, Ed Cohen, wanted to fly us to New York and meet right away.

We prepared for the meeting, scheduled for March 10, 1989,

as if it were the Bar Exam. We were getting close to do-or-die time on whether we could proceed with a full year City Year program. We studied General Atlantic's annual report, and noticed they had a creative, independent style. None of the partners wore ties in their photos, their bios included their interests and activities outside of work, including public service, and they emphasized that their investment strategy was to focus on great people and management teams as well as good ideas. We hoped we could impress them with our commitment as well as our City Year model for national service.

They escorted us into a room with a Persian carpet on the floor, exquisite art on beautiful wood-paneled walls, and everyone seated in a haphazard circle, some in plush easy chairs, others on carved, antique looking, wooden chairs. The three of us were directed to a couch. Most of the partnership—about ten of them— had gathered to meet with us. They asked us probing questions about the program, the diversity of the corps, the kind of service projects we had done, and our plans for the future. They asked about our backgrounds and what motivated each of us to want to start City Year. They also drilled down very specifically on where our fundraising stood. We put the best spin on our situation we could, emphasizing that each of our summer team sponsors were considering a $100,000 team sponsorship, none of them had said yes, yet, but none had said no either, and Bank of Boston had specifically told us they would be the second $100,000 gift if we could get a first one and General Cinema committed that they would be third if we could get two other commitments. We also stressed we had already received more than one hundred applications for a corps of only fifty, so the demand to do City Year was there. We gave them copies of some of the applications so they could read for themselves the motivation behind the young people wanting to make a difference through City Year. We admitted we felt we had to raise the money before we could start accepting corps members into the program, and that we feared losing some by making them wait too long before we could accept them. We ended our pitch by asking if they would consider being a half-team sponsor by making a $50,000 gift. We reckoned that since the foundation was based not in Boston but in New York, that figure was the most we could reasonably ask for.

Ed Cohen asked us to leave the room. He said they wanted to talk about our proposal for a while and might be able to give us a response later that day. In fact, it was barely fifteen or twenty minutes later when they asked us to come back, but at the time seemed much longer as we waited anxiously. Ed had a smile on his face and he proceeded to tell us they would give us a $100,000 three-to-one challenge grant. He explained if we could get three other companies to sponsor a team at $100,000 each, General Atlantic would sponsor a team at the full $100,000 level. Ed also said we had to match the challenge within ninety days, as they knew we needed to select our corps in time to be able to launch the program in September. He also offered to talk to any of our potential sponsors to share with them directly General Atlantic's commitment. It was a pivotal breakthrough.

We thanked them all, politely trying to maintain our professional composure. Out on the street, we gave each other high fives, hugs, and screamed. After months of tension and worry, we believed in our hearts City Year would now happen. Back in Boston our first call was to Ira Jackson. He indicated that Bank of Boston would probably come in as the second team sponsor with a $100,000 grant. Within days, Ira confirmed it. With two team sponsors at $100,000 we called General Cinema. Within weeks they also committed to sponsor a team for $100,000. We needed just one more to meet the General Atlantic Challenge. The Equitable came through, so we called Ed Cohen to tell him that we had met the challenge grant. It had taken only forty-five days since the meeting in New York. Ed was excited and happy for us and pleased that Echoing Green's "venture philanthropy" challenge grant approach had worked. He agreed to join our board, would also serve as Chair, and has been an extraordinary advisor, champion, and friend for more than two decades.

Bain and Company also let us know that they would sponsor a team. So we had exceeded the General Atlantic Challenge grant with four gifts of $100,000 each, secured in just sixty days. The puzzle had been completed. City Year's first full year program would now be a reality.

▼▲▼

The first year experience was intense, sometimes comic, always revelatory, and demonstrated that no matter how much you plan, you cannot control events. You just have to ensure that your organization is robust enough, clear enough in its shared mission, to roll through them.

First the comedy. We spent three hours at one staff meeting debating whether the corps members should be allowed to wear their own hats. Like other service programs, both civilian and military, we had decided to have full City Year uniforms. This, we hoped, would build a sense of esprit de corps. The uniforms also helped us brand City Year and make us identifiable to the children and communities we served. With Lonni's leadership, we got the uniforms completely donated. But, we had not gotten City Year ball caps for everyone, so some of the corps members, as a way to express themselves and their own individuality, started wearing their own hats. We didn't have an official policy on this and we soon learned that whenever we didn't have an official policy, the corps would jump right into the void with their own approach. Some on the staff thought we should just let it go and have the corps members wear whatever hat they wanted. Others thought this was a fundamental issue and that the whole point of having a uniform was to be, well, uniform.

So we called a special after-hours staff meeting to discuss this issue. We were trying in those early days to run City Year by consensus. Michael and I were the official co-directors of the program, but we tried to empower all of the staff by including everyone in the major decisions. We started the meeting at 7:00 pm and finished after 10:00 pm, with everyone tired and more than ready to go home. We just couldn't come to any consensus. People felt strongly on both sides of this issue and we just kept going around in circles. Finally, we resolved that Michael and I would discuss it and come up with a decision since we couldn't get everyone to agree. (We ultimately decided that having a uniform was very important to City Year and thus, we would not have people wear their own hats. The issue of hats was also particularly important as many different gangs in Boston in those days identified themselves through the hats they wore, another reason we took this issue seriously.) We would later laugh at ourselves for taking three hours of valuable staff time to simply discuss the hat issue. As time went on, our decision-making improved. People would be empowered to make decisions within their area of responsibility with oversight from their supervisor. For major organizational decisions, Michael and I would take input from folks, but then ultimately take the responsibility for the decisions. Everyone was happier with that approach as it didn't waste people's time and it provided more clarity around the decision-making process.

A much more difficult situation was thrust upon us and the entire city of Boston just a few weeks later. Charles Stuart was riding in his car with his pregnant wife, when he reported the car was stopped by an African-American man who tried to rob them and shot Stuart and killed his wife, Carol, and unborn child. The crime outraged everyone in Boston and people demanded that the killer be found and brought to justice swiftly. Pictures of the victim and of Charles Stuart grieving and recuperating in the hospital blared repeatedly across the TV news and front pages of the newspapers. Pressure on the mayor and the police chief grew daily to find the killer. The police stormed through the African-American neighborhoods of Boston in an unprecedented manhunt, randomly stopping African-American men, searching them and demanding information.

Boston is a city of strong ethnic neighborhoods. It has a checkered and difficult racial history going back to the days of busing in the late 1960s and early 1970s, when the city grew increasingly divided over the issue as some political and civic leaders played on racial prejudices and fears to advance their own political agendas. City leaders, including Mayor Flynn and leaders in the clergy, civic, and community groups, had worked hard to heal those divisions. But the Stuart case and the initial response to it brought all of the racial tension and division right back to the forefront of city politics and discussion. Reactions to it were largely split right down racial lines with white leaders and citizens saying the police tactics and media focus were totally justified due to the horrible nature of this crime, and black leaders and other leaders of color saying that an entire community's civil rights were being violated without any due process or sense of fairness or perspective. People who had worked for years to heal divisions literally stopped talking to each other, or would only communicate through accusations and counter accusations via the news media. The whole city seemed like it was coming apart.

This incident hit all of us hard at City Year. Part of the reason we had decided to start City Year in Boston was precisely because of Boston's history of racial division and tension. We felt that if we could make a very diverse youth service corps work in Boston, we could point to it as a model. We strongly believed that national service could be used to help complete the civil rights movement because while changing laws can change people's behavior, you can only affect people's hearts and minds through direct experience. But as the city started to come apart along racial lines, we wondered if City Year might start to come apart as well before we even had a chance to make the whole thing work.

We decided to be proactive and to confront the issue of the Stuart case firsthand by using time on one of the Friday leadership development days. As we often did in situations like this one, the first call we made was to Charlie Rose, a member of our Board, and the Director of Youth Services for the City of Boston. Charlie has a unique understanding of how to work with young people and an extraordinary ability to connect with people from all walks of life. He helped us pull together a set of leaders from diverse backgrounds to speak to the corps about what was going on in Boston around the Stuart case. He also helped us design a group of workshops to give the corps members a chance to speak honestly about their reactions and to share their ideas as to what should be done.

We should have had more faith in our corps members and in City Year. We had started the full-year program, as we had the summer pilot, with an overnight retreat that was a combination of boot camp and summer camp. It gave us a chance to share the philosophy, values, ideas, and ideals behind City Year. We also did a fair amount of team building, Outward Bound–style exercises, and some workshops on working with diverse people. That opening retreat was designed for people to get to know each other and to start building strong relationships that we knew would be necessary to break down the natural barriers that people experience when put together in a very diverse group. Regular team meetings were part of the program design to cover everything from how the service project was going to interpersonal team dynamics.

The Stuart case came less than two months into the City Year program, but the values and ideals had already taken hold. During our "community meeting" open discussion, corps members from different backgrounds talked openly and honestly about their feelings. African-American male corps members shared how they felt branded and violated by the police storming through their neighborhoods and randomly stopping any black male that remotely looked like the alleged killer. Others shared their sorrow over the loss of the mother and her prematurely born baby. Revealingly, the discussion turned to how most of the city's leaders were not leading responsibly. Everyone seemed to be accusatory, pointing fingers, laying blame, but not working together to lead people through this crisis.

I told the corps how impressed I was with the tenor and tone of the discussion, how they were listening carefully to each other and learning from each other—trying to walk in each other's moccasins. I suggested that in our own small way, we needed to do our utmost to show how a diverse community could react to this crisis, and try to be leaders who reached out across the divides to build bridges. I also shared my hope that, twenty years into the future, if Boston faced a similar crisis, a group of City Year alumni would come together and help to lead the city through it, because they understood each other's point of view and had a shared common experience through serving Boston.

By the end of that leadership development day, the corps resolved that they would not let the Stuart case tear our community apart. They also resolved to do what they could individually through their personal example and leadership to try to help people navigate through the dangers of the Stuart case.

Based on Charles Stuart's description, the police dragnet ultimately led to the arrest of Willie Bennett, whom Stuart picked out of a lineup on December 28. But the case took a sinister turn, when Matthew Stuart, Charles's brother, came forward to say that Charles himself was the murderer. As the police started closing in on him, Charles Stuart jumped to his death off the Tobin Bridge in Boston on January 4, 1990. The fact that Stuart himself was the killer and he had fabricated the whole incident, falsely accusing an African-American man, led to another round of recriminations and finger pointing. Leaders in the African-American community demanded apologies for the rush to judgment by the police and the extraordinary tactics they had used in trying to track down the alleged killer.

▼▲▼

I wanted to believe City Year could be a place where every single corps member could ultimately succeed if they were given the right amount of attention, support, and love. I eventually realized this was somewhat naive. The City Year corps was an intensely diverse group. We brought together former gang members with well-off suburbanites. Young people who had dropped out of high school served alongside graduates of Harvard. A number of our corps members had not succeeded in school or other programs.

We had developed a clear set of rules and expectations. If corps members had enough violations on their "contract," they would be dismissed from the program. We also had a "second chance" opportunity, whereby after completing forty hours of volunteer community service on their own, a dismissed corps member could reapply for admission to City Year. Readmission wasn't guaranteed. Ultimately, Michael Brown and I had final sign-off on all dismissals and readmissions. The system was put to the test when, one day, Jon Amsterdam, the Director of Field Operations, came into my office and said that he thought Manny [not his real name] should be dismissed from the program without a second chance to reapply. He explained that while on a service project Manny had refused to follow directions from first his team leader, and then from Jon and, ultimately, took a swing at Jon. Manny was a popular kid in the corps. He had a winning personality and a certain charisma that made everyone like him. He was also from a troubled background, and City Year seemed to be his best chance to get his life back on track.

I asked Kristen Atwood, who, as our recruitment director, knew each of the corps members intimately, to join me in conducting an investigation and to make a recommendation as to what we should do. Manny met with me and Kristen, and pleaded for a second chance. He said that City Year was all he had and he didn't know what he would do if he was dismissed. He acknowledged he had been wrong, and promised that he would behave better going forward. Manny had otherwise been doing well at his service project, was making strong progress towards getting his G.E.D., and everyone on his team petitioned that he be given a second chance.

Ultimately, with Kristen's support, but over the objections of Jon, I agreed to give him a second chance to reapply. Manny was extremely grateful as were his teammates. He did his forty hours, reapplied, and was readmitted.

Others on the staff, in addition to Jon Amsterdam, did not support my decision; in particular was Gordon, a graduate fresh out of Harvard who had joined the staff as a special projects assistant, supporting the organization in a variety of ways. He had spent some time working as a corps member at the San Francisco Conservation Corps under the tutelage of the legendary Robert Burkhardt. Gordon insisted that City Year would never work until I got comfortable with the need to hold corps members accountable and ultimately dismiss some from the program. He said, until that happened, we would never have clear expectations, some corps members would consistently try to "game the system," and it would undermine the effort to consistently enforce the rules and expectations for everyone. In order for the program to work for the vast majority of our very diverse corps, some of the corps members ultimately just wouldn't make it and I just had to recognize that and get comfortable with it.

I realized how right he was one cold December night when City Year was asked to help with the Boston homeless count. Many of the corps and staff volunteered for this assignment, even though we would be up until about 4:00 am.

We gathered at City Hall around 10:00 pm to get our instructions and to be broken up into smaller teams that would be deployed across the city. Manny was one of the corps members who had volunteered. He showed up and immediately began acting in an unruly and obnoxious way. He was clearly drunk. First his team leader, and then Jon, tried to calm him down, and to get him to go home. But he was having none of it. I thought that Manny and I had a good relationship, so I decided to intervene before Manny's behavior disrupted the training for everyone. He started swearing at me, and as I gently but firmly tried to grab his arm to lead him out of City Hall, he turned and took a swing at me, trying to hit me in the face. He was drunk and his movements were impaired and I easily dodged the blow.

At first, I was deeply offended that, after all of the support and chances that he had been given, he would act in this way. Later, I realized he had a drinking problem and City Year just wasn't equipped to help him with that. Manny needed to be healthy enough to serve as a role model for the children and communities we served. He simply wasn't. Although Manny came to see me the next day, apologized profusely, said he was drunk, that he didn't mean for it to happen, and repeated that City Year was all he had, and again promised he would never do it again, we dismissed him. This time, I made it clear that there would be no second chance.

I told Manny we all still believed in him, but he needed to get into a program to help him with his alcohol problem and his anger issues. He had natural leadership ability and a unique ability to connect with people—both children and adults—but he needed to want to use that talent. It was up to him. He had already been given too many chances at City Year.

The following month, another incident with a corps member helped me understand further the limitations of City Year. While recruiting for the founding full year corps, Kristen came across a wonderful young woman, Ida, who was living at the Long Island homeless shelter. Ida had had a very rough childhood, and had ended up on the streets before finding her way to the shelter. Meeting Ida, you would never know at first the hardships she had suffered. She had a generous personality, an absolutely beautiful smile, and a real desire to seize the opportunity that City Year provided for her to get her G.E.D. and get on to a better life path. We wanted to have a very diverse corps, thought Ida was very special, and that City Year could also be her route out of homelessness. Ida struggled somewhat at first. Long Island Shelter is in Quincy, more than ten miles away, so she had to get up extremely early to be on time for morning Physical Training (PT) which began sharply at 8:00 am every morning in front of the Federal Reserve building. The service work was demanding and required her and the other corps members to stay focused on the task at hand. But, with support from her teammates—all of whom fell in love with her—Ida seemed to be making it. Many of us put in extra time with her.

Ida really seemed to enjoy City Year, even though she sometimes complained about how hard it was for her. She kept saying how much she was looking forward to getting out of the shelter and into a regular living situation. And then, in January, Ida informed her team leader she was pregnant and was going to quit

City Year to get ready to have her baby. Kristen and I met with Ida right away to see if there was anything we could do to keep her in City Year.

Ida told us she appreciated City Year, but she just had to get out of the shelter. Originally she was way back on the waiting list to get into regular housing. But she had learned that if you were going to have a baby, you would move to the front of the list for regular housing as they didn't want babies being born into shelters. Only eighteen years of age, she was dating an older man who promised to take care of her after she got pregnant.

Although Ida was excited to be a new mother, Kristen and I and others on staff and in the corps were heartbroken. Ida was very special and we thought she was doing well, especially given the odds that she faced. At first, we tried to figure out if there was a way for Ida to continue with City Year, have her baby, and keep participating. But, she just didn't want to. She was focused on her relationship with her baby's father, moving into her new housing, and getting ready for the arrival. There was nothing we could do.

The whole situation was intensely frustrating. It made me realize that sometimes government policies designed with the best of intentions—in this case, the desire not to have babies grow up in shelters—can lead to unintended consequences, like incentivizing a young woman who was on a path that might lead her to success, to veer off into pregnancy.

Ida's situation, coming so soon after the blow-up with Manny, ended my innocence. I came to realize we couldn't "save" everyone, no matter how much we surrounded them with love and support. Everything first depended on the individual corps member's own wants, desires, motivations, and willingness to do what it would take to seize the opportunity that City Year provided. If they didn't want to do it, or couldn't for some reason live up to the admittedly demanding expectations and standards of City Year, there was not much we could do.

Eighteen years later, in spring 2008, Kristen Atwood happened across Ida. We soon got together for breakfast at Sorella's, a diner in the Jamaica Plain neighborhood of Boston. Ida looked terrific with that same beautiful big smile and an infectious laugh. We exchanged hugs and both of us had a tear in the corner of our eyes. Ida told the story of her life after she left City Year: the older man who had gotten her pregnant and made all of these promises to her, quickly abandoned her. But Jim, a corps member from her team, from the suburban community of Weston, attended Lamaze classes with her and was there for her baby's birth. She had been determined to give her daughter a better life than she had. She shared that City Year inspired her to do that. She repeatedly thanked us and said participating in City Year, being surrounded by people who loved her and believed in her, and having the chance to do service for others, had given her the confidence to turn her life around. She was so proud that her daughter was now going on to college. She was settled in a new relationship and very happy and also had a son, whom she named Lazarus because he had almost died in the hospital as a newborn. I was overjoyed to reconnect with Ida and learn how well she was doing. She made me realize that maybe the seeds of success do get planted, even if it is not apparent at the time.

In addition to raising the money and engaging our sponsors, and leading, managing, and building a diverse organization, we also worked on developing meaningful service projects that would have a tangible impact on people and neighborhoods in greater Boston. We chose to do both "human" service projects whereby we would be working with people and "physical" service projects where we would do manual work such as transforming a vacant lot into a playground or community garden.

Just as our financing model depended on strong corporate partners as team sponsors, our impact model depended on strong service partners—either community-based non-profits or schools who would utilize a team of ten led by a City Year staff person to help them achieve their mission. Michael Brown dubbed this the "yeast in the bread" strategy, whereby our City Year team would act like the yeast to help an organization accomplish something it otherwise could not do. We designed a service partner application whereby groups that wanted to host a City Year team would detail how they could utilize us, what the project would entail, what training was needed, and the difference we could make. Lisa Ulrich led a terrific outreach effort to groups across greater Boston with help from the Team Leaders and other City Year staff and volunteers. We ultimately selected partners based on the impact we could have and a mutual understanding of how best to deploy the City Year team.

Our service projects that first year included developing awareness curricula for school students on pressing issues that included environmental preservation, domestic violence, and HIV/Aids prevention. The corps members working with trained professionals would help to design the curricula and then we would take them to a variety of schools in Greater Boston. We developed our very first school partnership program with the Blackstone K-8 School in the South End of Boston, whereby we placed the City Year team in the school full-time to do everything from serving as teachers' aides and tutoring children who were behind, to designing recess activities, organizing field trips and special activities for the students, and contributing to a positive climate and culture in the school. Corps members also came up with the idea to organize "school vacation" camps, that would provide activities for the children during winter and spring school vacations as most of the students came from either two working parent homes or single parent homes without resources to pay for child care or provide activities during those weeks. We organized the first-ever after-school program at Urban Edge, a local Community Development Corporation (CDC), led by a dedicated community leader, Mossik Hacobian. This was a breakthrough: It was one of the first efforts by the CDC to go beyond "bricks and mortar" work, to providing human services for its residents, and contributed to an expanded vision for what CDCs could provide. We also provided comfort and assistance to people living with HIV/AIDS, through helping to prepare meals and regular home visits. And we worked with senior citizens, through groups like the Council of Elders, through companion visits and physical renovation projects, to improve the facility and grounds where the elders lived.

On the physical service side, we carried out a number of renovation projects that included painting, murals, and basic rehab work for groups like the Mass Avenue Baptist church in Cambridge. We also rotated teams through organizations like the Boston Recycling Center and the Greater Boston Food Bank so that our corps members could learn about the issues of hunger and the environment, while helping to organize the tons of donated food or recyclable materials that moved through these organizations on a regular basis. We did landscaping and renovation work at the Franklin Park Zoo, as well as special tours for school kids. We partnered with Boston Urban Gardeners (BUG), led by a real citizen hero, Julie Stone, on a variety of projects. Boston Urban Gardener's mission was to preserve greenspace in the rapidly developing and geographically tight city of Boston. Julie had a very small budget and staff and saw City Year as a way to extend her efforts both through our full-time corps members and other volunteers we could help her recruit.

The most ambitious project we took on with Julie and BUG

was preserving the Berkeley Street Garden in the South End neighborhood of Boston. The garden was a primary source of food for the elderly Chinese immigrants in that community but it was also considered an unsafe eyesore. It became a regular spot for the homeless and drug dealers, and over the years the elderly gardeners employed a variety of mismatched objects to mark off their plots. It was a tangled mess and hard to navigate. The South End was experiencing significant gentrification at this time and there was great pressure to flatten the garden and turn it into parking space and upscale condos. (When I first heard about this potential project from Lisa, that old '60s ballad rang in my ears: "Pave paradise and put up a parking lot…" and agreed we just had to take this on.) Through Boston Urban Gardeners, and in collaboration with a few of the local gardeners and a local representative of the Chinese community who ran a store nearby, Mr. Yee, Julie and BUG, were working to craft an aesthetically and environmentally feasible solution to preserve the garden. This included building safe paths, tearing out old trees that blocked the views , redefining the plots and fencing it off. It was a huge project—the garden extended a full city block and was the second largest in the city—and required a tremendous amount of manual labor. Once City Year agreed to partner with Julie, BUG and the local community, the city prevented the parking lot plans and approved the renovation design. More than twenty years later, every time I drive by the Berkeley street garden I feel a twinge of pride.

Finally, on the service front that initial year, we organized a number of "signature service" projects whereby the entire corps and staff and invited volunteers from our corporate sponsors and friends of City Year would all work together on one big project such as building a playground in one day, or completely renovating a shelter. And we recruited Eric Schwarz, an organizational genius who I had met during the Hart campaign, to design and develop the City Year Serve-A-Thon, a one-day event in which we would recruit thousands of volunteers to do physical service projects all across Greater Boston while also raising money by getting friends to sponsor them for each hour they served.

In reflecting on that first year's service efforts, we realized City Year corps members were particularly good at working with children. They were old enough to be strong role models—the kids would look up to them as superheroes—and the uniforms and creatively designed City Year Logo, even gave them a special feeling of being cool. But the corps members were also young enough that they could strongly relate to the kids. They knew about music, where the kids liked to hang out, and how to connect with them in a way older adults often couldn't. The diversity on the teams was a powerful resource as well. There were always at least some corps members who were from the same backgrounds as the children we worked with, and they could help facilitate connections and understanding for everyone.

We also realized that focusing the teams on a couple of major projects rather than moving them around would enable us to have a higher impact and build deeper partnerships with our service partners. We wouldn't take on as many projects, but the ones we fulfilled would be stronger. Finally, over time, we realized that having philanthropic partners fully sponsoring the cost of our teams and then offering City Year teams as a completely free resource to our service partners was sometimes a major mistake. Some service partners did not fully value the resource because they had no skin in the game, and we didn't get as much direct and negative feedback when we were not performing at the highest levels, because partners might worry we would decide to pull this free resource if they complained too much. It made it extremely difficult to build City Year as a sustainable organization as we had to fully fund the budget without any resources coming from the organizations that most benefited from City Year. The old eighty–twenty rule applied to our fundraising. Every year, we would get to about eighty percent of our budget funded, and then spend the last few months in a struggle to raise that last twenty percent. If we had built a model from the beginning that generated even just twenty percent of our budget from service partnership fees, the organization would be much more sustainable.[9]

▼▲▼

City Year's first year was full of trial, error, inspiration, and success. It came to an end in June 1990, when more than 650 people packed our 11 Stillings Street warehouse office for our first official graduation. It was a scorching day, and there was no air conditioning, but there was so much excitement that no one seemed to notice. It had been a very good year, a hard year for sure, with many lessons learned, but all in all, very successful. Our national service demonstration had worked. We had done important service work and demonstrated that young people could be a tremendous community resource. We had shown that service truly could unite young people from different backgrounds and that the private sector was willing to lead and support service in a powerful way. We had also shown that young people are not just the leaders of tomorrow: given the chance, they can lead today.

In recognition of our accomplishments and impact, Senator Ted Kennedy, whose life work and family tradition were synonymous with public service, had agreed to join us as our first graduation speaker. Kennedy entered to cheers from the hundreds of family members, supporters, volunteers, and friends who had gathered for this big day in City Year's young history. He quickly picked up on the energy in the room and started cheering enthusiastically as the City Year Corps was called out one final time and he joined them in our trademark PT exercises.

After listening to some remarks from our two corps members serving as MCs and a testimonial from a service partner, Senator Kennedy was called to the podium. He looked down at his prepared speech and you could see the wheels turning in this naturally gregarious and astute politician's head. His prepared text wouldn't do. He knew the subject of public service instinctively; he didn't need a prepared speech. He tossed the speech aside and spoke from his heart with warmth, passion, and inspiration.

After congratulating the corps and their parents on their dedication and work with City Year, and thanking the corporate sponsors and service partners and staff, Senator Kennedy explained that the City Year corps members stood in a long line of young people making change for the better. He reminded the audience that it had always been young people who had pushed for change in America. That it was young people who had answered President Kennedy's call to "Ask what you can do for your country…" and signed up in droves to serve overseas through the Peace Corps. It was young people who rode the freedom rides, sat in at lunch counters, and marched and protested for civil rights. It was young people who walked the snowy streets of New Hampshire to end the Vietnam War. It was young people who drove the women's movement and the environmental movement, fighting for equality and a healthy planet. And now, it was young people once again, who were serving through City Year and other programs like it across the country. Kennedy pledged to get back to Washington to see that the National and Community Service Act he had introduced just that year in the Congress to expand programs like City Year would be enacted into law. When he finished, the crowd rose to its feet and gave a prolonged standing ovation. Everyone felt that we were participating in a little part of history. We could not have asked for a better speaker to put our work in context or to validate the corps members' dedication and achievement. The City Year ripple was headed toward Congress.

4

AN "ACTION TANK"

Since dreaming up City Year, Michael Brown and I had traveled the country visiting other programs and many of the leading national service advocates and practitioners. We not only talked to strong believers in national service, but also to skeptics and outright opponents. We discovered that even among true believers, there remained a number of questions as to how national service would really work and whether it could fulfill its ambitious promise. We thought a unique contribution we could make to the burgeoning service movement would be to develop a new type of organization, something even beyond a "model program." We called it an "action tank." The key to "action-tanking" is to combine the best of what a "think tank" does—generate and promote policy ideas and proposals—with what a direct service organization does—put ideas into action and achieve demonstrable results. From the beginning, this was our theory of change. (For the Ten Principles of an Action Tank, see Appendix A, p. 255.) Thus, City Year was created to be an organization that would not only develop a model national service program as a demonstration, but that would also try to leverage that model to impact national policy. Or, to put it into the language of the popular movie of the time, *Field of Dreams*, we said, "If we build it, they will come."

As an Action Tank, we wrestled with several fundamental questions that were at the center of the debate on national service in the mid-1980s:

Should national service be seen as primarily a "jobs" program or as a citizenship enhancing and democracy-building program?

How should young people be viewed—as a client or a resource?

Who should serve? Should national service be a targeted program—either for the disadvantaged or the well educated and economically elite—or should it be for everyone?

What kind of service work should be done? And could young people who did not have a lot of formal work experience do important, impactful, and meaningful service work?

Who should pay for it? Should national service be designed as a purely government program or is there a strong role for the private and non-profit sectors?

Should national service be one-size-fits-all or, as Franklin Thomas, President of the Ford Foundation, argued for in a 1984 speech, "let a thousand flowers bloom?" And, related, should the role of the federal government be to develop one large federal program, or to help support and grow a set of local, state, and national programs run by non-profit organizations?

Michael Brown and I had developed strong views on these issues and felt that City Year could provide answers to many of them. So, we founded City Year with several core principles that remain at the center of the organization today. When we were in law school, we had a professor named David Rosenberg who taught us federal litigation. Professor Rosenberg said the key to a successful litigation effort was to figure out what your "core theory" was, why justice was on your side, what the essence of your argument was. And then, once you do that, you need to narrate that "core theory" through every single thing you do with that case. A strong core theory is both a sword and a shield, both moving you forward offensively and a defense against opposition, or attacks.

The core theory behind City Year was and is the notion that a democracy requires big, active, powerful, robust citizenship. So it was a founding principle for us that while national service can do many things, it must be about making citizenship meaningful, giving every person the feeling that they are part of a cause larger than themselves and building a stronger democracy—assuming "the highest office in the land." We emphasized that our rights came along with responsibilities. For example, we only have a right to a jury trial because other citizens take their responsibility to give up their time to serve on a jury, seriously. City Year corps members were continually challenged to think of themselves as active-duty Big Citizens, as were our private sector funders. And we knew we could only succeed if we could engage large numbers of volunteers to help us make City Year happen.

With City Year, we also wanted to show that young people are the resource, not the client. They can be powerful and can change the world. Even without extensive prior work experience or years of training, young people can do meaningful and impactful service work. Whether it is transforming a school's culture and climate, and playing a leadership role in helping students who are significantly behind in reading and math to catch up, to designing and organizing an after-school program, to transforming vacant lots into community gardens and playgrounds, young people can make a tremendous difference.

One of the great things that national service can and must do, is to give every young person a chance to be a civic activist. Through service, a young person can discover abilities and talents she or he may not realize they possess. City Year has consistently brought graduates of the program onto the City Year staff in all facets of the organization. Currently, both the President and the Sr. Vice President for Site Leadership—two of the top eight jobs in an organization with more than 2,000 full-time people—are held by City Year alumni. In addition, about half of all current City Year sites have been founded with executive directors who had served as City Year corps members themselves.

City Year has, from its inception, been both an intensely diverse program and a proving ground that national service can be a meeting place for all comers, giving people from widely different backgrounds a shared, powerful service experience. As City Year developed, we realized that diversity was a first step toward true "inclusivity," where everyone not only has a seat at the table, but feels equally valued and empowered to contribute and participate.

Becoming a truly inclusive nation remains a great challenge for America, even in 2010. A national service program, created on a scale that links people from different backgrounds to work together for the common good and on the common ground of service, is one of the best ways for America to travel the path from diversity to genuine inclusivity.

When we started to replicate City Year in other communities across America, if they were not succeeding in enrolling a diverse corps, we did not support opening the program. We had to make sure we spent time and energy training and programming to ensure a genuinely diverse community of City Year could work well together. We held both an opening and mid-year retreat, and used Fridays as leadership development days. We also developed a set of techniques to make a diverse group function well. They are simple but effective. One such is "NOSTUESO," an acronym for No One Speaks Twice Until Everyone Speaks Once. Another is the "Strong Circle" whereby a team circles up shoulder-to-shoulder when starting their day, or debriefing a project, so that everyone can see each other face-to-face: no one is inside the circle and no one is outside. Michael Brown's insight was that if we gave these techniques a name, we could then train people in them and develop them as useful tools that corps and staff could use, hence "power tools."

We developed a whole set of diversity and inclusivity workshops. One of my favorites we called the leadership compass. This workshop gets at a non-traditional kind of diversity, but often it's the one—especially in a team-based workplace like City Year—that is the most challenging, and focuses on how people approach solving a problem and accomplishing their work. This workshop—inspired by Native American tradition—asks people to identify their most comfortable work style using the directions of the compass. The east is for visionaries, people who approach a problem by first looking at the big picture. The south is for empaths, people who first try to understand where everyone else on the team is coming from as they approach a problem. The west is for analysts, people who want to think everything through and prepare a detailed plan before commencing any work. And the north is for action-oriented people, who have a strong bias to get going right away. What the workshop teaches is that often conflicts in the workspace come from different styles of problem solving. Conflicts often arise between people on opposite sides of the compass. Eastern visionaries often get frustrated by western analysts who pepper them with circumspect questions, and vice-versa. Northern action-oriented people often become frustrated by southern empaths who keep raising concerns about the overall status of the team, when the norths want to charge ahead. Finally, the leadership compass teaches that every successful team needs a balance of all four directions and that every successful leader needs to cultivate all four directions within themselves to reach their fullest potential. We ultimately took all of these various lessons learned, founding stories, power tools, and the key ideas behind City Year and put them into The Idealist's Handbook—essentially a City Year manual we give to all new City Year staff and corps members and use for regular trainings.

As to who should pay for national service, we believed strongly that it should be a public–private partnership. When we started City Year, all of the leading service organizations we studied were entirely or predominantly government funded. The Peace Corps, for example, was a federal government program. The conservation corps were usually started and primarily funded by state or local governments and fee-for-service contracts. The private sector was barely involved, but with City Year, we wanted to send the message that the private sector has an essential role to play in any ongoing national service system. We believed that, given more than seventy percent of people work in the private sector, we needed to engage that sector if national service was going to be truly transformational.

We learned from Michael's experience with New York's City Volunteer Corps that it was extremely difficult to build a public–private partnership model, when starting with a large budget from the city. So, we decided to launch City Year entirely with private funds because we anticipated it would be easier to evolve into a public–private partnership from a private sector base. We wanted to be entrepreneurial and quickly learn from our mistakes and build on our successes. Private funding allowed for more flexibility and innovation. Private funders are also very results-oriented: they want to see the impact of their investment. So, the private sector required us to demonstrate tangible and measurable success. We also felt we could learn a lot from people in the private sector as to how to launch, develop, and grow an organization, and we discovered that many people in the private sector were looking for more ways to be involved in the community. Finally, when we started City Year, there was no federal source of funding designed specifically for national service programs—inspiring such a program was a main goal of our action-tank strategy. Ultimately, to achieve our goal of universal voluntary national service that would engage at least one million people annually in full-time service, there would have to be federal funding involved because the annual cost was expected to be in the region of twenty billion dollars. We anticipated that, if a federal program for national service was developed, we would transition City Year from a purely privately funded organization, to a public–private partnership.

The fifth principle underlying City Year is meaningful social change comes from the grassroots and works its way up. Although Michael and I had once thought one big federal program was ideal, as we learned more about the various models for service that were bubbling up around the country in the 1980s, we became convinced that the federal government should instead support local, state, and national models and help to grow the ones that worked the best. As we worked to build City Year from scratch, we learned how important it was to engage local stakeholders, local champions, and local partners to ensure a high quality and sustainable program.

The sixth principle behind City Year is the need for a strong organizational culture built on core and clearly stated values. As a powerfully mission-driven organization, with such a diverse population, and the goal of being an action tank, developing a strong and unique culture was essential to make the program and organization work. Wearing uniforms, establishing founding stories, sharing leadership lessons encapsulated in a booklet called "Putting Idealism to Work" that Michael pulled together, "power tools" and our own City Year jargon, and a variety of City Year workshops that we developed—all contributed to building a very strong City Year culture. As we started to replicate the program across the country, we realized that, as much as anything else, we were replicating our culture, and thus it was key to always seed new City Year programs with some veterans who understood the City Year way of doing things and what City Year, at its essence, was about.

▼▲▼

In many ways, Boston was a providential location for a national service experiment. Boston was large enough to be conspicuous, but small enough to be manageable. It had a history of the private sector helping to lead civic causes and efforts, like the Boston Plan for Excellence to promote and improve public education. And it also had a history of racial strife: We wanted to show that national service could help overcome such social conflicts. Boston, as the birthplace of American democracy, also had great appeal to an organization dedicated to promoting strong, active duty citizenship. Finally, Boston also had one other great asset—its senior senator, Ted Kennedy.

The first real action-tanking we did—the first time we used the local activities of City Year to try to change public policy nationally—was to engage Senator Kennedy in our efforts. It was not hard. As early as the mid 1960s, Senator Kennedy had authored legislation to establish a national teaching corps; we were pushing on an open door when we reached out to him for advice, support, and help. Senator Kennedy took a strong and early interest in City Year. In the fall of 1989, just as we started our first full-year program, Senator Kennedy held a field hearing on national service at the Kennedy Library, and featured City Year as a new model program. And he served as our first graduation speaker at the end of that first City Year.

In the late 1980s, there were a number of national service bills and proposals pending in Congress, and Senator Kennedy ultimately rolled them all into new comprehensive legislation—the National and Community Service Act of 1990. Senator Kennedy had a history as a legislator of finding programs that worked at the state and local level and then trying to enact federal legislation that could both expand their efforts and learn from them. He did this in several areas, including, for example, community health centers and community development centers. He took the same approach in crafting national service legislation. In addition to looking at City Year as a model, he incorporated lessons learned from a pioneering school-based service learning program developed by Carol Kinsley in Springfield, Massachusetts, and a middle and high school after-school service program, the Thomas Jefferson Forum, started in Boston by Jeff Coolidge. The legislation also included support for youth corps programs many of them conservation corps— that had sprung up around the country. It supported service efforts on college campuses and had a section for national demonstration programs, thanks to Senator Sam Nunn's efforts.

Nick Littlefield, Senator Kennedy's staff director of the Health, Education, Labor, and Pensions (HELP) committee, worked very hard to get this legislation enacted. And we were fortunate in that a former law school classmate of mine and Michael's, Shirley Sagawa, was given responsibility to be the lead staff person. Shirley, who would go on to play a central leadership role in crafting every major piece of national service legislation over the past twenty years, did a terrific job of weaving together the various proposals into one coherent overall program. She has been rightly called a "founding mother" of the modern national service movement.[10] When the *New York Times* published an article about City

Year as a model national service program, Senator Kennedy had copies made and he personally gave them to senators and congress members, telling them "this program is in my home state. I know it well. It works. This legislation will help make it possible for programs like this to develop in your state and your districts."

While we were working closely with Senator Kennedy, we also reached out to the Bush administration and, in particular, Gregg Petersmeyer, the first ever White House Director of the new Office of National Service. We were honored and excited when Petersmeyer agreed to meet with Michael and me within thirty days of the new Administration taking office. The three of us hit it off immediately. Petersmeyer is extremely thoughtful and patriotic, and we shared a passion for America's founding ideals and values, and the role service could play in helping America reach its potential as a democracy. Petersmeyer confirmed that President Bush was deeply committed to service and wanted to build off the "thousand points of light" all across America's communities.

We explained the ideals and values behind City Year and said we thought they lined up exactly with what President Bush was promoting. Petersmeyer responded that the President would love a program like City Year, because it came from the grassroots, was being led by social entrepreneurs, and was grounded in American values. But, he revealed that the President was skeptical about the notion of "paying volunteers" and was more interested in traditional volunteerism. We argued that if you wanted to have a truly diverse program in which people committed to work full-time for a year, you would have to pay them; otherwise your program would be limited to a very small slice of America that could afford to volunteer full-time for free. We explained that City Year corps members were given a stipend that was less than minimum wage, and then, only upon completing a year in the program would they earn a college scholarship. We also pointed out that the Peace Corps paid a small stipend and the all-volunteer military paid people, as well. Nonetheless, it was a significant difference of opinion, even principle, that we could not immediately resolve. Ultimately, we did what we always did when meeting new people whom we were trying to convince of the value of City Year's approach to national service—we asked Petersmeyer to come visit City Year so he could see firsthand what we were doing and how it worked.

It took fifteen months, and several more visits to D.C., before Petersmeyer came to visit City Year in Boston in April of 1990, but it was well worth the wait, as he dedicated most of an entire day to us. He joined us for a service project, met some key City Year stakeholders, met with our staff leaders, and, most important, he spent more than two hours in a "roundtable discussion" with City Year corps members.

Ahead of Petersmeyer's arrival, we explained to the corps members that President Bush had expressed concerns about "paying volunteers" even a small stipend to serve in a full-time youth service corps, and they could affect policy for the entire country if they could convince Petersmeyer that without a small stipend, no one, except the very rich, could serve their country full-time for a year or more. We asked the corps members to just speak honestly about their experience and explain why they had decided to dedicate a year of their lives to service through City Year, what the impact of their service projects was, how City Year had affected them, and the value of being with a very diverse group of young people.

When Petersmeyer emerged, after thanking the corps members for their time and their service to Boston and our country, he sat down with us and said: "OK, I get it. I get it. This was a terrific discussion. The lower income young people made it clear that they weren't doing City Year for the money, but without the stipend, there was no way they could afford to do this full-time. Even the more upper income corps members said something very important. One corps member told me he could count on his parents to pay for his college education, but that by earning the college scholarship through City Year, for the first time in his life, he feels like he is earning something on his own and his parents are treating him differently because they really respect what he is doing. The corps members also impressed me with the clear leadership skills they are developing and the impact they are having in the community through their service projects. I'm going to go back to the White House and speak to the President and encourage him to support this idea."

True to his word, Petersmeyer went back to the White House and fought hard to convince President Bush to support the National and Community Service Act of 1990 that Senator Kennedy was moving through the Congress. Many others around the president didn't think he should sign the legislation. But President Bush trusted the strong advice of the person he had put in charge to lead the service effort from the White House. City Year was not at all the only reason Petersmeyer strongly encouraged President Bush to sign the new service legislation, but that visit, and the action tank that we had developed, definitely played a role.

In November, President Bush signed the National and Community Service Act of 1990, the first new federal legislation supporting national and community service since 1964, when Volunteers in Service to America (VISTA) became law. The legislation included in it the principle of allowing programs to "pay volunteers." The big innovation of this new law was, rather than setting up a new federal program to develop a one-size-fits-all approach to national and community service, it established a Presidential Commission charged with both developing an overall approach and making recommendations as to how national and community service should be supported in America. The commission also had to establish a competitive grants program that would support various streams of service including: service learning in schools, higher education service programs, youth corps programs, and national demonstration programs, such as City Year. As City Year had been used as a model for the legislation, and because of our action tank strategy and our goal of significantly growing the organization first in Boston and then around the country, we decided it was important for City Year to apply for funding under this new legislation and convert our organization from being purely privately sponsored, to a public-private partnership. But, our board also decided that we should commit to remaining majority privately funded so that we would not become dependent on federal money.

I was honored when President Bush nominated me with Senator Kennedy's encouragement, to serve on the Commission on National and Community Service, a position that required confirmation by the Senate. To a twenty-nine-year-old civic entrepreneur, it was an extraordinary opportunity to learn from and work with an outstanding group of national leaders, and also to see how national policy could complement and advance the growing grassroots service movement. We elected Tom Ehrlich, the President of Indiana University, to serve as our Chairperson and I was honored when my fellow commissioners selected me, along with Shirley Sagawa and former Congressman Pete McCloskey, to serve as Vice-Chairs of the Commission. The National and Community Service Act of 1990 and The Commission on National and Community Service were breakthroughs for the service movement. The Act provided important resources—for demonstration projects and to build capacity through training and technical assistance grants. The Commission also completed a national service strategic plan that we passed along to the Clinton Administration before it took office. The successful work of the commission would lay the groundwork for the Corporation for National and Community Service and the AmeriCorps program of the Clinton years.

The 1991 visit of presidential candidate Bill Clinton to City Year was City Year's second big breakthrough as an action tank. It crystallized a policy idea that he cared deeply about, and gave him personal and political ammunition—something tangible to point to that was working. Our dream when we first started City Year was to help inspire a President to enact a national service program that would include many of the founding principles underlying the design of City Year. It was a dream we shared with a growing service movement of grassroots leaders across the country. People we deeply admired as colleagues and friends and who worked hard through various programs and efforts to help inspire a new national commitment to service. Once President Clinton was elected, that dream started to be realized. President Clinton himself confirmed the value of the action-tank approach to change on a return visit to City Year's headquarters in Boston, a decade after his first visit:

> When I came here ten years ago, I was looking for some evidence that this kind of unformed idea I had that young Americans ought to have a chance to serve in their communities, ought to have a chance to earn some money for college, and ought to be given some way of reaching out across all the lines that divide us, that there was some way we would do it. And I showed up here at City Year and heard about the program...and then, in 1993, I signed a bill creating the community national service program, AmeriCorps. And it would not have happened if I hadn't chanced upon City Year.

President Clinton, and his special assistant for National Service, Eli Segal, took an innovative approach to developing his national service policy. The law they sponsored merged the Commission on National and Community Service with the old federal ACTION agency into the new Corporation for National and Community Service, which like the Commission, would be governed by a presidentially appointed board of directors. In addition, the corporation, rather than establishing one new federal program, would set standards and guidelines and continue to give funding to a wide number and variety of local, state, and national programs, most run by not-for-profit organizations. Because President Clinton had been a governor and knew the value of having states play a leading role in the development and delivery of a new service program, the legislation also required each state to establish its own State Service Commission in order to be able to apply for new federal funding for programs in their states, thus ensuring that governors and individual states would be strongly invested in the program's implementation and success. There was specific support for service learning in schools, college, and university-based service programs, and for full- and part-time national service programs. All of these would come under a new federal brand, named AmeriCorps. Programs would receive government funding and have to meet a set of requirements and standards, but would still operate independently. They would be united under the umbrella of AmeriCorps. City Year would remain City Year, but we would also proudly say we were an AmeriCorps program.

We were excited that President Clinton used a number of the key underlying principles of City Year in designing the AmeriCorps program. Specifically, AmeriCorps' model of engaging young people for a year or more, its commitment to providing opportunities for diverse Americans to serve, providing members stipends and educational scholarships when they completed their term of service, allowing non-profit organizations to deliver the program (rather than one federal agency, like the Peace Corps), and asking the private sector to provide matching dollars were all written directly into the legislation founding AmeriCorps and the Corporation for National and Community Service.

City Year was not at all the only organization that played an important role in bringing about AmeriCorps. And it was exciting to join with others, including Public Allies, Teach for America, Youthbuild, Youth Service America, Campus Compact, The National Youth Leadership Council, COOL, and the programs in the Corps Network among many others, to work to influence the Clinton Administration and Congress as they designed this new federal effort that built off of what was happening at the grassroots level, across the country. We were getting outside of our own organization and joining a larger movement for change, something we had dreamed about when we first started working on national service in college.

In a short period of time, City Year found itself a key part of national policy-making on national service. It was vivid demonstration of the benefit of public–private partnerships, and confirmed what Michael Brown and I had always believed: that any comprehensive solution to our big social challenges needed to engage all three sectors: the government sector, the private sector, and the non-profit sector.

5

SOCIAL ENTREPRENEURS AROUND THE WORLD

Entrepreneurship, according to the French Economist Jean-Baptiste Say, is the "rearranging of economic resources out of an area of lower utility into an area of higher productivity and greater yield."[11] Social entrepreneurs, by contrast, practice rearranging resources out of an area of lower *public* utility, into an area of higher *public* productivity and greater *public* yield. Carl Schramm, President of the Kauffmann Foundation, which focuses on entrepreneurship, offers this definition: "Entrepreneurship is the process in which one or more people undertake economic risk to create a new organization that will exploit a new technology or innovative process that generates value to others."[12]

J. Gregory Dees, professor at the Fuqua School of Business at Duke, and a leading scholar on social entrepreneurship, defines social entrepreneurs as people who "play the role of change agents in the social sector by adopting a mission to create and sustain social value (not just private value), recognizing and relentlessly pursuing new opportunities to serve that mission, engaging in a process of continuous innovation, adaptation, and learning, acting boldly without being limited by resources currently in hand, and exhibiting a heightened sense of accountability to the constituencies served and for the outcomes created."[13]

Bill Drayton, the visionary and brilliant founder of Ashoka, is in many ways the godfather of today's global social entrepreneurship movement. Ashoka, which identifies and supports social entrepreneurs all over the world (with more than 2,000 "fellows," so far), describes them as follows:

> Social entrepreneurs are individuals with innovative solutions to society's most pressing social problems…Rather than leaving societal needs to the government or business sectors, social entrepreneurs find what is not working and solve the problem by changing the system, spreading the solution, and persuading entire societies to take new leaps…every leading social entrepreneur is a mass recruiter of local change-makers—a role model proving that citizens who channel their passion into action can do almost anything. Just as entrepreneurs change the face of business, social entrepreneurs act as the change agents for society, seizing opportunities others miss and improving systems, inventing new approaches, and creating solutions to change society for the better. While a business entrepreneur might create entirely new industries, a social entrepreneur comes up with new solutions to social problems and then implements them on a large scale.

Ashoka cites as leading examples of historical social entrepreneurs: women's rights crusader, Susan B. Anthony; early childhood educator, Dr. Maria Montessori; founder of modern nursing, Florence Nightingale; John Muir, co-founder of the Sierra Club and creator of the National Park system; Vinobe Bhave, founder and leader of the Indian Land Gift Movement; and Jean Monnett, the visionary behind the European Coal and Steel Community (ECSC), an early inspiration for the European Union, among others.

Ashoka is also popularizing the phrase "citizen sector" and "citizen organization" as opposed to the non-profit sector, or non-governmental organization (NGO), sector as a way to emphasize that it is citizens acting for the common good who are the heart and soul of this sector. Ashoka argues the fullest measure of citizenship is when one or several people join together to cause positive social change.[14]

After several years as co-founder and CEO of City Year, I had met many inspiring social entrepreneurs from across the U.S. The not-for-profit sector was *thriving*, and pragmatic idealists were venturing to take on numerous challenges. It was thrilling to be part of a growing community of people who shared a commitment to changing the world.

The Echoing Green Foundation, which was providing critical support to many of the newer up-and-coming social entrepreneurs, brought us all together for annual conferences at the Colonial Inn in Concord, MA. These gatherings gave us a chance for renewal and reflection and to share ideas and knowledge. They helped us strengthen our sense of community and gave us a relaxed forum to discuss how we could work together on similar challenges and opportunities. For me, they provided a chance to deepen relationships with old friends and make new ones among an extraordinary group of people. For example, Wendy Kopp, the pioneering founder of Teach for America, attended, as did Bill Drayton, and Billy Shore, founder of Share Our Strength, a national hunger relief organization.

Steve Denning, one of Ed Cohen's partners at General Atlantic Partners, which had created Echoing Green, also joined us, and he shared a piece of business wisdom that I have never forgotten: "If you want to have a successful, growing organization—you have to always be on the lookout for talent and *hire ahead of your needs*."

It was at the Echoing Green conference in June of 1992 that

I first met Vanessa Kirsch. Vanessa had founded Public Allies, a national service program similar to City Year that trained diverse groups of young leaders ages eighteen to thirty through an intensive apprenticeship program with placements in not-for-profit organizations and government agencies. Public Allies' goal is to find the unknown community-based "leaders in the rough" and give them the training, skills, and experience, to become lifelong change agents. Vanessa was passionate, brilliant, beautiful, and exuded extraordinary energy for changing the world. I was immediately smitten. Later, I would tell people, I met the competition and decided my best answer was to marry it.

We were inspired by the potential of the times. The early 1990s seemed to promise a more peaceful and optimistic era, as institutional antagonists suddenly faded away. The Berlin Wall came down on November 9, 1989, without a single shot being fired. The Soviet Union disintegrated in a gift to the world on Christmas Day 1991. The Iron Curtain fell, the "evil empire" was eliminated from the face of the earth, and millions began the transition from dictatorship to democracy and freedom. Yitzhak Rabin and Yasser Arafat, bitter enemies for decades, shook hands and seemed to have started a fragile Middle East peace process. Nelson Mandela traveled a miraculous journey from prisoner to president. Democracy and free market economics swept the globe. Sworn adversaries in Northern Ireland began initial steps toward reconciliation. The world was introduced to the Internet, and became smaller and smaller and more connected.

There was an explosion in civil society all over the world. Professor Lester Salamon, Director of the Institute for Policy Studies of Johns Hopkins University, documented this phenomenon in a seminal article he published in *Foreign Affairs* in the summer of 1994, "The Rise of the Non-Profit Sector":

> A striking upsurge is under way around the globe in organized voluntary activity and the creation of private non-profit or non-governmental organizations...the scope and scale of this phenomenon are immense. Indeed, we are in the midst of a global 'associational revolution' that may prove to be as significant to the latter twentieth century as the rise of the nation state was to the latter nineteenth century.

Salamon's article sparked my imagination.

I had studied government, history, foreign policy, the Middle East and South Africa at Harvard less than a decade before, and no one I can remember foresaw anything at all close to this degree of sweeping change that had just erupted. We had not understood the potential for dramatic social change and improvement around the world. Vanessa Kirsch and I had been dating and together we decided to find out what the global revolution could teach America. We both took a leave of absence for a year, and set out to discover what a uniquely optimistic moment had made possible. We wanted to gain firsthand insights into what and who was driving this change and what could be learned from their experience. We were particularly interested in trying to meet young leaders from all sectors and discover their views of the future.

We spent a couple of months preparing for our trip, reaching out to everyone we knew in the foundation community, government, private sector, media, and non-profit world to help make introductions for us in the twenty countries we planned to visit. Then, on November 20, 1995, we got on a plane headed for Tokyo. We spent the next nine months traveling by plane, car, bus, van, train, kuumbi, camel, subway, boat, and mostly foot, nonstop through twenty countries and more than eighty-five cities, towns, and villages interviewing hundreds of social entrepreneurs, business, governmental, and non-profit leaders, young people, and citizen activists. Our mission was to learn as much as we could about how the world was changing, where new leadership was coming from, how civil society was developing, and whether the idea of national service was working or could work in other countries.

Our journey took us from Japan to South Korea, China, Thailand, Vietnam, Indonesia, Nepal, India, South Africa, Israel, Egypt, Turkey, Greece, Italy, San Marino, Austria, Hungary, the Czech Republic, Russia, and finally, Germany.

Whether it was in a village in Vietnam, a Banjar (district) in Indonesia, a boardroom in Hong Kong, the courtyards of Calcutta, a township in South Africa, Moscow's neighborhoods, or the Old City of Jerusalem, we were inspired by the passion people felt for their country and communities. It soon became obvious that all over the world, people shared a similar sense of obligation to common purpose, even though the challenges their communities faced varied hugely.

Traveling in the Mekong Delta, our guide was Dr. Chau Ba Loc, the Assistant Dean of the Can Tho University Veterinary School, in Vietnam. Dr. Loc was the lead representative of the Heifer Project in Vietnam, which we were visiting as part of a delegation from Share Our Strength, on whose board I served. Dr. Loc was just one of hundreds of fascinating, extraordinary, unsung citizen heroes we met. He was tall and thin, but his wiry appearance masked a deep strength. His lined face hinted at the challenges he had overcome and the wisdom he had gained. But he had a spring in his step and boundless energy. Dr. Loc was among the most spiritual, enlightened, and wise people I have ever met. His mission was to help the poorest of the poor, while also inspiring his veterinary students to commit to a cause larger than their own self-interest. We spent seven days and nights together traveling through villages in Vietnam, down the Mekong Delta, right up to the Cambodian border.

Dr. Loc told us that during the war he had been firebombed out of his home three times—and had to start over completely each time. He lost some close family members. To my astonishment, he had no bitterness towards America. The way he saw it, Vietnam had been fighting for independence for 1,000 years against the Chinese and the Japanese. The war involving the French and then the Americans was simply the last, most recent chapter of that much longer struggle. He described how he felt the need to look to the future. He told us if he and his countrymen remained bitter about the past, it would trap them and prevent Vietnam from reaching its full potential.

In addition to his duties as Dean at the Can Tho University Veterinary School, Dr. Loc was the leader of the Heifer International program in South Vietnam. He believed passionately in the Heifer program and, in particular, its philosophy of helping the poor help themselves, not by giving them a fish but by teaching them to fish. Heifer works on the concept of "passing along the gift." A family is given a goat or a cow to take care of and use to produce milk. That goat or cow can often be the difference between eating and starving.

But, the family does not retain ownership of that cow or goat until they have nurtured it to the point where it produces a calf or baby goat that they must then "pass on" to another family, who must then do the same. This teaches the family to take very good care of their animal and also gives them the chance to earn their gift. It is not a handout. Traveling through villages in Vietnam, where people lived on less than one dollar a day, and also through similarly poor areas of India, Indonesia, South Africa, and elsewhere, one of the biggest lessons we learned was that nothing given for free is completely valued. The best way to fight poverty is to help people help themselves. As Anton Soedjarwa, a leading social entrepreneur from Indonesia, explained to us, "If you take away poor people's desire to fight by simply giving them handouts, you leave them with nothing, because their fighting spirit is all they have."[15]

In Vietnam, I reunited with old friends from when I was resident at Harvard's Currier House, Jerry and Monique Sternin, who were leading the efforts of Save the Children, in North Vietnam. Jerry and Monique helped to develop a unique approach to solving the problem of childhood malnutrition through the concept of positive deviance (PD), a method that I came to understand could be applied to find a solution to virtually any problem or challenge. When they arrived in Hanoi in 1990, the US government had a full embargo against the government of Vietnam. Vietnamese officials told them they had six months to demonstrate impact. At the time, an estimated sixty percent of children under the age of five suffered from moderate to severe malnutrition.

Most people in a situation like this would focus on what wasn't working—the children who were malnourished and what was wrong with them. Jerry and Monique took exactly the opposite approach. They realized that the reason other intervention attempts had failed was because they brought resources into the community that weren't sustainable. They needed to find a solution within the community itself, by focusing on what *was* working: the children from poor families who, in spite of their limited resources, were healthy and adequately nourished—the positive deviance. They discovered that while the basic staple of the diet for everyone in the village was rice, the children that were healthy had mothers who would mix in with the rice some small shrimp and crabs that they could gather from the rice paddies, as well as sweet potato greens that were easily found in the village. These mothers also fed their children four times a day, rather than two times a day as was the practice of the majority.

Jerry and Monique took time to understand why some families

fed their children these healthy foods, yet others did not. They learned that conventional wisdom identified these foods as lower class or "common," despite their nutritional value. Jerry and Monique devised a program where mothers would learn about and begin to use these healthier foods together. They would gather in one woman's house, and everyone would be asked to bring with them small amounts of available nutritious foods. Mothers would cook together and feed their children together over a period of several weeks.

In the two-year period following Jerry and Monique's implementation of the positive deviance method, child malnutrition dropped in these villages by sixty-five to eighty-five percent. What's more, a follow-up study by Harvard School of Public Health found that children not yet born when Save the Children left these villages were at the same nutritional status as their older siblings. The healthy diet had become an enduring part of the culture.

▼▲▼

Positive deviance should be implemented on a grand scale. We often used this concept at City Year when we were trying to solve a particularly vexing challenge, and more often than not, it helped provide the key to a successful solution. President Clinton was fond of saying:

"There isn't a problem in America that isn't being solved by someone, somewhere in America." It's a simple but powerful statement. As I became part of a larger community of social entrepreneurs, I realized almost instinctively they would seek out and develop positive deviance solutions.

We met inspiring people like Jerry and Dr. Loc in every country we visited. In Thailand, we were hosted for a week by Dr.

Soonthorn Antarasena. Dr. Antarasena chaired the Department of Otolaryngology at Rajvithi Medical Center in Bangkok and was one of the leading Ear, Nose, and Throat specialists in all of Thailand. He was a devout Buddhist and had a quiet, unassuming manner. Upon first meeting him, you would never know how extremely accomplished he was. Dr. Antarasena felt a strong obligation to use his gifts not only to achieve personal professional success, but to make a meaningful difference for the less fortunate of his countrymen. So, he used his position to help establish the Rural E.N.T. (Ear, Nose, and Throat) Foundation of Thailand, for which he served as president. The mission of Rural E.N.T. is simple and straightforward—work for the public and work for the advancement of ear, nose, and throat medicine.

As one of the leaders in his specialty, Dr. Antarasena was in high demand as a teacher for young medical students, interns, and residents. And he wanted to instill in his students the same commitment he felt to contributing to his country and world. So, as a requirement for getting to train with him, Dr. Antarasena required his students to dedicate one long weekend a month (usually three to five days) to join him in a traveling clinic to poor villages across Thailand to provide free ear, nose, and throat care. The services ranged from simple checkups to full surgeries. On a given day, they would see between 300 to 500 outpatients, with about ten percent of them needing surgery. Even though this meant a more demanding schedule and time commitment on the part of the medical students, Dr. Antarasena was always oversubscribed.

We spent five days traveling across Thailand with Dr. Antarasena and his students, starting on New Year's Day morning, rising at the crack of dawn each day, and finishing after sundown so they could see as many patients as possible. The contrast between the villages we visited and the bustling, modern, traffic-plagued capital city of Bangkok was tremendous. In terms of medical facilities, the best villages could offer was a bare-bones community clinic or basic rural hospital. So, Rural E.N.T. brought its own mobile operating room with them. The children in the villages, in particular, were tremendously excited to see these traveling doctors outfitted in their official white coats. They were greeted like heroes everywhere we went. The impact on the medical students was profound. They relished the opportunity to make a difference for their fellow Thais while also improving their skills and knowledge. They told us that even with the extra demands, their work with Rural E.N.T. was their favorite part of their medical experience. They each felt privileged to be able to train with Dr. Antarasena, and it was clear that even more important than passing on his medical skills, he was passing on his values. Dr. Antarasena told us that among many countries in Asia, Thailand was relatively prosperous and his vision was that he could expand the work of Rural E.N.T. from Thailand to neighboring needy countries including China, Laos, Cambodia, Vietnam, and Bhutan, both as a way to serve people and build bridges among Thailand and its neighbors.

I will never forget Calcutta. We landed late at night in its simple airport hoping our luggage had made it, too. The baggage retrieval space was a stark, bare room, where everyone gathered in a jumbled crowd waiting to find their luggage, which was just strewn on the ground in no organized manner. As we followed the crowd, a government official in a sharp uniform tried to cut to the front of the line. Immediately, the crowd stopped him. "Who do you think you are? Get to the back of the line right now! This is a democracy! You don't have any special privileges here," they all stated in unison like a chorus. We waited to see what would happen, the official surveyed the agitated crowd, and sheepishly followed their bidding and moved to the back. Right away, we knew we were in a special country.

Calcutta is an assault on the senses. As in other parts of India, the colors are bright, the people energetic, and the noises of the city ring all night long. True to its reputation, the poverty is extreme and visible. The most painful to witness are the children, too many maimed, clad in ragged clothes, crawling along the streets begging for even just one or two rupees. (At the time we were there, equal to about two to five cents.) The number and condition of the most disadvantaged is overwhelming. Even idealists such as Vanessa and me wondered what could possibly be done to relieve so much pain and suffering.

We had read that Mother Teresa's mission was open to anyone who wanted to visit and if she was there, she personally greeted visitors and volunteers daily. However, she traveled extensively. There was a simple wooden sign posted outside the door. It slid back and forth to show one of two options; it read either Mother is In or Mother is Out. We made our way to the mission, and amazingly, the sign indicated she was In. With anticipation, we gently opened the door and made our way inside. We were given a tour and learned about the extensive work of the mission and then were asked if we'd like to meet Mother Teresa. We gathered with about forty other people who were waiting patiently. We had a chance to talk to many of them, most of whom had been volunteering at the mission for some time and had never had a chance to meet Mother Teresa. They came from all over the world and were inspired by her deep commitment to the poor and dispossessed. We felt a little guilty: here we were, on our first day in Calcutta, not having volunteered in the mission at all and we were among these privileged few. But before we could agonize about it, she came down and patiently greeted and personally blessed every single one of us. She was extremely tiny and somewhat frail, but she had a powerful glow and spiritual energy around her that was palpable, and she was unlike anyone I had ever met before. (The only other person who had that same kind of spiritual energy I've met since is Nelson Mandela.) We quietly took our leave from the mission, amazed at our amazing good fortune.

Thanks to Sushmita Ghosh, at the time President of Ashoka for Northern India, who hosted us, we met extraordinary social entrepreneurs across India, who took the challenges of Calcutta and India as an inspiration to apply their skills to make a difference.

Debashish Nyack, an architect by training, saw opportunity where most would see only despair. From his training and love of history, he knew that Calcutta had a rich architectural history, with some of the most beautiful courtyards one would find anywhere in the world. But over time, these courtyards had fallen into significant disrepair and had been abandoned as the local economy worsened. So Debashish established Heritage, to help reclaim these courtyards and boost tourism while organizing local community residents to provide for them jobs and empowerment.

Debashish is part architect, part community organizer, part historical preservationist, and part evangelist. He spent a day taking us around Calcutta, showing us neighborhoods and historic sites you could never find in a travel book. During our tour, we walked through crowded streets and along hidden, maze-like roads, and then all of a sudden arrived in a stunningly beautiful courtyard concealed behind a decaying exterior. Debashish explained how he was able to inspire local residents, many jobless and some homeless, to join in a community preservation effort to renovate and restore this and other courtyards in the area, while providing a source of revenue through tourism. This effort also built a spirit of pride among the residents and strengthened their bonds of community. From his studies, Debashish knew that many old cities had similar architectural landmarks in need of preservation, across India and other parts of the world. His model was based on a virtuous cycle of community empowerment and employment through historic preservation that could reverse the cycle of urban decay that plagued too many urban centers in the developing world. His passion, combined with the success he'd already achieved, made us realize he was on to a very powerful vision.

In India, we also met Ashraf Patel, the founder of Pravah, which means "flow," an organization designed to educate Indian youth from privileged backgrounds of both Hindu and Muslim descent, to become sensitized to the needs of the more disadvantaged in India's society. Pravah's goal is to instill a strong sense of active citizenship among its participants. Ashraf herself is a product of a mixed religious marriage. Her father was a civil engineer and a Muslim, while her mother was a college professor and a Hindu. So, she was raised to see the value of both religious viewpoints. While on her honeymoon, religious riots broke out after Hindu fundamentalists destroyed the Babri Mosque in Ayodhya in Uttar Pradesh. Shocked by these riots and with her justice nerve turned on, Ashraf decided to leave her highly paid job in corporate finance to bridge gaps in Indian society among people of different religious, socio-economic, and educational backgrounds. She decided to focus on high school and college age youth as having the best chance to develop a generation that could lead Indian society in a new direction. To accomplish her objectives, she used both community service opportunities and workshops designed to expose her participants to different cultural, religious, and economic situations. Her goal was to develop Pravah as a model and then have its programs adopted across Indian society. We were struck at how similar her work was to what we were doing in America with City Year and Public Allies. We felt like we had found a soulmate, half the world away.

▼▲▼

One of the most powerful parts of our travels was the time we spent in South Africa, learning about the tremendous change that had occurred since the fall of apartheid.

We arrived in Johannesburg in the middle of March 1996, while South Africans were in the process of ratifying their constitution, and it was the most exciting display of citizen participation and engagement in democracy I had ever experienced. After leaders of the constitutional process finished a draft constitution, they released it to the entire country and asked for comments. More than a million comments were given by citizens, NGOs, business leaders, and civic groups of all sizes and from all corners of the nation. Virtually every night, TV public affairs programs were dedicated to debating and discussing the constitution. Everyone had an opinion about what South Africa's constitution should be, from young people in townships to business leaders to civil society leaders. The people voiced it should not only help South Africa overcome the legacy of apartheid, but should be a model for the whole world.

One of the principles underlying this new South Africa was the African concept known as Ubuntu. Loosely translated, it means sisterhood or brotherhood and that a person is a person only because of other people. That no one lives in isolation and that we must all recognize that we are part of a larger community with both benefits and responsibilities coming from that community. Given our work with City Year and Public Allies, we fell in love with this notion of Ubuntu immediately. In a single word it communicated a philosophy at the heart of our work.

During that month, we learned there was a strong movement for a national service program in South Africa. I became convinced City Year should attempt to create a program in South Africa as a way to learn from this extraordinary country, culture, and new democracy, as well as do our small part to contribute to this inspiring transformation. Five years later, in April 2001, at the invitation of President Mandela and President Clinton, we traveled with President Clinton to South Africa to begin the process of establishing City Year in South Africa. Then, in February of 2004, thanks to the leadership and dedication of board co-chairs, Rick Menell and Murphy Morobe, the City Year South Africa program finally opened its doors. It had been nine years since my first visit. Like establishing City Year itself, it was a dream come true—and a reminder that change often takes time.

While we were in South Africa, we had the opportunity to spend a day in the Alexandra (Alex) Township in the heart of Johannesburg. It occupies one square mile, and in 1996, it had more than one million inhabitants. A friend arranged for us to meet with Linda Twala, one of Alex's outstanding civic leaders. Linda ran a full-service community center that provided opportunities for young people and senior citizens, and initiated a number of community development efforts. He seemed to know everyone in town. Because a big part of our journey's focus was to get a sense of young leaders' views of the changing world, Linda arranged for us to meet with about twenty-five young people from Alexandra.

Before our meeting, Vanessa and I strategized how we could best connect to this group and learn from them. We decided to use some techniques that we had developed in our work with young people back home. We began with the "human knot" exercise—we broke into three groups of about ten each, asked each group to form a circle, and then people linked hands across the circle to create a "human knot." They then had to untie themselves without letting go of one another's hands. There was much joy and laughter as people stepped over and under arms and clasped hands. Somehow all three groups managed to untie themselves without breaking their link to each other, which did not always happen with this exercise. It was human-scale problem solving, and everyone enjoyed it. We were off to a good start.

We brainstormed the assets that Alexandra possessed, especially when it came to young people, as well as the challenges the community faced. We used this as a way to encourage discussion about their hopes and dreams for the future. We found that, in general, even though these young people weren't materially well off, they had an extraordinary spirit; they were inspired by the transformation of their country and were determined to contribute to the new democracy emerging in South Africa. Their strongest desire was to have access to excellent education. And while they found significant obstacles, whether enough electricity or good job opportunities or a lack of strong educational opportunities in their township, they also recognized their ability to make a difference. We found them to be remarkably uncynical and utterly optimistic. This may have been a result of the recent transformation under the extraordinary leadership of Nelson Mandela and others in South Africa who had helped usher in the profound change, but whatever its origin, it was wonderfully inspiring.

During our meeting, this group of young leaders decided it would form its own youth council, and invite others to join it, so that the young leaders could work on some of the challenges they had identified. Vanessa and I were scheduled to be interviewed on the local radio station following our session. Instead of doing it alone, we brought two of them with us—after all, it was their community. They used that opportunity to announce their idea for a new youth council, and to invite others to participate. Several weeks later, we received an email that included the newly agreed mission statement and initial goals for the

Alexandra Youth Council. It was inspiring to see progress being realized.

South Africa was full of outstanding people like Linda Twala and the young leaders from Alex. One of the most accomplished social entrepreneurs we met was Dr. Garth Japhet. After years of practicing medicine and dealing with issues of HIV-AIDS, domestic violence, substance abuse, and other medical conditions, Garth became convinced there must be a better way to reach people than just one-by-one in his practice. He also wanted to focus on prevention and not just treatment. So, he came up with the idea of producing radio and television programs built around health related themes. With this insight, Soul City Productions was born. The power of Soul City is that they recruit young South Africans to write the scripts and star in the programs, so they have a relevance and authenticity that connects with their intended audience. Soul City has consistently been one of the top three programs in South Africa. Its success led Garth to develop Soul Buddyz to reach an even younger audience of children. Along with the television and radio programs, Soul City produces training and workshops for young people so they can internalize the message and prevention techniques directly. Garth is passionate about using his skills to confront the many health challenges in South Africa and across the continent. He keeps developing more entrepreneurial ventures and spinoffs to achieve his goals. I was excited when we were reunited in 2001 thanks to the Schwab Foundation's program on Social Entrepreneurship. We caught up on each other's progress and our visions for the future. Garth was working to expand Soul City to other African countries and was even more passionate and committed to his work as he successfully navigated the complicated political climate regarding the issue of HIV-AIDS in South Africa. The timing of our reunion was fortuitous, as we were just beginning City

Year's work in South Africa. Garth became a valuable source of insight as to how to work successfully in South Africa, and referred a number of outstanding young leaders to us.

▼▲▼

From South Africa, our journey took us to Israel, Egypt, and the West Bank. We arrived in Israel in April, one month ahead of the elections for Prime Minister. In conjunction with the election campaign, there had recently been some terrorist acts. The threat of violence was palpable, and everywhere you would see young people in uniform, patrolling the streets. We were struck by the power of national service. We had the privilege of talking to a number of these young people, both at friends' homes and at more formal gatherings. Older people in Israel took their young people more seriously and listened to their opinions and points of view more carefully, I believe, because these same young people were literally defending their country. We soon realized they had a level of maturity and sense of purpose that was greater than the average young person in the United States.

I had always been a believer in the concept of national service as a way to unite the country, instill a sense of purpose and common mission and commitment to causes greater than your own self-interest, but in Israel, it all became very real and tangible for me. Military service is a much different commitment than civilian service, and in Israel it is compulsory, with an option for conscientious objectors to perform civilian service as an alternative. I believe in a voluntary service system with civilian and military options. But in terms of bringing people together from different backgrounds and uniting the country through a shared rite of passage, and empowering young adults with a sense of mission, I experienced in Israel the tremendous impact that a comprehensive national service system can have on its participants and the country.

We had similarly eye-opening and inspiring experiences in virtually all of the countries we visited because we met extraordinary people—big citizens, leaders, and change agents all—everywhere we went. And while these people came from various cultures and backgrounds, had different histories, experiences, stories, and spoke different languages, they had one powerful thing in common: a commitment to the greater good and a unique brand of hope.

They were driven not by the momentary euphoria that some experienced when the Berlin Wall fell, or Mandela was released from prison. Nor was it a naive sense of joy, or simple optimism about the future. Rather, it was a deep and pragmatic feeling and determination to do what was right.

Vaclav Havel best captured the spirit of hope we witnessed over and over, when he said (*Disturbing the Peace: A Conversation with Karel Huizdala*; New York: Knopf, 1990):

> Either we have hope within us or we don't, it is a dimension of the soul, and it's not essentially dependent on some particular observation of the world or estimate of the situation...Hope in this deep and powerful sense, is not the same as joy that things are going well or the willingness to invest in enterprises that are obviously headed for early success, but rather, an ability to work for something because it is good, not just because it stands a chance to succeed...Hope is definitely not the same thing as optimism. It is not the conviction that something will turn out well, but the certainty that something makes sense no matter how it turns out.

The essence of our trip was meeting person after person, in country after country, who embodied and embraced this special sense of hope for the future. People who acted on the certainty that something made sense no matter how it turned out.

Hope drove twenty-eight-year-old Seung Ryong Park, who had moved his life from South Korea to North Vietnam to work with returning refugees. He wanted to learn about the communist mindset and how Vietnam dealt with reunification, because he dreamed of helping to lead South Korea to peaceful reunification with North Korea. Hope inspired Christine Loh, a legislative councilor in Hong Kong, who was fighting for democracy in Hong Kong as it transitioned from British to Chinese rule. And, Aditi and Ajay Mehta, a young Indian couple from Udaipur who worked in local government and with the NGO, Seva Mandir, respectively, and were passionate about empowering Indian citizens from disadvantaged backgrounds to achieve both economic success and to participate fully in India's democracy. Francesco Cesario, Managing Director of Timberland Europe, was leveraging the resources and expertise of his company to launch a new foundation and Italian youth corps, even though Italy has little experience of the private sector playing much of a role in addressing social issues, having relied heavily on the church and the government to meet those needs. Mechai Veravadya, known as the "Condom King" of Thailand, applied his business expertise and developed a set of restaurants called "Cabbages and Condoms," with the profits going to support family planning and AIDS prevention awareness. Nilda Bullain of the Civil Society Development Project was training young leaders from Warsaw, Prague, and Budapest, in how to start and grow new NGOs as a way for young people to become leaders in these new democracies. Nadia Seryakova, of the New Perspectives Foundation in Moscow, was passionate about developing young people and ensuring that their perspective was included and their voice heard in Russia's new democracy.

Each of these people, and so many others who we had the privilege to meet, when asked why they chose to do these things, had a common answer: because they felt it was the right thing to do. They saw a need and had to try to meet it.

In addition to meeting extraordinary people all over the world, we also recognized some trends that were beginning then and have since grown in importance. While we were traveling, President Clinton famously stated in his 1996 State of the Union Address: "The era of big government is over."

We realized this was true not just in America, but all over the world. Partly driving this civil society revolution was a growing frustration with government and bureaucracy everywhere, amplified by corruption scandals breaking out all over the world. From South Korea, Thailand, and India to Turkey, Egypt, Russia, and elsewhere, we read headlines of people's frustration with bribery scandals, government kickbacks, and the powerful taking advantage of insider access. While we were in South Korea, there was a major scandal unfolding whereby a number of people died when a major building collapsed due to shoddy construction. It was revealed that one of South Korea's powerful business groups known as "Chaebol" had paid off government bureaucrats to waive the normal building standards and inspections. People everywhere wanted to streamline government bureaucracy, move power to citizens, and engage the private sector more deeply in helping to solve social problems.

While the growing interest in civil society was the basis for great optimism, the bad news was that, all around the world, the non-profit sector was treated as second class in terms of resources and access to talent (especially among younger people, who were getting more and more opportunities in the private sector with the globalization of the economy). Everywhere we traveled, we found the greatest hurdle facing people committed to developing civil society, was access to resources. Countries in the developing world and the newly emerging democracies of Eastern Europe lacked the philanthropic system of America. Resources to sustain efforts and get them to scale for significant impact were rare if they existed at all. As the *Chronicle of Philanthropy* reported while we were traveling in Russia in 1996:

> Nobody knows for sure how many charities have sprouted in Russia in the years since the Communist system started to weaken, but the best estimates suggest between 17,000 and 35,000 were created in the past decade. Perhaps nowhere is the fragility of those charities more evident than in their effort to win donations. Many groups have pursued fundraising enthusiastically, but they say the seeds of philanthropy fall on hard times.
>
> Russians who can afford to give are often wary of charity scams, fearful of their own finances, and annoyed that they rarely receive accolades for their donations.

This same analysis applied to virtually every country we visited. Moreover, the inability of non-profit organizations to leverage their work and bring it to scale[16] stood in sharp contrast to the global reach of private sector firms we saw in every country we visited. It was on this trip Vanessa first began to develop the idea for her organization, New Profit Inc, which is like a venture capital firm for the non-profit sector. As we traveled and visited interesting programs and projects in country after country, led by the most inspiring people one could ever hope to meet, we were struck by how little information sharing there was among these programs. People were constantly reinventing the wheel. It was very hard to scale up and replicate their models. There were extraordinary people doing incredible work, often against great odds, everywhere we went, but their efforts were often a drop in the bucket compared to the scope of the problem. Or, whatever breakthrough idea they had come up with, and breakthrough organization they had developed to implement it, was isolated, and the lessons learned and new approaches were not being shared with people confronting very similar problems in other parts of the world.

The Rural E.N.T. Foundation could be replicated anywhere there were doctors and people in need of medical care. But it wasn't. MTV or an MTV-like spin-off, was on TV in almost every country we visited, while Soul City was limited to South Africa. Jerry and Monique Sternin's breakthrough work in North Vietnam needed to be applied in villages all over the world. But it wasn't. By contrast, Coca-Cola had figured out how to get Coke to any and all corners of the globe. We saw McDonald's and Kentucky Fried Chicken franchises everywhere. And in virtually every country we visited, we were able to put our American bank card into the local bank machines in that country, and even if we could not read the language on the screen we could withdraw local currency that would be deducted from our bank balances back home, thousands of miles away. When it came to delivery and ability to scale, the private sector had and still has much to teach most not-for-profits, which is why we have long believed that private involvement in social entrepreneurial activity is essential: uniting the entrepreneurs and entrepreneurial efforts of both sectors is where breakthrough change will come from.

Too often, what philanthropic support could be obtained was focused more on starting up a new idea or organization, or responding to a foundation's program guidelines, rather than figuring out how to replicate and grow a successful existing effort, or how to change government policy as a result of that successful innovation. Thus, New Profit, Inc. would be dedicated to working with successful social entrepreneurs and providing them with both significant "investment philanthropic capital" and strategic consulting and management advice so as to take their organizations and innovations to scale.

The other thing we realized as we traveled was that the idea of "national service" could work anywhere in the world. In virtually every country we visited, there was some kind of service effort going on. It is human nature for people to support and help each other. The growth in the NGO sector globally led to a growth in social sector and service organizations. Young people we met with in country after country were intrigued by what we had done with City Year and Public Allies, and expressed a strong desire for similar opportunities in their countries. With the end of the Cold War, the invention of the Internet, and the world becoming smaller and more interconnected, this emerging generation would be the first that could think of themselves as global citizens. The experience of our trip revived my earlier enthusiasm for a new global service corps and global service effort to unite young leaders from a variety of continents and countries to work together on pressing issues of the day as a way to instill a sense of global citizenship on the basis that we share this small planet and, at the end of the day, are all in this together. It also got me excited to explore what City Year could do internationally to both contribute to this effort and learn from people in other countries.

Vanessa and I still often talk about our trip around the world—the extraordinary people we met and efforts for change we witnessed. As anyone who has spent significant time abroad will tell you, you never appreciate what America stands for, the freedoms we have, the opportunities in front of us, and the uniqueness of America, as you do when you are overseas. As we traveled, we also felt a sense of responsibility to communicate the values and ideals of America. We felt as though we were "citizen ambassadors." Many of the places we went—villages, banjars, townships, and more—were not typical places for Americans to visit. In these places, we encountered an overriding curiosity, not about who we were as individuals, but about the country we came from and what it stood for. We realized that the ideals of America and the example that it sets are among its greatest resources, especially in the eyes of people around the world. The importance of these ideals—equality of opportunity, service, freedom, justice for all, citizen-led democracy, a sense that we're all in this together—and our collective work in trying to live up to them, would later be challenged in a visceral way after we returned home.

▼▲▼

In 1996, the world seemed heady with democratic optimism and the potential for transformational change. There were major elections that year in Australia, Taiwan, Turkey, Spain, India, Italy, Israel, among the Palestinians, Russia, Northern Ireland, the Czech Republic for parliament, and the United States. We even learned from Tony Saich, then the director of the Ford Foundation in China, and now a professor of policy at the Harvard Kennedy School, about an important nascent effort to introduce local elections at the village level in China. The Communist party hierarchy saw those elections as the best means to hold local party and village officials accountable.

The Cold War may have been over, but it wasn't yet clear what would replace it, as evidenced by continuing referrals to the "post–Cold War" world. No one could name the new era, as its contours had not yet been established. And while we did pick up initial rumblings about frustrations with globalization and a sense that some were benefiting much more than others, we did not see that the era of optimism might end with almost the same abrupt suddenness that it began. That was still to come. When it arrived, the lessons of our travels in good times seemed, if anything, more valuable, more central. Every country needed social entrepreneurship and big citizenship at a local, community, and national level. It became more, not less, vital when the storm clouds gathered.

6

SAVING AMERICORPS

What the federal government gives the federal government can also take away. In the discussion about public-private partnerships, the example of AmeriCorps shows both what can be achieved and how abruptly it can also be mortally threatened.

On June 6, 2003, the Corporation for National Service announced they were delaying their grant announcements until June 16. I soon learned the delay was due to a devastating eighty percent cut in the AmeriCorps program for the coming year. The cuts were not made because any one of the more than 1,000 AmeriCorps programs operating all across America had been accused of doing anything wrong or improper. They weren't made because programs were reviewed as inadequate or ineffective. They weren't made because these programs lacked support at the state and local level. Instead, the cuts were a result of partisan politics and mismanagement in Washington and, ironically, because there had been an outpouring of people wanting to serve after 9/11. There was absolutely no warning that the cuts were coming. Programs that were educating disadvantaged children, providing needed after-school programs, preserving our environment, building houses and playgrounds, caring for our elderly, immunizing children and more—faced closure or massive reduction, without any notice or explanation.

When I first heard about it, I couldn't believe the news. After 9/11 President George W. Bush had called on all Americans to dedicate two years—4,000 hours–over the course of their lives, to service. He established the USA Freedom Corps to organize and lead this effort and had promised to *grow* AmeriCorps by fifty percent. Instead, out of the blue, the program was getting a drastic cut, tantamount to elimination.

After fifteen years of fighting to get America to embrace national service in a new way, it was unfathomable to realize it could all be wiped out in an instant, with no warning, no explanation, and no good reason. I immediately thought of the tens of thousands of young people who had committed themselves to a year of service and who had put off college or other work opportunities, or for whom AmeriCorps was the best chance to get their lives on track. Thousands of schools and community-based organizations and hundreds of thousands of children all over America were depending on these dedicated and idealistic volunteers.

The service movement, which by 2003 had more than 1,000 AmeriCorps programs and 50,000 members, reacted to the news by instinctively feeling we had to fight this with everything we had. William James, in 1910, famously described national service as the "moral equivalent of war"; and that is what we felt was needed in response to these cuts.

Upon hearing the news of the cuts, I realized we needed a team of leaders to work together and combine our efforts if we had any chance at all of turning this around. AnnMaura Connolly, City Year's Senior Vice President for Public Policy, and an essential leader in the service movement since her days as a Jesuit Volunteer Corps member right out of college, joined with me to coordinate the effort. We immediately reached out to people. Wendy Kopp signed up. So did Rob Waldron of Jumpstart and John Gomperts of Experience Corps. Shirley Sagawa and Deb Jospin, who had worked with Eli Segal to found AmeriCorps, joined us. Dorothy Stoneman, the indefatigable founder of Youthbuild, played a lead role, as did Paul Schmitz from Public Allies, Eric Schwarz from Citizen Schools, Sally Prouty from the Corps Network, Bill Basl, the legendary head of the Washington State Service Commission, and Wendy Spencer, who held the similar position in Florida. Many other important service leaders enthusiastically agreed to join forces.

We also recruited an advisory group of national service champions who had great experience in Washington and excellent bipartisan connections. Eli Segal, City Year's board chair since 2002, was essential. Eli, AnnMaura, and I emailed and talked round the clock. David Gergen was invaluable with his inside knowledge of how Washington worked, outstanding communication skills, and a fundamental belief in us and the cause of national service. Former Transportation Secretary Rodney Slater possessed excellent strategic judgment and the ability to work with people from both sides of the aisle. He gave us consistently excellent advice and help. Jeff Swartz, CEO of Timberland, reached out to other business leaders and to important Republican Senators Judd Gregg and John Sununu. Joe Banner, co-chair of the City Year Philadelphia Board and president of the Eagles Football Team, leveraged his important relationships with leading Republican Senators Santorum and Specter, as well as with local Philadelphia media. Harvard Professor Rosabeth Moss Kanter gave us invaluable strategic advice as did David Cohen, Senior Vice President at Comcast. And Don Fisher, the founder of the GAP and a strong champion for Teach for America, reached out to his many lead contacts in the Republican Party.

Three prominent Republicans played essential roles. Marc Racicot, the former Governor of Montana and former Chair of the Republican Party, was absolutely instrumental. For a period of time I was in daily and sometimes hourly contact with him. As someone who was universally respected in the Republican Party, Marc's willingness to champion our cause was invaluable. He had nothing to gain by this, except his belief that what he was doing was right and good for the country. Ultimately, he would take the case all the way to Speaker Hastert and President Bush himself. Stephen Goldsmith, the innovative former Mayor of Indianapolis, and the Chair of the Board of the Corporation for National Service, also played a crucial role. He spent hours and hours of volunteer time meeting with Republicans on the Hill and in the White House, trying to work out a resolution to the crisis. And John Bridgeland, the founding Director of the USA Freedom Corps and an assistant to the President, also went way above and beyond the call of duty to ensure that people at the highest levels of the White House knew what was happening. Bridgeland convinced his colleagues that they needed to fix the problem. These three musketeers worked very closely together to convince their Republican colleagues they needed to come through for this valuable program and all of the people who were depending on it.

The campaign to save AmeriCorps aimed to be both a grassroots and a "grass tops" movement. We simultaneously reached out to the tens of thousands of citizens—the grassroots—who had participated in and benefited from AmeriCorps, while also engaging notables from all sectors of our society—the grass tops—who had firsthand experience with the impact and benefit of AmeriCorps programs.

From June 6, when we first learned of the cuts, until July 31, when the Congress left Washington, DC, for their summer recess without restoring funding, the Save AmeriCorps campaign, supported by an emergency grant of $150,000 from the Omidyar Network delivered:

> One hundred editorials from major newspapers all over the country;

> Forty-four governors from both political parties led by Massachusetts Governor Mitt Romney (a former City Year Board member) and Pennsylvania Governor Ed Rendell wrote to President Bush and congressional leaders to ask for the restoration of AmeriCorps funding;

> 147 mayors, led by Mayor Menino of Boston, and Republican Mayor Tom Murphy of San Diego, sent a similar letter;

> A full-page ad in the *New York Times* and *Financial Times* signed by more than 250 business and philanthropic leaders called on the President and Congress to restore AmeriCorps funding;

> "Save AmeriCorps" rallies were held in cities all over America;

> More than 50,000 citizens signed an on-line petition to Congress and President Bush;

> 228 Congressmembers—a majority—signed a letter calling for emergency AmeriCorps funding;

> Congress passed the Strengthen AmeriCorps Act, which resolved a six-month dispute on the AmeriCorps trust fund, that effectively reduced the funding cuts from eighty to fifty-five percent.

With the help and leadership of Senators Bond, Mikulski, Clinton, Kennedy, Reid, and McCain, and with support from Senators Stevens and Frist, among others, the Senate voted seventy-one to twenty-one for one hundred million dollars in emergency funding for AmeriCorps.

We also had assurances from the White House that they had worked out a deal with House Appropriations Committee Chairman Young, for the House to work with the Senate to ensure that a final compromise emergency funding bill would include one hundred million dollars for AmeriCorps programs.

But then, it all unraveled. Congressman Tom Delay, the House Majority Leader at the time, and an outspoken opponent of AmeriCorps, decided that the compromise would not go through, despite a majority of the members of the House having signed the petition calling for one hundred million dollars in emergency funding. Congressman Delay used a parliamentary maneuver to prevent a vote on the substantive matter. In a flash, all of the work we had done, and the funding to save AmeriCorps and keep thousands in service, just vanished.

I was extremely frustrated and upset. I called some good friends and mentors for advice. Gary Hart encouraged me to keep fighting and had some prescient words: "Alan, don't let Tom Delay stop you. Eventually he will get what is coming to him. You cannot operate in Washington the way he does and last forever."

After conversations with Vanessa and others, we came up with a strategy that had always served us well at City Year: the best way to save AmeriCorps was to let it speak for itself. With other principals from the service movement, we decided to convene one hundred hours of round-the-clock, nonstop testimony on Capitol Hill in Washington, DC in a kind of citizens' hearing in order to show Congress and the White House the power and impact of AmeriCorps. We would take a page from the Frank Capra movie *Mr. Smith Goes to Washington*, and see if we could similarly inspire and move Washington to act.

Some people within City Year, and some outside, thought I was a little crazy. They were justifiably concerned about the toll that the campaign thus far had taken on City Year. They wondered, with some good reason, why was I spending so much time trying to save AmeriCorps, when City Year itself was at risk? City Year's grant from AmeriCorps was to be cut by 55%, a loss of more than $8.5 million dollars, or more than 25% of the total budget. In each of the fourteen cities that City Year operated, we had established the organization as a public-private partnership, with private philanthropy being matched by federal money, thus losing federal funding put the entire model at risk. The City Year program for 2003–04 was scheduled to start in just three weeks time. We immediately had to make very hard decisions and calculations about how many corps member positions and service projects we would have to cut. Many at City Year thought the time I was pouring into the Save AmeriCorps effort and the use of considerable organizational resources could be better spent on trying to raise more private sector money for City Year so we could somewhat mitigate these funding cuts.

But, for me, it was not really a hard choice at all. The reason we started City Year was to help inspire a nationwide commitment to national service through a program like AmeriCorps. We were honored and proud to serve as a model for AmeriCorps. And, much more important than the almost seven thousand people who had spent a year in service through City Year by 2003, were the 250,000 people who had served America through AmeriCorps. If City Year survived, but AmeriCorps disappeared, the net loss to the country would be huge.

Given the pushback I was getting on the one hundred hours idea within City Year, I did what I often did at times when I was trying to make a tough decision. I went to see Hubie Jones, a key mentor from the very first days of City Year, and a giant in the Boston social justice world, who, in addition to serving as Dean of the Boston University School of Social Work, had worked to found or co-found more than thirty-three non-profit organizations.

Hubie listened carefully and thoughtfully as he always does, and then he said to me:

"Alan, if I have learned one thing in my forty-plus years of advocacy for social justice, it is that you can never give up especially when you are in a fight like this one. Their whole goal is to get you to just stop and go away. They try to wear you down and wear you out. The only way you win is by making it clear that not only are you not going away, you are stepping up the pressure. Once they realize that you won't stop no matter what, that is when you win. Because, after all, restoring money for Ameri-Corps is something they should be doing anyway. It is clearly good for the country. It has such broad-based universal support. The hundred hours is a great idea. Yes, the folks at City Year are tired and concerned, understandably so. You need to acknowledge that. But, you can't quit, not now, not ever."

As usual, Hubie sent me away, re-centered and re-energized, clear about what I had to do.

To pull off the one hundred hours hearing, which would involve the personal testimony of more than 700 people who would travel to Washington, DC from across the country, we needed to raise some significant resources extremely quickly. We put together a budget and determined it would cost about $250,000 in total, given we had only about a month to organize it. We approached our long-time lead funder—Atlantic Philanthropies—which had been a strategic leader among philanthropic organizations in funding national service programs thanks to the dedication of Chuck Freeney, Joel Fleishman, and Angela Covert. Forty-eight hours later, we received a phone call saying they had approved a grant of $200,000. We then approached the Omidyar Network and they quickly came through with the other $50,000 we needed. So, we were off and running.

The hundred hours of testimony, which we branded as Voices for AmeriCorps, was magical, exhilarating, and exhausting. People came from forty-seven states, from Alaska to Mississippi, and the whole event had the feel of a reunion even among people who were meeting for the first time. We were united in our commitment to serve our country and to being heard on Capitol Hill. After months of struggle to get Congress and the White House to pay attention to the need and value of AmeriCorps, we felt empowered that we were finally taking the issue into our own hands and doing what citizens had done from the very beginning of our country—speaking truth to power. To ensure that our message was clear, we made up "step and repeat" placards that we placed behind the speakers, emblazoned with the words—Service, Patriotism, Citizenship—to express our cause. During the day, we alternated between Senate and House caucus rooms in which hearings are normally held. In the evenings, because of security concerns, we could not use the Congressional rooms, so we held our citizens hearing in a building near the Capitol. Audience members included AmeriCorps alums, leaders of organizations that had benefited from AmeriCorps programs, and a broad array of supporters of the AmeriCorps program. Momentum built during the week and more and more Members of Congress joined compelling grassroots citizens in testifying. When the final witness wrapped up, we had recorded 108 hours of testimony because so many came in to join the effort. We knew that we had done what we needed to do to make our case.

And it worked. Not only did Congress restore all of the funding for the Corporation for National and Community Service in the next year's budget, they added, per President Bush's urging, a one hundred million dollar increase in order to fulfill his promise to grow AmeriCorps from 50,000 to 75,000 members. Even Congressman Delay signed off on this agreement and got, in exchange, some reforms to the AmeriCorps program that were reasonable.

The methodology we used in Saving AmeriCorps—building a broad-based coalition, getting agreement on a policy objective, reaching out to and effectively engaging grass tops leaders and grassroots citizens, and leveraging the media and the Internet—made me think that this could be a new strategy to drive progress. While one organization, like City Year, acting as an "action tank" could help to inspire a new public policy, as we had with AmeriCorps, what the Save AmeriCorps effort made clear to me, was it would take a large coalition doing "meta-action tanking" to be able to impact and move the larger public policy system. No one organization could do it alone. "Meta-action tanking" required leveraging the combined resources of the entire field of service—board members, funders, political leaders, media contacts, constituents, and beyond—as our only hope to prevail. Once we did combine efforts and resources, we were almost unstoppable. All of us in the service movement who had joined forces to fight these cuts realized, as Benjamin Franklin famously said about his fellow revolutionaries, that "unless we hang together, we will for certain hang separately." The question I began contemplating was, could this same methodology be used "offensively" to proactively promote a bold new policy agenda and not just defensively in response to threats to an existing program.

It was apparent that the national and community service field had to become much more engaged in helping to promote national service policy. We all had the expertise, the passion, and the connections from the grassroots to the grass tops. We could not simply rely on leaders in Washington who have a long list of issues to care about and focus on to drive the service agenda. If we were to have any hope of achieving our mutual vision of a country where citizen service was an ethic and opportunity for Americans of all ages, we all had to continue to work together to make it happen. As a step toward that effort, we decided to permanently establish Voices for National Service—whereby the leading organizations that had made up the Save AmeriCorps coalition, pledged to continue to work together to help impact national and community service policy in the country. Voices is now the leading organization representing the national and community service field. It conducts annual visits by program leaders to Capitol Hill and works on important advocacy efforts around national service policy and appropriations.

Another lesson learned was, for an effort like this to succeed, you need dedicated champions. We were blessed to have an extraordinary group of leaders who stood strongly with us to bring about the Save AmeriCorps victory. Senator Kennedy, as the author of both the National and Community Service Act of 1990, and of the legislation that created AmeriCorps, was completely committed to the effort. He detailed his extremely talented staff member, Jane Oates, to work with us full-time on everything from intricate legislative strategy to ensuring that we could secure rooms in the Senate for our hundred-hour hearing. Senator Mikulski—the "Godmother" of national service—was masterful, even in the minority, working so closely in a bipartisan way with Senator Kit Bond to both expeditiously resolve issues around the national service trust fund and secure the one hundred million dollars in emergency funding that the programs needed. Her committed chief of staff, Jenny Luray, was available to us round the clock.

Senator Clinton, who had played a lead role in the development and championing of the AmeriCorps legislation, participated in strategy calls, did outreach to other members of the Senate, and also testified at our hundred-hour hearing. During her testimony, she shared the previously unknown fact that when

President Clinton left office, as per custom, he made one request of President Bush: "When I took office, your father asked me to keep his Points of Light initiative going. I was happy to do that and I not only kept it going, I grew it. I'm asking you to keep my AmeriCorps program going, as I know that both of our families are deeply committed to service." Senator Clinton recounted that President Bush had promised he would definitely do so, that he knew of AmeriCorps' great work from his days as Governor of Texas, and that he was "strongly committed to it."

Senator Clinton's testimony immediately became big news. It added to the drumbeat demanding that President Bush stay true to his promise to push the Republican Congress to save Ameri-Corps. It also showed both Senator Clinton's commitment to AmeriCorps and her acute understanding of how to use her unique bully pulpit as a nationally known Senator from a major state.

Senator McCain also played an important role. He not only testified at our hundred-hour hearing, he also wrote a column in *Newsweek*, in which he stated:

> The administration has withheld support for legislation that Sen. Evan Bayh and I introduced to increase AmeriCorps. We did win administration approval for a plan to encourage short-term enlistments in the military in exchange for education benefits, and to begin funding national-service programs that help communities with their homeland-security challenges. But beyond this modest support, his administration has neglected to match the President's rhetoric with concrete steps to keep his promise.[17]

In addition to Senator McCain, other Republican Senators including Senator Norm Coleman and Senator Lisa Murkowski, testified at our Save AmeriCorps hearing. On the House side, the bipartisan co-chairs of the House Service Caucus, Congressmen Harold Ford, Jr., Chris Shays, David Price, and Tom Osborne from Nebraska, worked hard to get their colleagues to support the funding to save the AmeriCorps program. Each of them testified at the Save AmeriCorps hearing, too. Chris Shays sent every single one of his staff people to spend at least two hours listening to the testimony of service leaders, participants, and supporters from all over the country.

Lawmakers who weren't able to join us definitely heard from their constituents as the more than 700 people that came to Washington from all over America to testify, also spent time visiting their members of Congress and making the strong case as to the value and impact of the AmeriCorps program. Having strong bipartisan support was absolutely essential to securing the increased funding for the AmeriCorps program and putting it back on a path to stability and growth.

The campaign to save AmeriCorps was almost military in its planning and execution. Every day was intended to bring a new focus and a new assault on those who were trying to shut the program down. It has become a case study in the Kennedy School.

The Save AmeriCorps campaign was a turning point for me as well as for the national service movement. Though I didn't realize it at the time, it was what ultimately led me to move on from City Year. On the one hand, I experienced the extraordinary power of grassroots citizen action and a coalition working together. Thanks to thousands of people organizing and mobilizing, rallying and pledging, testifying, and advocating—our Congressional leaders and President Bush not only restored funding for the AmeriCorps program, but gave it more than a one hundred million dollar increase for the following year, both to make up for the cuts and to grow the program by fifty percent as President Bush had promised in his 2002 State of the Union address.

But, once the pressure stopped the following year, when we

had all gone back to our real jobs, the AmeriCorps program was cut again by almost twenty-five million dollars, and then the following year, it was cut again by twenty-three million dollars. So, in just two years, we had lost almost half of the gain we had achieved through the Save AmeriCorps effort.

Because these cuts occurred gradually and not in one fell swoop, it was hard to generate the counter pressure to get them restored. And once again, everyone was focused on running their organizations, especially because they had to make up for the years of significant funding cuts.

So, while I experienced the power of immediate grassroots action in a crisis, I came to realize its limitation: once the action and pressure stopped, Washington went back to business as usual.

It made me pause, and reassess how I was spending my time. The Save AmeriCorps campaign rekindled my interest in politics, policy, government, and in participating in larger movements for change. We only succeeded because we put together a comprehensive and coordinated strategy that leveraged all of the resources of our collective networks. It was exhilarating to see that, through our collective action, we were able to completely turn around what at first seemed like an impossible situation. I also got a chance to work closely with leading senators and their top staff, people whom I deeply admire. And I came to realize that while there was broad support for national service in the Congress, it wasn't that deep apart from a few notable champions.

David Gergen also contributed significantly to my thinking about other ways to impact policy and politics in our country. At the inaugural New Profit Gathering of Leaders in February 2005, Gergen gave the keynote speech. He said he greatly admired what we in the social entrepreneurship movement were doing. We were often inventing new solutions and new ideas, and getting real results that greatly impacted the lives of people for the better. But, he also challenged us and said that if we weren't bolder, we would be marginalized. He warned us that while we were spending all of our time slowly building our organizations, and growing our collective budgets by millions of dollars, to affect thousands of people, our political leaders in Washington were spending tens and hundreds of billions of dollars and affecting millions of people; sometimes, when they found out about it, applauding our work, but not really taking it seriously. Gergen went on to challenge us all to start engaging more directly in politics and government. He counseled that we needed to do more to educate and involve our elected officials in our work and share the solutions we were developing. He also argued that some of us needed to actually run for office and get into politics directly. Otherwise, we risked our movement being viewed as nice, but not essential. Coming right after a hotly contested election year, Gergen's words had a great impact on all of us.

City Year survived losing more than fifty-five percent of its federal funding that year, and managed to keep all of our local City Year programs open. We cut back the size of our corps by twenty-five percent from 1000 full-time members to 750, by stretching everyone to spend more time raising private sector money for one-time gifts to get us through the crisis year. For the following year, we succeeded in growing our corps back to more than 1000 corps members and fully restoring all of the service projects we had committed to do. As things at City Year started to stabilize after a tumultuous couple of years, I began to think it was time for me to take another sabbatical from City Year. It had been ten years since my last leave.

When Eli Segal became the City Year board chair in 2002, he had advised Michael and me that at this stage in City Year's development, our principal goal should be to institutionalize City Year and ensure that its leadership team was strong enough that it could survive either or both of its founders leaving. We worked together on a plan of action to make that happen. Eli coached me to work to continue to empower everyone in the organization and give them the room and opportunity to lead strongly and run with the ball. Eli also taught me I should spend my time doing the things that only I could do, and if there was something I was doing that someone else in City Year could or should be doing, I should give it to them. It wasn't always easy to adapt, but it is an extremely valuable leadership lesson. Time is everyone's most limited and valuable asset and the way to strengthen a team is to empower them with clear responsibility and authority. Everyone on the team should be doing what they can uniquely do.

I felt incredibly blessed to have Eli's coaching and leadership. Eli, a consummate entrepreneur himself, was a tremendous board chair, mentor, coach, leader, and friend for me. He always had a wonderful twinkle in his eye, and would slowly rub his hands together as he thought through challenging situations. He was deeply idealistic, but also smart and pragmatic, often saying "you campaign in poetry, but govern in prose" and "don't let the perfect be the enemy of the good." Eli also had a wonderful intuition about people and a deep belief that young people could change the world. He mentored literally hundreds of young people and made a strong personal difference to all of them.

With about a year before my planned sabbatical, Eli, Michael Brown, and I focused on the key goals the organization needed to accomplish. These included completing the next five-year strategic plan, strengthening and diversifying our leadership team through the recruitment of a new CFO and Senior Vice President for Civic Leadership and Program, finding a new permanent home and launching a capital campaign for a City Year building, and continuing to run the organization well day-to-day with a focus on refining our service model and impact and keeping the organization financially sound and secure.

We anticipated that 2005–06 would be a consolidatory year, in which we did not expand to any new sites or anticipate significant growth. Then Hurricane Katrina pounded the Mississippi and Louisiana coast.

Like everyone else in America, we watched with horror as lives were washed away across the Gulf Coast, and a beloved American city, New Orleans, was submerged. We needed to find some way to help. Jennifer Eplett Reilly, one of our original City Year co-founders, lived in Baton Rouge, LA, and she experienced the devastation of Katrina viscerally. Jennie described how people were in dire straits and they needed us to do whatever we could to help. We had opened City Year New York in direct response to 9/11; now Jennie asked if we could start City Year in Louisiana as a response to Katrina. She offered to lead the effort.

City Year's senior team brainstormed what we could offer. We ran the gamut from sending some volunteers immediately to help with the relief and recovery effort, to trying to start a new City Year program on a rapid timetable. Finally, we agreed we would try to launch a new City Year program in Louisiana in an unprecedented one hundred days, something we had never done before, as the process usually takes at least two years.

We discussed the idea with Eli and he was enthusiastic. Soon after, we were at the Clinton Global Initiative and had a chance to propose it to President Clinton. He asked what it would take. We knew we would need to raise two million dollars right away. On the spot, he committed a million dollars from the newly formed Bush-Clinton Katrina relief fund and suggested we announce it at once. City Year's Board established a special set of guidelines we would need to meet in order to open City Year Louisiana on this aggressive timeline and we all got to work.

We called in to all of our local City Year Executive Directors and reached out to major supporters. The response was incredible and heartwarming. Everyone wanted to help. The most important and limiting factor was whom we could recruit on such a short timeline, to be the founding corps members. We knew that, given the challenges surrounding Katrina, we couldn't open with a corps of totally new people. We needed a core group of City Year alumni—people who had already worn the City Year uniform, knew what City Year was about, and had veteran service experience so they could hit the ground running. We sent out an email to our alumni network asking who was willing to completely uproot their lives within a matter of weeks. Within forty-eight hours, we had a hundred City Year alumni ready to serve. At that point, we knew it would happen. And with Jennie Reilly's tireless leadership as the Founding Board chair and some heroic work by City Year staff member Wyneisha Foxworth, who had uprooted from Philadelphia to move to New Orleans, and Michael Flood, a City Year alum who returned to City Year to serve as Co-Director with Wyneshia, and the alumni who signed up for a second tour of service, we opened City Year Louisiana with fifty full-time corps members in less than one hundred days from when the Board approved our going forward. These staff and corps members went way above and beyond the regular City Year commitment as they often put in sixty-to-ninety-hour weeks doing relief, recovery, and rebuilding work.

City Year Louisiana would be a permanent legacy of the willingness of people to come together, work together, and serve after a devastating disaster.

With the successful launch of City Year Louisiana accomplished, I returned to the larger set of goals we had agreed on.

▼▲▼

The next time I spoke to Eli, he told me he had lung cancer.

And then my whole world turned upside down.

After several rounds of tests, doctors discovered that Eli had mesothelioma, a terrible form of lung cancer caused by exposure to asbestos. Eli's family never determined where he could have been exposed; some thought perhaps the public schools in New York when he was a boy, but we couldn't know for sure. The bottom line was that, all of a sudden, he went from being a terrifically healthy, active, and energetic sixty-two-year-old, to someone fighting a devastating and debilitating disease. Eli was diagnosed in the middle of November 2005 and passed away on February 20, 2006, President's Day, just three months later. It all happened so quickly, it didn't seem real. For so many of us, Eli's passing was a wrenching loss. As his daughter, Mora, movingly said at his funeral service, "Eli had two kinds of friends—best friends and close friends." Fittingly, we officially opened City Year Louisiana just two days before Eli passed away. With President Clinton in attendance, the opening was dedicated to Eli, who had fought so hard to make it happen.

Those of us who were close to Eli—a large group—took his death hard. The suddenness of his passing brutally showed how short time can be for any of us. For me, it clarified the decision to move on permanently from City Year and take up new challenges.

I realized it would be fairer to Michael and to the organization if I just decided to leave, rather than take another sabbatical, and delay for a year what would probably be the decision not to come back. City Year had emerged stronger than ever from the Save AmeriCorps crisis and I didn't want to slow down its momentum. My leaving would clear up any ambiguities. It would give Michael and the senior leadership team a chance to move boldly and aggressively forward, as opposed to having a year that would have some uncertainty around it. And it would also force me to focus on what I was going to do next without the safety net of just falling back on returning to City Year.

Michael was more excited than ever to double down on City Year and lead the organization into its next phase of growth, impact and sustainability. He had a strong vision for City Year's future and got right to work with our outstanding senior leadership team and dedicated Board of Trustees.

I was lucky and extremely gratified when I was selected as an Institute of Politics (IOP) Fellow at the Kennedy School of Government for the fall 2006 semester. The Kennedy School was dynamic, interesting, and fun. I quickly realized that at the IOP I was surrounded, as I had been at City Year, by idealistic, talented, and committed young people who would share their energy and dreams with me. I taught a study group on Changing the World through Social Entrepreneurship and National Service, and my time at the Kennedy School just flew by. It felt like a perfect place for me to go to as part of my transition from City Year, which I left officially on October 15, almost exactly twenty years to the day when Michael and I had written our first plan for City Year in preparation for a meeting with then-President of Harvard, Derek Bok.

7

SERVICE NATION

Be the Change was the organization I conceived that would act as a platform for campaigns of social change on a national scale. The name was inspired by Gandhi, who said, "You must be the change you wish to see in the world." The idea of it was to tackle systemic challenges, initially in the areas of service, opportunity, and fighting poverty, and education to change the landscape in which civic entrepreneurs and innovators operated at a public policy level. Be the Change would try to unite the service and social entrepreneurship movements with ordinary citizens to create a powerful coalition for change that would fashion bold, comprehensive, bipartisan policy blueprints to solve big problems, and then mobilize a national grass tops and grassroots movement to make it all happen. It would use those movements as a base to try to build larger citizen support and engagement around key issues confronting our country.

I also sought to bring the methods that had worked during the Save AmeriCorps campaign to the new organization. These included coalition building, getting agreement on an agenda that a broad base could buy into, and then working together on a comprehensive media, legislative, and presidential engagement strategy. I had learned through Save AmeriCorps that while one organization like City Year, designed as an action tank, could help to inspire a policy innovation, it would take a broad-based coalition—working together on a common agenda and utilizing its collective networks and contacts to grass tops leaders in the public and private sector, its media contacts, and its citizen base and networks—to affect the system as a whole. This strategy had worked defensively through the Save AmeriCorps effort. Now, I wanted to see if the same strategy and change methodology could work proactively. I called this approach "meta-action tanking," as the key was getting a broad-based coalition to combine efforts and leverage its collective resources. But while it was one thing to get organizations to work together when they were faced with elimination, it was quite another to get them to work together on a collective goal when they were not facing an immediate and grave threat to their existence.

I knew how demanding the day-to-day pressures at City Year had been. I knew how overtaxed and understaffed most nonprofits were. Part of the case I made to my colleagues was that I was developing an organization that would make it much easier for them to participate in a larger movement and allow them to escape the "social entrepreneur's trap."[18]

It was a thrill to be launching something new, and to have a chance to be creative and entrepreneurial again while also engaging in the broader world of policy, advocacy, and movement building. At the same time, starting over was more than a little daunting. When I started City Year with Michael Brown, I was twenty-six and single. I could survive on pizza and live in a barebones apartment. Now I was forty-five, Vanessa and I were married, and we had a child, a mortgage, and other responsibilities. But I loved the freedom that being an entrepreneur provided, and with Vanessa's support, I believed I could use my track record at City Year to get going.

The first big breakthrough for me, which eased my worries considerably, came thanks to Josh and Anita Bekenstein, two extraordinarily generous philanthropists who are major supporters of City Year as well as numerous other good causes. Josh is a very smart businessperson who has a huge heart that is filled with passion about making a difference in the world.

As part of reaching out to a number of good friends to get their advice about my future plans, I asked Josh if we could get together for lunch. He agreed and we met at Bain Capital, his firm. I shared how I wanted to move from being solely a civic entrepreneur, to more of a political and policy entrepreneur.

Josh listened patiently and thoughtfully, and asked excellent questions while also providing insightful advice. We talked about how hard it seemed to make change through our political system. Josh asked what my thinking was in terms of how to get started and what issues I would like to take on. I described what I had learned from City Year: I needed to find a partner and start building a team. I wanted to work on issues where I thought the system was either stuck in some way, or there was potential for a big breakthrough. The initial focus for the organization would be service, poverty, and education. After some more conversation, Josh stunned me by saying, "I like your idea a lot, Alan. It is high risk, but also high reward. There is a chance that you won't succeed with your ultimate goals, but if you even come close, you could have a big impact on the system as a whole." He then went on to say, unprompted, that he and Anita would be willing to commit a major multiyear founding challenge grant to help get Be the Change lauched. He explained that he wanted to offer the money now when I really needed it, rather than wait when it would not have as much of an impact.

I sat back in disbelief. I hadn't planned to ask Josh for any money; I really just wanted his feedback and ideas. Instead, his incredibly generous offer meant I would have desperately needed startup funds to launch Be the Change immediately. Josh was not just writing me a check over lunch, though. He wanted to structure the gift for maximum effect and leverage. He said that he and Anita expected me to match their start up gift with other commitments so that their funding would be leveraged to help make Be the Change sustainable. Another fundraising lesson I'd learned over the years was that it is very hard to get that first big gift, but once you get it, it is much easier to get the second and third. Or, as Holly Davidson once said to me: "It takes a polar bear to catch a polar bear."

The seed money allowed me to hire a small permanent team that consisted of Lisa George, Tim Zimmermann, Emily Cherniack, Greg Propper, and Ethan Gray—the proverbial five to six people that it takes to start anything—and we started to focus on the first major campaign that Be the Change would undertake. During the early months, I went on an extensive listening tour, talking to various friends and colleagues to share my thinking and vision for this new organization, which, increasingly I looked at as a hybrid of a think tank, action tank, coalition organizer, and movement builder. I received tons of excellent advice, but the pivotal moment occurred in August 2007, when I visited John Bridgeland, known to his friends as Bridge.

Bridge listened carefully to the vision and strategy for Be the Change and then suggested that national and community service should be its first big issue. He recommended I start by trying to organize a major national summit on the issue. He had recently organized just such a summit to fight the high school dropout crisis, which had been a big success and galvanized a coalition of organizations, as well as education leaders, to target that specific problem. Bridge is one of the world's nicest guys, has a keen intellect, and remarkable political instincts. He had served as Domestic Policy Advisor in George W. Bush's White House, and had been the key person to help launch President Bush's Freedom Corps in the aftermath of the 9/11 tragedy. He was a true believer in the power of service, and had great relationships with both political leaders and major Washington organizations, like the AARP. So when he said he would be eager to work with me, I knew I had found an excellent ally.

Because I knew the service field well and had a strong track record there, I could move quickly by reaching out to many of the key players and organizations of the Save AmeriCorps campaign. I had been thinking anyway that service would be a natural initial focus because it can have great impact in so many policy areas, including education and poverty, two areas I knew we would want to grow into. I contacted AnnMaura Connolly for advice, and she agreed that the time was ripe for a major new campaign to take the issue of service to the next level and was enthusiastic about working with me on it. The 2008 presidential campaign offered the opportunity for a major breakthrough on service because there were significant service champions in both parties running for President. My priorities now fell into line: launch a major service campaign going into the 2008 presidential election, with the aim of generating legislation that would take service to a new level in America and ensuring it passed in the first year of the next presidency.

From my work with City Year and many other social entrepreneurial organizations, I knew the importance of getting early "wins" and of demonstrating immediate results and impact in order for a new organization to establish credibility and traction. Taking on the cause of service, given my experience and relationships on this issue, provided the best chance for an early win. If we did it right, we could demonstrate how a new methodology for effecting change could work. And if we could do it successfully, we would make a big difference and hopefully generate the resources and support we needed for similar efforts in other areas. The newly hired staff agreed, and Be the Change was ready to launch its first major campaign. It was exciting, and felt right. The seed that would become Service Nation had been planted.

A few weeks after we had settled on service as our founding campaign, Michael Brown shared with me that *Time* magazine was planning a major cover story on national service and that he and AnnMaura were working on it with *Time*'s managing editor, Rick Stengel. This was a great breakthrough. Stengel was a true believer in the power of national service. He came to it as a constitutional scholar and believer in American democracy. Before *Time*, he had served as the executive director of the National Constitutional Center and also had collaborated with Nelson Mandela on his autobiography, *Long Walk to Freedom*. Stengel has a particular appreciation for the power of civic engagement, and like me and Michael, sees national service as a vehicle to help make the great promise of our Constitution and the American Dream real for all citizens.

As it happened, Bridge had worked with Stengel on the drop-out summit. *Time* was a major presenting sponsor and ran a cover story on the issue. *Time*'s upcoming service cover was slated to run September 13, 2007, just as the presidential campaign was heating up, and we figured we could pitch Rick and *Time* on a similar package for 2008: a cover story that would be a nice follow-up to the first one, tied to a major summit. Bridge, Michael, and I agreed a meeting with *Time* was a top priority. I widely circulated an invitation to leaders in the service movement—many of whom had been on the front lines of the Save AmeriCorps campaign—to join me at an initial planning and strategy session in Washington, DC.

By October, Bridge, Michael, AnnMaura, Greg Propper, and I had met with Rick Stengel and Ed McCarrick, the worldwide publisher of *Time* magazine. Ed had lots of good questions about cost,

Time's role and other details, but in principle, Rick and Ed expressed serious interest in getting involved in a summit that would accompany another service cover story. That gave real momentum to our incipient campaign. We quickly started signing up coalition partners and there was great enthusiasm for uniting once again in a larger effort to propel the national and community service mission. People agreed it was time for our movement to go on the offensive, and the presidential election offered a tempting window of opportunity. We planned a major national summit and a comprehensive policy blueprint that would capture all the best service strategies and ideas for increasing service opportunities, scaling up service programs and organizations with proven impact, promoting social entrepreneurship and innovation, and elevating service as a core ideal in our culture. Once we had that blueprint, we could take it to presidential candidates, leaders on Capitol Hill, the media and public, with the goal of building a powerful, bipartisan movement in support of bringing about a new era of service in America.

If we managed to win backing for our ideas from whoever won the 2008 presidential election, we would need a sound, and well-developed, legislative strategy to have any hope of moving major new service legislation in the first hundred days of the next presidency, which was our secret stretch goal. So I reached out to Shirley Sagawa, who was the leading expert on national service legislation, to join our effort. She readily agreed and would go on to play an indispensible role in helping to craft and pass legislation. Thus far, only Senator Chris Dodd, a Peace Corps, National Guard, and Army reserve alum, had unveiled a major new proposal for national service. Dodd was running for president, and he wanted to make a major proposal on service a centerpiece of his platform. So he began reaching out to service leaders in the spring of 2007 to help him shape a proposal. Mary Ellen McGuire, a member of his Senate staff who had moved over to his campaign, reached out to me for advice and I was happy to help.

Based on the input Mary Ellen and Senator Dodd received from the service leaders they consulted, along with Dodd's own direct service experience, Dodd put together an extraordinarily comprehensive and visionary proposal. It included growing AmeriCorps to one million people a year from the current 75,000; a new opportunity for baby boomers to serve through "encore careers"; elevating the CEO of the Corporation for National and Community Service to Cabinet status; a new Summer of Service opportunity for teenagers; and growing the Peace Corps more than three-fold to 25,000 people a year. All of us in the service field were thrilled with its boldness. I was honored to be included in the group of service leaders that was asked to contribute ideas, and didn't worry too much about the partisan nature of the exercise. I had a policy of working with any leader—Democrat or Republican—who wanted to develop new ideas on national service. With our hopes of making national service a centerpiece issue of the 2008 presidential campaign, we were excited to see a candidate put forth such a grand proposal.

Because Dodd was such a long-shot presidential candidate, unfortunately, his proposal did not get the attention it deserved. But subsequently, Dodd's proposal and his personal leadership became integral to the Service Nation campaign and the Serve America Act. The *Time* cover story on service, however, sparked renewed interest in national service, and eight presidential campaigns asked for briefings on the issue from John Bridgeland and Bruce Reed, who had served as President Clinton's Domestic Policy Advisor and was now president of the Democratic Leadership Council. We also held out hope that the service issue would eventually gain traction because a number of leading presidential hopefuls on both sides of the aisle had been strong supporters. Senator McCain, in June 2001, had teamed up on a comprehensive bipartisan bill with Senator Evan Bayh, to grow

AmeriCorps from 50,000 people a year to 250,000, and he chose the City Year annual convention in Chicago to first introduce his new proposal. Governor Mitt Romney had served on the boards of City Year and Points of Light. Governor Mike Huckabee was a strong believer in national service and often spoke during his stump speech about the need to offer more young people the chance to serve in exchange for college aid.

On the Democratic side, Senator Clinton had helped to devise and save the AmeriCorps program. Senator Edwards had also supported AmeriCorps in the Senate and had started the One America effort to get his supporters to do regular community service as part of his campaign. Senator Obama had started his career as a community organizer, and his wife, Michelle, was the founding Executive Director of the Chicago Chapter of Public Allies, one of the models for the AmeriCorps program that my wife, Vanessa, had founded back in 1991. Governor Richardson strongly supported AmeriCorps as well, and would eventually propose that we establish a new "GI Bill," in which a person who served for two years could get four years of support to attend any State university. Senator Biden had also been a strong supporter of AmeriCorps and the Peace Corps in the Senate.

Helping push the issue in front of the candidates and the primary voters was a terrific new organization called Serve Next, co-founded by two young City Year alumni, Zach Maurin and Aaron Marquez. ServeNext's goal was to get every presidential candidate to sign a pledge to grow AmericCrps by 100,000 (bringing the total to 175,000), and to double the Peace Corps. Their strategy was to recruit AmeriCorps alumni to politely but persistently bird dog the candidates in New Hampshire at town meetings, and film their response (which would quickly get uploaded to YouTube and spread virally through Facebook). By early fall, they had succeeded in getting every single Democratic

Presidential candidate and Governor Mike Huckabee to sign their pledge. Senator McCain had a policy of not signing pledges but welcomed ServeNext aboard his bus for filming, and was already on record with his legislation supporting an increase in AmeriCorps to 250,000. So, thanks to the creativity and dedication of ServeNext, significant growth in AmeriCorps became part of the presidential primary campaign agenda. It was amazing what a small group of idealistic young people could do. They not only used the opportunity that the New Hampshire presidential primary provided to meet the candidates face to face, but understood how to use the latest technology to pressure the candidates to embrace their agenda. For example, John Edwards had committed to sign the ServeNext pledge, but had not done so. Finally, after they filmed him promising to sign and uploaded the video to YouTube, he did.

To add to the momentum, Senator Barack Obama went beyond signing the ServeNext pledge, to give a major speech on service and social entrepreneurship, in Iowa on December 5 (he was introduced by Harris Wofford, who included a strong endorsement in his introduction). Vanessa's organization, New Profit Inc., had organized a broad-based coalition called America Forward to promote the ideas of social entrepreneurship and innovation with all of the Presidential candidates. It was so exciting for both of us to see these two movements of service and social entrepreneurship coming together powerfully under Senator Obama's leadership. Senator Obama's speech was an elegantly forceful call for all Americans to step forward. "We need your service, right now, in this moment—our moment—in history," Obama told a young audience. "I'm not going to tell you what your role should be; that's for you to discover. But I am going to ask you to play your part; ask you to stand up; ask you to put your foot firmly into the current of history." Obama said, if elected, he would increase Ameri-

Corps to 250,000, expand service programs for older Americans, double the Peace Corps, and put a new emphasis on social entrepreneurship by establishing a White House Office for Social Innovation, among other things. What really caught my attention, however, was that Obama didn't just lay out a new proposal, he pledged to make service "a cause of my presidency."

Again, as I had been for Senator Dodd, I was honored to be asked to serve as part of an outside advisory group to work with Heather Higginbotham and Carlos Monje of Obama's campaign staff in developing and reviewing his national service plan. They did an excellent job reaching out to many leaders in the service community. After the Iowa speech, Senator Obama incorporated his commitment to national service as a major part of his stump speech. As Bill Clinton had found in 1992, a new call to service resonated deeply with audiences across the country.

The way the politics of service were shaping up on the campaign trail, it made it all the more important that a national coalition and a strong policy blueprint was ready. To unveil it all, and reinforce the idea that service should be a central theme of the next presidency, we committed to September 11–12, 2008 as the dates for the Service Nation summit. We were excited to incorporate the idea of 9/11 being an official day of service and remembrance as part of our policy agenda, as many of us in the service movement had long advocated for that as well. David Paine and Jay Winuk of My Good Deed, and the other leading 9/11 family groups, would go on to play a very important role in our coalition and in reaching out to the eventual presidential nominees in support of the summit.

We wanted the summit to be a major event, which meant that we needed—in addition to whichever candidates won their party's nomination—to inspire the attendance of leaders of every sector of American society, from the civic and faith-based community to corporate CEOs, to the military and educational community. That meant we needed all-star co-chairs to lead the summit. After Rick Stengel we first reached out to Caroline Kennedy.

I was enthusiastic about Caroline. I had met her several times through Senator Kennedy and the work of the Kennedy Library in Boston and the Institute of Politics at the Kennedy School. She had edited a wonderful compilation of America's most inspiring and important writings about citizenship and service, called "A Patriot's Handbook." She was a regular contributor to *Time*, and had written an essay about the enduring power of the Peace Corps in the recent issue on service. Caroline had done her own public service by dedicating herself to the cause of public school reform in New York City, working closely with Mayor Bloomberg and Schools Chancellor Joel Klein. We all felt that Caroline would be a compelling public voice for our summit, and an ideal person to help lead this new effort for a major expansion of national service. Caroline had agreed to speak at the dedication of City Year's new permanent National and Boston Headquarters in October, so we had just the right moment to tell her about this new effort and ask her to join it.

Caroline, who is remarkably modest, easy to talk to, and down to earth, first asked, "Are you sure I'm the right person for this?" We assured her that for many reasons she was. She then said that she was honored to be asked, and affirmed she was totally committed to national service. She loved the Peace Corps and Ameri-Corps and thought that there wasn't anything more important for our country. A couple of weeks later, Caroline officially confirmed she was excited to join us and serve as a co-chair for the summit.

To fully leverage the experience and talent available, we decided that Be the Change, Civic Enterprises (Bridge's outfit), and City Year would work together to help pull together Service Nation. (Greg Propper had come up with this name after endless internal agonizing and lists of contenders. As a lifelong devoted member of Red Sox Nation, I immediately embraced it.) Eventually, we would add Michelle Nunn and the Points of Light Institute as another coordinating organization. Michelle brought deep experience from her almost two decades as a leader in the service movement and also represented a very important "stream of service"—community volunteering.

We knew that success depended upon uniting a large coalition of organizations that represented both the leading service organizations, but also "natural allies," organizations that embraced a new policy blueprint and major new commitment to national and community service. For example, the American Jewish Committee, just the year before, had pulled together an excellent task force and published a major report on the need for a dramatic new effort around national service as a way to strengthen our democracy and meet pressing needs. They enthusiastically signed on from the very beginning. America's Promise, led by Chair, Alma Powell, and CEO, Marguerite Kondracke, emphasized service as one of their five key goals, and also joined up, with Alma Powell agreeing to be a co-chair of the summit. Roxanne Spillett and the Boys and Girls Clubs used service as part of their core youth development strategy and played a leading effort in our coalition and grassroots campaign. And Bridge had been talking with the AARP, which was excited to push a new proposal for service, especially for baby boomers, who were looking for new opportunities to stay involved and serve. Colonel Rob Gordon, who had an outstanding twenty-six-year career in the Army, including a year as a White House Fellow working with Eli Segal to establish AmeriCorps, and who was now a Sr. Vice President at City Year, connected us to a group of retired military leaders who had formed an organization called the Critical Issues Roundtable. This group, led by Alan Salisbury and

Tony Smith, had developed their own blueprint for a major civilian national service program to sit alongside the military service system.

One of the key objectives our growing coalition identified right away was the need to cultivate some bipartisan champions to promote ambitious new service legislation in Congress. The names that readily rose to the top of the list were Senators Kennedy and Hatch. Senator Kennedy was an obvious choice since he had authored every major service bill, going back to the National and Community Service Trust Act of 1990. Additionally, he chaired the Health, Education, Labor, and Pensions Committee in the Senate, where new legislation would originate. We saw Senator Hatch as a natural ally for Senator Kennedy. As a Mormon missionary, he had done two years of service as a young man. He was also an original co-sponsor of the 1990 Service Act, and he and Senator Kennedy had worked across the aisle on a number of issues, including children's health insurance, the Ryan White Aids Bill, the Americans with Disabilities Act, and others.

We knew we could talk to Senator Kennedy easily; we had worked with him closely for almost twenty years. As we wondered how best to approach Senator Hatch, something funny happened, which made me think this was all meant to be. Chris Campbell, Senator Hatch's legislative director, called my office in December and said he wanted to get together to talk about national service because Senator Hatch wanted to develop a major new proposal that would give everyone in America a similar life changing service experience to the one he had experienced as a missionary. It was an amazing synchronicity. Getting to Senator Hatch was one of our absolutely essential objectives, and here he was reaching out to us!

In the Mormon faith, service is a rite of passage, and Chris Campbell indicated that Senator Hatch had initially even considered a mandatory program. He had changed his mind, which I agreed with because service is so much more meaningful if it is voluntary, but Campbell emphasized that his boss really wanted to do something big, bold, and transformational for the country. Campbell said that Senator Hatch was deeply committed to this, explaining that he was concerned that America was becoming too divided, and he saw service as a way to help unite the country while also unleashing citizen energy as opposed to government bureaucracy to address major problems. Senator Hatch hoped a major new service initiative would foster a sense among citizens that whatever our problems and challenges, we needed to face them together. He had a vision of getting a number of the longer serving members of the Senate together to unite behind this proposal, leaders who had been there long enough to remember the days when it was part of the regular course of business to work together in bipartisan ways. And as luck, or fate, or history would have it, Hatch wanted to begin by reaching out to his good friend, Senator Kennedy.

I wanted to speak to Senator Kennedy directly, as I had a sense he would get excited about this new effort, especially since Senator Hatch was ready to collaborate. Once I told him, after barely a pause, he replied, "Alan, I'm very interested in this. We can't get a new service bill passed until there is a new President, but we need to get working on it right away and get it all teed up, so as soon as there is a new President, we can get it passed in the very beginning of the next administration. I'd be delighted to work with Orrin on this. He and I have done some great things together. You should call Mike Myers, (Kennedy's Chief Counsel for the Labor Committee) right away and he will follow up with you. We can get this done. And I'm delighted that Caroline is involved."

Kennedy grasped exactly what it would take and how to get it done, and as we worked with him going forward, I came to appreciate even more why he was arguably the single most successful Senator of his generation. I lived by the Sun Tzu mantra that "every battle is won or lost before it is fought" and in that brief moment, Senator Kennedy could see the entire battle of new service legislation being played out and began the process of getting it done in the Congress. Like all great strategists, he was already projecting into the future and seeing around the corners.

No one was a bigger champion of national service in the Congress than Senator Kennedy, and if he made new service legislation a major priority, we had a much higher likelihood of ultimate success. His partnership with Senator Hatch would make the effort strongly bi-partisan and mean that regardless of whether a Democrat or Republican won the White House, we could move this new legislation.

It had been almost a year since the Bekenstein's initial founding gift and it was proving harder to match than I expected. Only Jonathan and Jeanne Lavine, longtime friends and supporters, had thus far come through with a very generous matching gift. Nor had we raised any specific funding for Service Nation. And until Kennedy agreed to team up with Hatch on a new legislative effort, we had little to point to that could indicate our advocacy efforts could be successful. Unlike City Year, where we could see daily impact through our direct service work, the fruits of our efforts in the advocacy space could not be immediately measured or at all guaranteed. Because direct service work could lead to tangible and often immediate impact, a number of leaders, participants, and supporters in the service and social entrepreneurship movements were wary about spending too much time and energy on advocacy. Having two legislative giants behind our cause inspired more people to make a deeper commitment to the Service Nation effort. I could hardly wait to tell Vanessa I felt we finally had true liftoff.

Within a week, Senators Hatch and Kennedy had conferred

and confirmed their partnership. AnnMaura Connolly and I briefed Kennedy's staff on the strategy for Service Nation. By this point, we had more than eighty major organizations in our coalition and forty of them were actively involved in our policy development process which we had opened up to anyone and any organization that wanted to participate. Plans for the September 11–12 service summit were coming along and we hoped it would be possible to complete the legislation in time to unveil it there so we could use the summit as a galvanizing event to help build support for it. Kennedy's staff confirmed that Senator Kennedy shared this goal and they would work hard with Senator Hatch to get it done. Kennedy was legendary for having absolutely the best and hardest working staff in the Congress. Working closely with Michael Myers, Emma Vadehra, Carmel Martin, and Eric Mogilnicki, over the next two years I would see on many occasions how well deserved this reputation was.

In addition to the summit that would convene about six hundred people, a central part of our strategy was to engage a broad grassroots base of citizens to advocate for a new call to service. So, leveraging our growing coalition, we planned to convene a National Day of Action, on Saturday, September 27, two weeks after the summit, where hundreds of events could be held all over America involving tens of thousands of people in service projects, service fairs, town meetings, forums, and other activities. That way, people who couldn't attend the summit could nevertheless demonstrate their support for a new era of service in their hometowns. While the summit focused on engaging the grass tops, the Day of Action would help to mobilize the grassroots and create an explosion of energy around the idea of service that would hopefully help us build the national movement we would need to win fast passage of major new service legislation, while also deepening the culture of service around the country.

By March, we were making strong progress along most of our goals—legislative, coalition, grass tops, and grassroots planning, and the Presidential nominating contest had narrowed to Senator McCain on the Republican side and Senators Obama and Clinton on the Democratic side, so we knew we would have strong service champions for both nominees. We had one major problem: we still had not raised any sponsorship funding for the summit or Day of Action. Ahead of an important meeting with Rick Stengel and Ed McCarrick, we needed to show at least some initial fundraising momentum. Our plan was to try to get lead sponsors who would commit anywhere from $100,000 to $500,000 towards the overall costs of the Service Nation summit and Day of Action.

I had approached James Jensen, a strategic philanthropist, to see if he would be willing to be the first gift of $100,000. James deeply understands the value of philanthropists making highly leveraged, strategic philanthropic investments as a way to catalyze major change. He called and committed to be our first sponsor right before our scheduled meeting with *Time*. Laurie Tisch, another strategic philanthropist based in New York, confirmed soon after that she would match the Jensen gift. I was grateful that, thanks to James and Laurie, we finally had some fundraising momentum, but we had only raised about ten percent of our two million dollar goal, and September was fast approaching. It was a start, but what we really needed given the scale of the summit and day of action we were planning, and the short timeline, was a major donor. The breakthrough came thanks to a conversation that Rick Stengel had with Vartan Gregorian, president of the Carnegie Corporation of New York.

On St. Patrick's Day, because most of New York City was off, Vartan Gregorian spent more than two hours with us, during which he listened carefully to our vision and plans. He had a complete knowledge of the history of previous national service efforts in America—both those that had succeeded and those that had failed. He said he was interested in having Carnegie play a leadership role in the summit, but advised that it needed to be an action-forcing event that would engage leaders from all sectors and networks. Vartan agreed to become a co-chair of the summit, along with Caroline, Rick, and Alma Powell. He asked us to submit a formal proposal that he would fast track for a June Board vote, and suggested that Carnegie would be a lead convener of the summit with a gift of $500,000.

Within days of this Carnegie meeting, Bridge and *Time*'s Ed McCarrick met with Bill Novelli, CEO of AARP, who signed on as a co-chair of the summit, and AARP jumped in with $250,000 in cash and a commitment to deliver one million dollars in additional in-kind support from their website, magazines, communications, and staff time. AARP also agreed to become a lead member of our growing coalition and to deploy their considerable advocacy capabilities to help move new service legislation once it was introduced. We had gone from no lead sponsors to several anchor sponsors in a matter of weeks. Partnering with AARP was an especially significant development, not only because AARP has deep experience and resources, but more importantly because retiring Boomers were a massive service-oriented demographic. In fact, many of us in the service movement felt the next big frontier for national and community service was to engage in large numbers the baby boom generation, which had come of age with President John F. Kennedy's idealistic call for Americans to ask what they could do for their country. With AARP's support and help, it became possible to more effectively tap this important new national resource. Also, AARP, with its capacity to mobilize millions of older Americans, was legendary for its ability to move legislation forward on Capitol Hill.

Support begets support. Target, which has long been a leading corporate sponsor of service initiatives and service organizations, also joined as a "Presenting Sponsor" of the summit, with Laysha Ward, President of the Target Foundation, serving as a co-chair. More foundations and corporations signed on as well, building a platform of support that would give us the resources to stage a truly meaningful summit and Day of Action. Part of our strategy was to find roles for as many strongly committed service champions as we could, and to engage them in the Service Nation effort. So, we also created a Leadership Council, which we could turn to for advice, media assistance, credibility, and networking. Eventually, we signed up some eighty-five key figures from every sector of American society. We wanted to get young people, in particular, very excited about what we were doing, so we were delighted when the music star Usher agreed to serve as the Service Nation Youth Chair. With the money we had raised, we created a Young Leaders program that would identify and recruit one hundred young service superstars, so they could attend the summit, offer their perspective, and share their incredible energy and idealism.

Then, wrenching news. Between January and May, I saw Senator Kennedy several times at events in Boston. Each time, he went out of his way to talk to me about the progress he was making with Senator Hatch on the new service legislation and reassured me that it was moving along and would get done in time for our planned summit in September. He also encouraged me to keep growing our coalition to build broad support for the legislation and gave me advice both about some partners we were enlisting and how to be successful with other members of Congress. His commitment to this effort was strong, enthusiastic, and invaluable.

But, on May 20, along with the rest of the world, I learned that

Senator Kennedy had been rushed to the hospital and been diagnosed with brain cancer. Having been through lung cancer with Eli Segal, I, like so many others, was devastated by this news. Senator Kennedy, even in his late seventies, was so full of energy and life that we all just assumed he would be with us for years to come. He was an indispensable leader, not just for the service movement, but to so many other progressive causes. Much depended on his unique leadership and ability to bring people together to get things done.

Characteristically, Senator Kennedy took the fight to his cancer. He chose an aggressive form of treatment that included brain surgery that entailed many risks. He emerged in good shape and good spirits, but his prognosis was uncertain. I was in DC soon after Senator Kennedy's diagnosis and had a chance to visit Michael Myers and Emma Vadehra from his staff. We shared our mutual concern for Senator Kennedy and how unique he was as a leader. Michael told me they were all doing their best under the circumstances, and that Senator Kennedy was focused more than ever on the new service legislation and determined to move it forward.

We got back to work, committed to make the summit as powerful as possible by recruiting A-list speakers and attendees. We started with New York City's mayor, Michael Bloomberg, since he was our host and a strong supporter of national and community service. He quickly agreed to be a keynote speaker. We then asked Governor Arnold Schwarzenegger, who just a few months earlier had become the first governor in the country to elevate his director of the California Service Commission, Karen Baker, to Cabinet status in his government. Governor Schwarzenegger and his wife, Maria Shriver, were leading national figures on the issue of service, and he agreed to keynote as well. Eventually, the speaker roster would include Senators Hatch, Clinton, Dodd and

Wofford, First Lady Laura Bush, the Chairman of the Joint Chiefs of Staff, Admiral Mike Mullen, Queen Noor of Jordan, and Congressmen Chris Shays and Rob Portman. We also reached out to Hollywood. Tobey Maguire agreed to attend the entire summit and say a few words. Tobey would go on to chair the Service Nation Ambassadors Council and recruit a group of leading celebrities to get behind the Service Nation effort. On the day itself, Jon Bon Jovi gave an impassioned plea for service and Alicia Keys brought down the house with an inspired speech and a beautiful a cappella riff on Sam Cooke's "A Change Is Gonna Come."

It was now June; the summit was just about three months away, when along came another little miracle. Vanessa gave birth to our second child, a boy, on Friday June 13. We named him Reece John Joseph Khazei; Reece, because it means "great enthusiasm for life," and John Joseph for his maternal great grandfathers. We were overjoyed. Even if it meant I once again was soothing a baby and sending emails at three in the morning. So I had several startups going—Reece, Service Nation, and Be the Change. And as crazy as it would seem to take on more, we decided to set our sights on one additional, blockbuster element: we wanted both the Democratic and Republican nominees for President to attend a nationally televised forum on service on the evening of September 11. Senators Obama and McCain had by that time emerged as the candidates. If we could somehow get both of them to participate in the summit, we would simultaneously engage the next president, and force the national media to take notice of the growing power and potential for service to help address an array of chronic social ills while uniting increasingly divided Americans in common cause.

Getting McCain and Obama to accept our invitation—despite the deep commitment both had shown to the idea of service—was not guaranteed. Both campaigns would need to game out the value of an appearance, as well as weigh it against the legion of other political events their candidate could choose instead. Thus far, the only joint appearances the candidates had agreed to for the general election were the televised debates. To make a joint appearance less risky, and more appealing to the campaigns, we purposely did not present the forum as a head-to-head debate (where the dangers to either campaign are magnified), but rather as sequential interviews with a brief joint appearance on stage in the middle. We hoped that if one candidate committed, the other would follow. So, we launched a full-court press to get them both to come. That meant, beyond a formal invitation from Service Nation, persuading everyone we knew with a direct connection to the candidates—or to their campaign staffs—to encourage them to unite around the cause of service on the evening of September 11th. The power of our coalition really kicked in. By this point our Service Nation coalition included more than one hundred major national organizations that collectively reached more than one hundred million Americans. A letter was sent to each candidate from the entire coalition, and dozens of influential leaders from the communities around each organization (whether it was a board member or a lead spokesperson) contacted them directly as well. We managed our own internal "war room" to keep track of the numerous contacts being made to each candidate and campaign.

Senator McCain signed on first, agreeing in early July. McCain's acceptance arrived in time for us to include it in our formal press announcement of the event. That helped give the summit credibility, as well as some news. Getting Obama to accept our invitation was not as easy as we had hoped, however. The campaign was swamped with opportunities for all sorts of events. Finally, in mid-August, just three weeks before the summit, we received word that Senator Obama would attend. It was just in time and helped cement the summit as a major media event that would draw national press and be broadcast live by all of the cable news networks, along with PBS. It would be the first joint appearance of both nominees of the general election as it would take place before the first debate.

With McCain and Obama onboard, the list of attendees snowballed. In addition to most of the people we had invited, many folks called out of the blue saying they would like to come. With every day, we had to make excruciating decisions about numbers, speakers, and attendees.

I was especially excited that, in addition to Chairman of the Joint Chiefs Admiral Mullen, Lt. Gen Ben Freakley would join us with an additional sixty military representatives: thirty young veterans who had served in Iraq and Afghanistan, and another thirty retired Senior Officers. I had long been convinced that to truly unleash the power of service in America we had to unite the worlds of military and civilian service. The summit would be a great place to begin to make that connection; led by retired Colonel Robert Gordon and Colonel John Tien, we had spent more than a year building bridges to military leaders, who were interested in what civilian service could do to help veterans reintegrate smoothly into civilian life, as well as what service organizations might be able to do for all the military families who were coping with the incredible stresses of war and repeated deployments. The military representatives were given a very warm welcome at the summit, and it was a real breakthrough for the service movement.

But as momentum built for the summit, we ran into a last minute crisis that threatened to derail everything. Senators Kennedy and Hatch had still not come to final agreement on the contours of the new bipartisan service legislation they were working on. We thought that once we secured both Presidential nominees everything would be smooth sailing. But we were a week away from the summit and the legislation had still not been finalized. It was a reminder that the legislative branch works on its own timetable. AnnMaura Connolly, Bridge, and I were in regular contact with Senator Kennedy's and Senator Hatch's staffs, trying to do whatever we could to finalize an agreement, reminding them that we now had a coalition of more than 120 organizations that reached one hundred million people who were excited about this new legislation and how high profile the summit promised to be.

We were on pins and needles, but kept up a positive face. There were some thorny issues that the two staffs just could not resolve. The final resolution came through direct negotiations between Senators Kennedy and Hatch just four days before the summit was to begin. The visibility of the summit, where it was widely understood Senators Kennedy and Hatch would be unveiling their new legislation, definitely helped bring them to agreement. But they sure waited until the very last minute. Sadly, Senator Kennedy was not able to join us on the day because of his health. Caroline represented him. In seeing Senator Hatch and how enthusiastic and excited he was to be at the summit, one would never know that just days before they did not have a bill to introduce. When I asked him how they had finally come to agreement, Senator Hatch told me: "You know, Teddy and I are like brothers. We fight a lot, but we love each other and always try to work things out. At the end of the day, Teddy gave me his word on an issue I cared strongly about and that was good enough for me." It was a vivid reminder of how strong relationships across the aisle are key to getting the business of the Senate done.

The Service Nation Summit contained many wonderful highlights. Senator McCain spoke movingly about his own military service and Senator Obama reiterated that he would make a new call to service a "cause of my presidency." For those of us who had toiled in the service movement for years, it was amazing to see more than ninety minutes of live national television in the midst of a heated presidential campaign devoted to the cause of national and community service. Both nominees agreed at the forum to become original co-sponsors of the Kennedy-Hatch legislation, which had been named the "Serve America Act." That meant that, regardless of the election result, the next president was on record as strongly supporting a dramatic expansion of national and community service. The only previous example of both Presidential nominees in the midst of a Presidential campaign embracing the same piece of legislation that we could think of was when Wendell Wilkie, the Republican nominee for President in 1940, supported President Franklin Roosevelt's Lend-Lease program.

The summit on September 12 was powerful. The Serve America Act was introduced by its forceful coalition of Congressional sponsors; New York Governor David Paterson announced a cabinet position for service in his administration; Bank of America, Goldman Sachs, PWC, and Target announced new corporate commitments to service. Five University Presidents—from Bentley, Duke, Tufts, Tulane, and U Penn—announced new commitments around service as well. Tobey Maguire, Alicia Keyes, Jon Bon Jovi, and Glenn Close added stardust, and *Time* magazine published their second annual cover story on service, detailing all the ways in which Americans could choose to serve. The Young Leaders added energy and idealism and reminded all of us how service could transform and unite the next generation.

Just two weeks later, we were fully at work for the Service Nation Day of Action. Thanks in part to a partnership brought to us by Sally Prouty and the Corps Network with National Public Lands Day, which fell on September 27 and was devoted to service projects restoring national lands, and the power of the coalition, the Day Of Action featured 2721 service events in all fifty states. More than 250,000 citizens and one hundred elected officials participated directly. The strength of the Day of Action was that it was designed to be de-centralized and to allow for local creativity and leadership. What some people did with that freedom was simply amazing.

In Denver, CO, returned Peace Corps volunteers, VISTA Alumni, the director of the Commission on Volunteers and Service, corporate leaders, and State Senator Romer spoke at the Colorado Summit on Service. In Detroit, MI, 200 volunteers participated in a Youthbuild Green Homes build and the Showdown in Motown talent show, judged by Mayor Cockrel. In Stowe, VT, AmeriCorps members serving at a senior center met with Gov. Jim Douglas and shared their experiences. In Charlottesville, VA, students and community members attended a public sector, non-profit, and service graduate panel, ServiceFest volunteer opportunity fair with more than forty organizations and speakers. In Dallas, TX, the Dallas Classic Gold Tournament raised $130,000 for Junior Achievement. In San Diego, CA, volunteers across the city participated in 130 service projects organized by San Diego Volunteers and Change Agent Jon Keyon. While the summit had secured the leadership participation of both presidential nominees, we used the Day of Action to secure the support of Michelle Obama and Cindy McCain. Both agreed to sign our Declaration of Service, a document we released at the summit and put on our website and social media pages so any citizen could sign. In essence, it was a way for any citizen to say she or he believed in the power of service. After that, we had to wait for the political process to play out with the election of a new president and Congress, which we eagerly hoped would right away take up the Serve America Act.

The question for Service Nation was how to help build momentum behind service and the Serve America Act, so that it would move quickly once President Obama assumed office. We were acutely aware that the first one hundred days is when a new president, buoyed by the election and inauguration, has the best chance to get new legislation enacted. While most elected officials support the idea of service, it does not always mobilize them to action like other issues, such as taxes, jobs, and health care, that most directly touch voters' lives. By January 2009, the nation was rapidly accelerating into the worst economic meltdown America had experienced since the Great Depression, so jobs and the economy were the overriding preoccupation of both Washington and the incoming president. Nonetheless, the Service Nation coalition, at a strategy session soon after the election, decided to seize the opportunity of the Inauguration, which fell the day after the Martin Luther King, Jr. holiday dedicated to service, as the place and time for our next big push.

Working to sustain service as a priority in the face of the economic collapse consuming the country was made easier by the fact that the leaders of the Obama transition team on service and social innovation—Sonal Shah, Michele Jolin, Paul Schmitz, and Cheryl Dorsey—were well known to most of us, and had asked me and some other service movement leaders including Vanessa Kirsch, John Gomperts, Geoff Canada, and Dorothy Stoneman to serve on the transition advisory working group on Social Innovation and Civic Engagement. It was also extremely helpful that Shirley Sagawa and Deb Jospin were asked to lead the transition review of the Corporation for National and Community Service, as they had extensive hands-on experience and knew everyone in the service field. A central topic during the transition process focused on the economic stimulus package. We argued that a major expansion of service would be an ideal part of the stimulus as it would create service jobs at a relatively low cost to the federal government, while also providing much needed support to the non-profit sector and enlisting citizens to meet growing needs. Ultimately, the Congress approved $200 million dollars for expanding AmeriCorps as part of the $787 billion stimulus package that was signed into law in the first month of the Obama administration. It was not as much as we would have liked, but at least AmeriCorps was included; the funding was seen as an initial "down payment" on President Obama's larger campaign pledge.

We also continued to work closely with Senators Kennedy and Hatch, and they agreed to re-introduce the Serve America Act on January 16, the Friday before the Inauguration. That way, it would get into the news cycle before the Inaugural weekend activities and Martin Luther King Day. And it would be "teed up," as Senator Kennedy had so shrewdly suggested it needed to be, for President Obama's arrival.

Publicly, Service Nation had set a goal of getting new service legislation enacted into law by September 11, 2009. But internally, we continued to work hard to make it within one hundred days. We teamed up with two other strong coalitions—America Forward and Voices for National Service—for a coordinated strategy and all-out push to try to accomplish this goal. The growing economic crisis strengthened the case for service. Every organization within the Service Nation coalition was doing work that in some way helped communities weather the economic cataclysm. As unemployment continued to climb rapidly, growing numbers of Americans looked to AmeriCorps and national service programs as a meaningful alternative to Wall Street or other jobs. At the same moment, social sector budgets were shrinking, putting AmeriCorps and service organizations on the front lines of the crisis.

On February 24, in his first joint address to Congress, President Obama put his cards on the table and the full weight of his office behind new service legislation, saying: "And to encourage a renewed spirit of national service for this and future generations, I ask this Congress to send me the bipartisan legislation that bears the name of Senator Orrin Hatch as well as an American who has never stopped asking what he can do for his country—Senator Edward Kennedy."

Many leaders from the service and social entrepreneurship movements were assembled at New Profit's annual "Gathering of Leaders" conference in Miami, watching President Obama on a giant television screen that had been set up for the address. At those words, a roof-raising cheer burst forth from the assembled crowd.

The Serve America Act is a landmark piece of legislation that uses the existing service framework as a foundation, and dramatically expands upon it. It expands AmeriCorps from 75,000 participants a year to 250,000 by 2017, and increases the educational award for the first time from $4,730 a year to $5,350 and puts it on a par with Pell Grants. With the growth, the legislation also establishes five new "problem solving corps" to use service as a strategy to address pressing national challenges: The Education Corps, Healthy Futures Corps, Clean Energy Corps, Veterans Corps, an Opportunity Corps to fight poverty. It also establishes a National Service Reserve Corps to deploy service alumni to respond to natural disasters. This is a civilian counterpart to the Army reserves.

The legislation also has a strategy to encourage more young people to engage in community service and service learning through:

> The **Campuses of Service** program, to recognize two-year and four-year public and private institutions of higher education that promote service-learning, community service, and public service careers.

> The **Youth Engagement Zone** programs, in which nonprofits, local educational and government agencies, institutions of higher education, or state actors partner to provide high-quality service-learning opportunities for secondary school students or out-of-school youth.

It creates the **Summer of Service** program to engage rising 6th- through 12th-graders in community-based service-learning projects during the summer months and to provide educational awards for those who complete one hundred or more hours of service.

And authorizes a **Service-Learning Impact Study** to assess the impact of service-learning initiatives created by the Act on student academic achievement, engagement, and graduation rates.

While encouraging young people, the legislation also establishes programs designed specifically for older Americans and retiring baby boomers through new Encore Service Fellowships, and allowing older Americans who serve at least 350 hours to earn educational awards of $1000 or more. They can also transfer these awards to a child or grandchild or mentee if they choose. And there are new Serve America Fellowships, to enable Americans of all ages to work with non-profits and faith-based organizations in internship and apprenticeship programs.

In addition to facilitating more full-time service opportunities, the legislation also encourages more volunteer service through the Volunteer Generation Fund to provide matching grants to organizations that focus on recruiting, training, and deploying volunteers, and a non-profit capacity building fund to support non-profits in developing high quality volunteer programs.

And, in recognizing the link between the service movement and the social entrepreneurship movement, the legislation establishes the Social Innovation Fund to be housed at the Corporation for National and Community Service. This fund focuses on providing grants to take high performing and entrepreneurial non-profits to scale through an innovative challenge grant program.

It also encourages more international service by making permanent the Volunteers for Prosperity program started under President George W. Bush that supports Americans serving abroad for periods of anywhere from three months to two years.

Finally, to deepen the culture of service in America, the legislation also calls for a new Call to Service Campaign, establishes a Civic Health Assessment to measure civic participation (much like the GDP measures economic output), and establishes September 11 as an official day of service and remembrance.

The exciting thing about the Kennedy Serve America Act is that it took the best of what Presidents George H. W. Bush, Bill Clinton, and George W. Bush did while adding new elements championed by President Obama and its Congressional authors. It did this not by establishing a major new government bureaucracy, but by building upon the not-for-profit and local and state efforts that were already happening all across America. It called for matching funds from the private sector for every program to make them more sustainable and accountable to local needs and conditions. It is a strongly bi-partisan bill and the vote for its passage reflects that. The architecture of the bill is such that the foundation is there to eventually bring us to the day in America when a commonly asked question when people meet each other will be: "Where do you serve?"—because service has become a common expectation and common purpose for all of us.

Once President Obama called for the Serve America Act to come to his desk, things began to move very quickly. The Service Nation coalition continued our work with Voices for National Service and America Forward with an aggressive advocacy campaign aimed at demonstrating to both the House and Senate that there was strong, bipartisan support for the new legislation. In a matter of a few weeks, sixty-one mayors, led by New York's Bloomberg and Miami's Diaz, sent a letter to Congress, testifying to the critical work service was accomplishing in their cities. Twenty-one governors, led by Governors Schwarzenegger and Paterson, sent a similar letter. More than four hundred nonprofit CEOs also weighed in, along with almost 200 private sector CEOs and 107 university presidents. We reached out to editorial boards, winning strong endorsements for the Serve America Act from the *Boston Globe*, the *New York Times*, and other papers, and we placed numerous op-eds. And the entire Service Nation coalition used its websites, along with Facebook and Twitter, to rally citizens to email and call their senators and representatives.

On March 26, I joined the Be the Change and New Profit staff in front of a television at our headquarters in the Monitor Company, less than two miles away from where we had first housed the inaugural City Year team. Senator Orrin Hatch strolled to the microphone on the floor of the United States Senate, and when he spoke his voice quavered with emotion and pride. The Senate had just voted seventy-nine to twenty in favor of the Serve America Act. Senator Hatch now moved to have the Senate vote to rename the legislation the Edward M. Kennedy Serve America Act in honor of his friend and legislative partner, who had worked so hard and masterfully to add this momentous service legislation to his considerable legacy. It would be the great senator's last bill and we were humbled and immensely proud that it bore his name.

As Orrin Hatch finished his remarks, the Senate spontaneously erupted in a standing ovation for Kennedy, who had joined them in the chamber for only the second time that year. Even senators who voted against the legislation were applauding. I hugged Vanessa, wiping a slight tear from the corner of my eye, overjoyed that we had finally reached this milestone after a twenty-five-year journey.

Once the House voted 275–149 in favor of the Serve America Act, it was truly done. Three weeks later, Vanessa and I joined

other leaders and champions from the service and social entrepreneurship movements at the SEED school in Washington, DC
for the signing of the bill into law. The event was especially moving because of Senator Kennedy's presence; only he and President Obama spoke. Senator Kennedy opened with a broad grin
by saying "this is a wonderful day!" He talked about his longtime
passion for service and how it brought out the very best of the
American people. It was that very same simple conviction that
had set us on the road a quarter century earlier.

8

A SHORT, SPIRITED SPECIAL ELECTION

A career as a civic entrepreneur and a movement builder, is not, evidently, the traditional preparation to become a member of the US Senate. I know this because, in 2009, the professions represented in the Senate (some senators had multiple identities) included:

Fifty-one former lawyers;

Forty former state legislators;

Twenty-seven businesspeople;

Twelve former governors, ten former mayors, and four former lieutenant governors;

Two doctors;

One Peace Corps alum, one veterinarian, one farmer, and one lapsed comedian.

I entered the contest to become the Democratic nominee for the Massachusetts Senate seat left vacant by Ted Kennedy's passing, because I believed it would be the best opportunity for me to continue to make a difference; Washington was stuck and needed new ideas and more independent voices who were not products of the existing political system. In the end, I didn't win the special election, but the experience of the campaign was hugely positive. At the outset, not only was I little known to the public at large, but even among some of those whom did know me, the support was of the "more in hope than expectation variety."

My reasons for running were several-fold.

First, through my work in the service and social entrepreneurship movements, I came to realize the big gap between people making change across our country at the grassroots level and our political leaders in Washington. Too many people in the service and social entrepreneurship world thought politics was dirty. And even those who wanted to engage were often intimidated to participate in advocacy efforts due to fears of being labeled "political" or of risking their funding. And too few political leaders were aware of the innovations of path breaking social entrepreneurs and how they could lead to a new approach to solving problems. Politics in our democracy at the end of the day is our collective effort to decide what is important. I had seen both the negative impact of politics when the AmeriCorps program was gutted in 2003 and the positive impact people could have through the Save AmeriCorps and Service Nation campaigns. My work focused on empowering people to make a difference and I had come to see that engaging in politics was essential. I hoped my running would help bring these two movements closer to the political and policy process.

I also wanted explicitly to challenge the way business is done in Washington. I chose not to accept any campaign contributions from special interest PACs or lobbyists, even though I was starting completely from scratch. If elected, I didn't want to be beholden to anyone except the citizens and voters. Instead, we would bring new people into the political process and demonstrate the potential of a grassroots campaign that relied more on citizens and volunteers than special interests.

I hoped to present a different vision for what a United States senator can do when that extraordinary platform is fully utilized. I had learned from a number of great senators—Kennedy, Hart, Tsongas, Clinton, Mikulski, McCain, Hatch, Nunn, and Wofford—that a senator has a unique capacity to impact the lives of people. Being a senator is much more than casting votes and giving speeches; the position has the potential to empower people to make a difference in their own lives and their community. Senators can play a leadership role in sponsoring new agendas and policies, while reminding us of the importance of the national interest. They can showcase innovative solutions that are happening at the local and state level and help to expand them across the country. Above all, they can support and encourage progressive citizen movements.

Finally, in the interest of helping to build a new kind of politics, I pledged to run a positive campaign as a civic entrepreneur and citizen leader, not a typical politician. I wanted the campaign to be fun and engaging for the people who joined it—to encourage more citizen involvement in politics.

Before I officially entered the race on September 24, 2009, Vanessa and I spoke with a number of good friends to get their advice and counsel. Many were enthusiastic, and pledged to help. Some were against my running. They pointed out the odds against winning were very steep. They said the frontrunner had overwhelming advantages in name recognition—which was essentially 98% across the state—and in support from party luminaries and special interest groups. The other candidates included a well-regarded congressman and a successful businessman who had virtually unlimited funds to spend. By contrast, I had no political base, no political organization, and no campaign funds.

Given the short special election, only about ninety days until the primary, they said it was impossible to conduct the kind of grass-roots campaign I wanted, and I risked never registering at all and potentially embarrassing myself. Dark horses, they argued, typically needed a longer, traditional campaign calendar to get known and gain any kind of traction. They also pointed out the toll campaigns take on families and personal lives.

But the friends encouraging me outweighed those against, and Vanessa and I had never made decisions based on the odds of success. We felt enough people were behind us that we wouldn't be taking this plunge alone. A supporter posted a Facebook page and within days "Citizens for Alan Khazei" had compiled more than 2,000 members encouraging me to enter the race. No sooner had I decided to go for it than the first poll came out: I registered one percent, which, allowing for the margin of error, might suggest that Vanessa and I were the only people who knew I was running at all.

So we embarked on a wild, improvised ride during which I was pushed in ways I had never been pushed before. I found increasingly that time was the campaign's most limited asset and the pressures to build an organization, raise money, pull together a policy agenda, meet citizens and voters, conduct press interviews, prepare for debates and forums, launch a grassroots effort, and deal with the daily fires that came up, were incredibly challenging. I found myself often thinking about President Kennedy saying that he loved the Greek definition of happiness the most—"using all of your talents and abilities along lines of excellence." I found I had to use everything I had, and then some, during the campaign.

The campaign's first goal was to gain credibility. We knew there was a risk that the press and pundits might treat me as a fringe candidate who didn't really have a chance of winning. So, we focused on demonstrating significant grassroots support, to make up for my lack of traditional political advantages. The first formal step in becoming a candidate was to take out nomination papers and get 10,000 signatures from registered voters to get on the ballot. The other candidates had simply sent a single staff person to quietly pick up their papers. We decided to have a group of volunteers take out the papers and begin collecting signatures right away. We were able to recruit seventy-five volunteers to take the day off and start the process. Most inspiring was that more than two thirds of them had never done it before.

The other candidates entered the race in front of a small crowd of thirty to fifty people. We staged a public announcement rally at noon on Boston Common with a goal of getting hundreds of people to turn out, one of several ambitious goals the campaign set. On September 24, a beautiful sun splashed day, more than 400 people gathered on Boston Common for the official announcement of my Senate candidacy. The feeling was electric and the response terrific. In the crowd were friends from every part of my life. As I looked out at the crowd, I felt like Jimmy Stewart at the end of *It's a Wonderful Life*. I particularly appreciated that Harris Wofford had flown up from Washington, DC, to officially endorse me and that Suffolk County Sherriff Andrea Cabral and Representative Smitty Pignatelli of Lenox, had agreed to serve as statewide co-chairs. They both took big political risks to do so. It sent a good message that I had some established political support.

We got good press coverage on the announcement that treated me as a serious candidate and, in response, Billy Shore, sent me a short email: "Strategic Objective number one accomplished: You're credible!"

▼▲▼

About a week after I entered the race, I got a phone call from Maxwell Kennedy, Robert Kennedy's son, saying he wanted to endorse me in the primary. Given that we were running to follow Ted Kennedy, this was a very big deal. I was grateful and excited. Max's wonderful wife, Vicki, was one of our very first City Year volunteers. Max flew out the following week and spent four days campaigning with me. We got another round of good media coverage and I had a ball traveling across Massachusetts with Max, who is a gifted, passionate campaigner. With the first milestone of launching the campaign and gaining credibility passed, we shifted gears to developing our comprehensive policy agenda and building out our grassroots campaign effort.

A central goal of the campaign was to demonstrate how civic entrepreneurs set about tackling problems. When we made policy statements, they were intentionally not the standard proposals from a Democratic playbook. Instead, we reached out to experts and practitioners, trying to find the best ideas and creative solutions, and then locating the policies both within the overall framework of Big Citizenship and a set of Citizen First principles that we developed. These were:

1. Start with the facts.
2. Consult with the world's best experts and practitioners.
3. Look for innovative solutions wherever they may be.
4. Develop programs to invest and grow what works. Stop wasting money on what doesn't.
5. Listen and understand other points of view.
6. Ask for citizen ideas.
7. Ask for citizen action to be a part of the solution.
8. Know what it costs and how to pay for it.
9. Ensure how to measure the cost and the benefits.
10. When necessary, build a movement to get it done.

By bringing together the experience and advice of a great group of outside advisors, the lessons we learned from the entrepreneurs and innovators we met during the campaign, and ideas from our supporters, volunteers, and engaged citizens, we developed comprehensive proposals for five major issues: Creating Jobs and Growing the Economy; Leading the Clean Energy Revolution and Addressing Climate Change; Comprehensive Health Care Reform, Quality, and Affordability; Pre-K through College Education Reform and America's Role in the World, and a New Approach to Afghanistan. We also produced position papers on all of the other pressing issues, from immigration reform to taking care of our veterans. Ultimately, we produced a 130-page book. It is one of the things that I am most proud of from the campaign.

As I was traveling the state, I heard more and more stories from people who were hurting in the terrible economy. People like Maria, an Italian-American immigrant, who came to Massachusetts, saved up and opened a restaurant in Hopkinton, only to lose that restaurant after being in business for more than eleven years because of the horrible economy. She broke down when I asked her to tell me her story, but she quickly pulled herself together and said: "Alan, I'm going to start over and rebuild. I'm talking with my friend Adrianna and together we are going to open a new restaurant." I was inspired by Maria's undaunted spirit to rebuild even in the face of huge adversity.

When I decided to run for the Senate, unemployment rates in Massachusetts and the rest of the country were approaching record highs. One of the reasons I ran was because I wanted to become "*the jobs Senator*." As the only entrepreneur in the race who had started an organization in a dorm room and grown it to a fifty million dollar not-for-profit enterprise, I knew firsthand the job creating power of America's entrepreneurs and small businesses.

Through our policy work and during my travels across Massachusetts, I learned more about and met with Massachusetts-based world-class entrepreneurs, who were creating thousands of jobs, addressing our country's greatest challenges, and creating new opportunities for our citizens. I encountered companies like En-erNOC, the innovative demand response energy company that supplies electricity to their customers by incentivizing others to be more energy efficient; schools like TechBoston Academy, where 97% of its low income students graduate and 94% go on to post-secondary education; new models to provide strategic and financial support to small businesses like NextStreet, a merchant bank for the inner city and Accion, which applies the principles of micro-finance to provide the access to capital that small businesses in Massachusetts need to grow; and Health Dialog, a company that empowers health care consumers with the information they need to make informed decisions about their care, improving the quality of care, reducing health care costs and creating over a thousand jobs along the way.

I put a major effort into developing a comprehensive economic plan that focused on jobs. Highlights of that plan included: a new jobs tax credit to stimulate hiring; dedicated support for small businesses; and clean energy and efficiency investment, including establishing a clean energy institute, a new Home Star program to weatherize homes and stimulate construction jobs, and passing clean energy legislation to create 1.9 million jobs. The plan also focused on stabilizing the housing market to keep Americans in their homes; growing non-profit job opportunities and supporting civic entrepreneurs through accelerating the Kennedy Serve America Act; and avoiding layoffs and cutbacks in schools, police, and firefighters through more state aid.

As I campaigned, I also met a number of people who had served, or had family members serving, in Iraq and Afghanistan. One was Mary, a nurse practitioner, whose son Charlie, had enlisted in the Marine corps two years earlier after graduating from college, because "he felt he had led a blessed and sheltered life and wanted to do something to give back to his country." Charlie had served in Iraq for the past year. He was offered a chance to come stateside for six months, but instead agreed to be transferred to Afghanistan because he didn't want to let down his "buddies" from his unit. Mary was as worried as a mother can be. Mary and parents like her led me to devote a lot of time to a major speech and policy on what to do about Afghanistan.

At the time, the Obama Administration was daily wrestling with whether or not to send an additional 40,000 troops to Afghanistan. One of my core theories for my campaign was to try to demonstrate the kind of senator I aspired to be through how I conducted the campaign and the positions I took and policies I developed. I spent several weeks thoroughly studying Afghanistan because I wanted to propose something I could strongly advocate for if I was elected. I reached out to as many experts as I could who represented a variety of points of view. Some were opposed to sending more troops, others in favor. I gained insights from Senators Gary Hart, Sam Nunn, and Harris Wofford, four star General Wesley Clark, Joshua Cooper Ramo, retired Colonel Rob Gordon, and Professor Linda Bilmes. I also consulted a number of my friends who had actually served on the ground in Afghanistan to get a frontline perspective, and I read General MacCrystal's report.

Ultimately, I came out strongly against sending more troops to Afghanistan and said we needed to move from a counterinsurgency strategy to a counter terrorism strategy, and set a timetable for bringing our troops home. I argued that the cost, first in American lives, and second, to our economy (more than 130 billion dollars annually) was not worth it for an effort that was very unlikely to succeed given the history of Afghanistan and the corrupt nature of the Karzai government. I was convinced we needed to put more of our energy and focus on Pakistan and developing a more comprehensive strategy for fighting terrorism and Al Qaeda in the 21st century. Along those lines, I suggested we needed a new twenty-first-century version of NATO focused on fighting terrorism globally—the major security threat we face—and increased economic and educational development aid for the people of Afghanistan and Pakistan.

I gave the speech before President Obama announced his decision to show the voters of Massachusetts that I was independent of party policy. When asked by reporters after the president's speech if I changed my views, I said no. I respect the president, and these decisions as Commander in Chief are the loneliest and hardest. I strongly support our troops and hope they succeed in the mission, but I remain deeply doubtful about the overall policy.

In addition to laying out a comprehensive policy agenda, we invested a lot of time, energy, and resources into building a strong grassroots campaign. We were the only campaign to open field offices all across the state, a significant investment as it diverted precious dollars from our television ad campaign. The political pros felt there simply wasn't enough time in the shortened calendar to wage a strong grassroots effort. But, to me, connecting with voters where they lived was a prerequisite to the kind of politics I believed in and wanted to promote.

Eric Schwarz arranged the citizen co-chairs of the campaign. Essentially, we invited anyone who was willing to play a leadership role to contact fifty to one hundred friends and voters directly and persuade them to support me and to get involved with the campaign. We ended up recruiting more than one hundred Citizen Co-Chairs and also organized more than 600 citizen leaders across Massachusetts. In addition to recruiting Citizen co-chairs, I met with democratic activists across the state and visited as many college campuses as I could, but not as many as I hoped.

The citizen co-chairs, activists, and students, were the backbone of the campaign, and, thanks to them, we were the only campaign that attempted a major door-to-door canvassing effort across the state. There are about one million registered Democratic households in Massachusetts. In a short campaign we had no hope of reaching them all. But it was important to try to get to as many as possible not only to advocate for the campaign, but to listen to the voters. We set an initial goal of trying to knock on 150,000 doors that would reach about 225,000 people directly in their homes and apartments. (With a projected small turnout in the campaign, we anticipated that as few as 225,000 to 250,000 votes could win the primary, and we wanted to reach at least that many directly.) By the end of the campaign, we had knocked on only about 50,000 homes directly, which was a frustration. I don't regret that we opted for a door-to-door strategy at all: it reflected who we were. It was my favorite part of the campaign because it showed grassroots democracy at its best, with citizens talking directly to other citizens about the issues and concerns they cared the most about. Many volunteers afterward told me, that even though they were at first a little intimated to do it, they ultimately really enjoyed it and, like me, learned a lot from talking directly to their fellow citizens.

The canvassing was a fun, as well as meaningful, part of the campaign. We also did regular community service projects across the state, organized by college students, to tangibly put into practice our theme of Big Citizenship. And we made creative use of new media outlets like YouTube, Facebook, and Twitter. I also enjoyed going from diners to small businesses, bowling alleys to churches. In particular, I loved connecting with young people like Henry, a junior at Lincoln-Sudbury High who has started a program for his classmates to raise money to support disadvantaged kids in low income schools. Henry told me, he came into a candidate forum undecided, but left ready to volunteer and go door-to-door over the last fifteen days of the campaign. Henry confided to me that he hoped to run for the Senate one day. I suggested that would be terrific, but that he might help me get elected first and not be in too much of a hurry.

Despite our intense early effort, polls the first month of the campaign indicated we had not broken through. My name recognition was extremely low: I was polling at about two percent. We had no choice but to look on the bright side: we had doubled our support. At this point in the campaign, there was only one televised debate scheduled to be held at the John F. Kennedy Presidential Library and sponsored by the new Edward M. Kennedy Institute. The debate would take place from 7:00 to 8:00 pm on Monday, October 26. The stakes were high, especially for a dark horse candidate who was being introduced to voters for the first time. We were strictly limited to sixty-second answers. That first debate was only seen by six percent of the electorate, but for me, it was a start. Additional momentum following the debate came from an unexpected boost when the *Boston Globe* wrote an editorial several days later headlined, "No PACS a Plus for Khazei," praising my position on not taking any money from PACS or lobbyists, and encouraging the front-runners to do so as well.

Then, two days after that, we received another breakthrough when Jonathan Alter wrote a *Newsweek* column titled, "Teddy's Rightful Heir" recommending me. The *Newsweek* article, was perfect timing, because we also launched our statewide canvassing effort that Saturday, October 31, bringing together hundreds of volunteers across the state who would go door-to-door. Thanks to the dedication of so many volunteers, we would canvass every weekend going forward until the primary.

The trifecta for the day came in one of the funnier moments of the campaign. One thing you quickly learn when you become a candidate for national office, is that your privacy is no longer your own. For Halloween, the *Boston Herald* had the unconventional idea to surprise all of the candidates to see what we were doing and what kind of candy we were giving out. That afternoon, as I was preparing to take my kids trick or treating, a *Herald* photographer and reporter showed up unannounced at our front door, catching me dressed up in my Johnny Depp *Pirates of the Caribbean* costume. As it turned out, I was the only candidate dressed in a Halloween costume and was rewarded with a big photo and nice headline in Sunday's *Herald*. We quickly put out a blast email linked to a banner headline on our website:

"Khazei Wins Halloween Primary."

With five weeks to go until Election Day, the campaign became even more intense. By now, I had gotten into a rhythm and loved campaigning and meeting citizens and voters. We were doing weekly policy events, where I would put out a major policy proposal by visiting a breakthrough organization in Massachusetts that was a model for the ideas I proposed. For example, we visited Year Up, an outstanding not-for-profit founded by Gerald Chertavian, that recruits disadvantaged inner city young people and prepares them for IT jobs with starting pay of over $30,000 a year. Eighty-seven percent of their participants graduate into these jobs. It is an outstanding success and should be used as a model for workforce development.

We also continued nonstop fundraising through call time and house parties. Although I had spent my career raising money for City Year and other non-profit causes, I had done it through a lot of meetings with people, putting together proposals, and building committees of volunteers to help organize fundraising events. I almost never raised money for City Year simply by getting on the phone. But I soon discovered that in the political fundraising world, call time is how it is done. I had to dial for dollars during every spare minute. From the very first day right up until Election Day, Vanessa and I spent hours and hours on the phones asking people for money.

We had surprised everyone when we raised over a million dollars by the first deadline of September 30 through a terrific volunteer fundraising committee led by Jim and Kristen Atwood, David Belluck, and Michael Alter. I was consistently overwhelmed by the generosity of so many friends from Massachusetts as well as across the country.

After our initial burst, fundraising got tougher. My name recognition was low and I trailed consistently in the polls. We had tapped out much of our initial network of good friends. In November, J.J. Abrams and Katie McGrath held a wonderful event for me in Los Angeles and Mayor Bloomberg of New York endorsed me and held a fundraiser at his home in New York City. We finally started our television advertising the first week of November. Both Congressman Capuano and Steve Pagliuaca had been on television from the first weeks of the campaign and Attorney General Coakley was on the air now as well. The TV buys dramatically increased our expenses. By the second deadline of November 18, we had raised a further $1.2 million—a million dollars for the primary, and another $200,000 in general election funds. By Election Day, our total was a little more than $2.3 million raised for the primary and another $500,000 in general election contributions which I returned after I lost the primary. But the other candidates had significantly more resources. Attorney General Coakley raised about $5 million for the primary, Congressman Capuano had about $3.7, million including transferring about $1.2 million from his congressional campaign account, and Steve Pagliuca spent more than $ 8.2 million, most from his personal funds.

The *Boston Globe* provided one of the lowest points and highest moments of the campaign. On Sunday November 22, the front page headline read:

Coakley leads, but electorate unsettled
In Globe poll, fifty percent remain undecided; Capuano running second, but far behind AG

The poll results among likely voters were: Coakley 43%, Capuano 22%, Pagluica 15%, and Khazei 6%. After more than two months of around-the-clock work by everyone on the campaign, this was discouraging news. Even though we had never put much stock in polls this poll definitely hurt the momentum of the campaign and affected our fundraising. We faced the disappointment by resolving to work that much harder.

Just six days later, approaching midnight on Saturday night, November 28, I was home after a long day campaigning, watching a documentary about Bobby Kennedy with my brother Lance, who had put his career on hold to move to Boston from Los Angeles, to help with the campaign. I got a phone call from Kelly Ward, my dedicated campaign manager. I couldn't imagine why Kelly would be calling so late on Saturday night. She told me the *Boston Globe* had endorsed me and it had just come out on-line. I was elated. I was up against two well-established office holders and an accomplished business leader who had outspent me on television ten-to-one, yet the leading newspaper in the state had selected me none the less. Lance and I shouted, hugged, and high fived. Vanessa was already asleep, but she woke up, came downstairs and joined in the celebrating. In our exuberance, we woke up my seven-year-old daughter, Mirabelle. She padded down the stairs half asleep. I brought her into my arms and sat her on my lap and she asked: "Daddy, what is all of the screaming about?" And her excited father responded: "Honey, the *Boston*

Globe just said your Daddy would be the best senator to follow Ted Kennedy." Mirabelle replied: "I already knew that. Can I just go back to sleep now?"

In addition to the *Globe*, other strong endorsements came in from leading media institutions and respected national figures during the last nine whirlwind days of the election. On November 30, General Wesley Clark endorsed me. Two more televised debates were held on December 1 and 2. Blue Mass Group, the noted progressive blog, endorsed me on December 2, and then came endorsements from the *Worcester Telegram and Gazette*, the *West Roxbury Transcript*, and Senator Sam Nunn on December 3, and the *Cape Cod Times* two days later.

Our message of Big Citizenship and the need for new approaches had begun to break through. Despite the slow climb out of single digits, we were enjoying momentum during the last week of the campaign. Our breakthrough came eleven weeks after we launched. From one perspective, it didn't take us long to gain traction, but from another it was very late in the game—just days before the election.

Given how short the special election was, I decided to spend the last four days nonstop campaigning. This included a forty-hour, straight-through-the-night marathon that began at the crack of dawn the Monday before the election in Lenox, MA, and finally finished right before the polls closed on Tuesday, December 8. Robert Lewis and Harris Wofford joined me for the entire stretch, while other friends and volunteers showed up for shifts. Harris had been an ongoing source of wisdom and encouragement throughout the campaign.

My final campaign stop was at the Florence Sawyer School in Bolton late Tuesday afternoon on Election Day. A group of eighth-grade students had written me personal invitations inviting me to come to the school. I've always believed in empowering young people, and since these students had written to me, I wanted to show up to send them a message: even as eighth-graders they could make a difference.

It was a great way to end the campaign. The students asked substantive and thoughtful questions, and I was relaxed, not to say a little weary, having campaigned all night. I tried hard to tell them they could be leaders today and they didn't have to wait until some ill-defined tomorrow or for any kind of vote before they started. Mirabelle joined me on stage and even made a couple of comments. She did such a great job that the teachers had her visit every second grade class and she spoke to each one to explain what the election was about, what a senator does, and why her daddy was running.

My daughter effectively had the last word on our campaign. She had provided one of the most personally satisfying moments earlier as well. Somehow, before I had decided to enter the race, the *Boston Globe* found out I was thinking about it and tracked me down on my cell phone. I immediately called Vanessa, who exclaimed: "But, we haven't even had a chance to talk to Mirabelle yet!" She had started second grade just the day before. We needed to explain everything to her and let her teachers and the school leadership know before they read it in the papers. So we sat down and asked her: "Sweetie, what do you think about Daddy trying to become a senator?" She responded without skipping a beat. "Daddy, I think that would be a great idea. If you become a senator, you can help me get my battery powered, gas-free, scooter built." I was proud of her for several reasons, quite apart from pure paternal pride. First, she had clearly thought that the position of senator was not remote or strange or out of reach for her dad or anyone else. And she was right. It should be a simple question of the electorate deciding whom they want. No one is excluded from candidacy, and political engagement should be as natural for all of us as the idea of it was to my daughter.

I loved her idea of what senators could do as well. She didn't imagine speech-making or even think in terms of passing laws: in her mind, a senator was a person who helped other people achieve their ambitions, overcome their challenges, and work to the general betterment of all. Simply put, a senator's work was to serve people.

All throughout Election Day, there was a great buzz among the campaign. We kept phone banking and emailing, trying to turn out every possible supporter we could. Vanessa even got on the phones around 6:00 pm—two hours before the polls closed— to chase down every last vote. She had been indispensable throughout, and was all in right up until the very last moment.

Finally, we made our way to the Parker House hotel where I had some interviews scheduled before awaiting the returns. The first results were not a surprise, but nonetheless, a disappointment. Martha Coakley, as she had from the beginning, was significantly in front, with Congressman Capuano second, me in third place, and Steve Pagliuca in fourth.

I had come up short for sure, but I was also gratified that we did break through, even if it came in the eleventh hour. We had journeyed from 400 people at our announcement to 90,000 votes eighty-five days later, and, as a percentage of the electorate, our support more than doubled that final two weeks of the campaign. I was satisfied we had given it everything we had. Because we were sensing upward movement that last week, there were times during our forty-hour marathon that I thought, maybe we would pull off an incredible upset, but that was, perhaps, my lack of sleep talking more than anything else. I had no regrets. I had run the kind of campaign I had set out to run: positive, issue focused, grassroots and with a vision for the kind of senator I hoped to be, and the kind of governing philosophy and agenda I felt were needed in tough and good times alike. We had brought many new people into politics and contributed to the overall tenor and tone of the debate. While I had lost this battle, I still had faith that an era of common purpose and renewal was coming because of the big citizens I had met all across Massachusetts.

So, what did I learn?

First, I am extraordinarily blessed to have an amazing family and friends. The overwhelming feeling I had throughout the campaign and still have as I reflect back on it, is one of enormous gratitude. I still do not know how to properly thank my enormously dedicated and talented staff who, ably led by the legendary Teresa Vilmain and indefatigable Kelly Ward, worked round the clock, as well as the hundreds of people who volunteered hours and hours of time. Lisa George got a leave from her job and came all the way from Australia to serve as my Chief of Staff. One friend, who had broken up with her fiancé, decided to sell her engagement ring and donate the money to the campaign. I was staggered by that. Friends from all parts of my life made phone calls, raised and gave money, went door-to-door, housed staff and volunteers, organized events and flew to Massachusetts for days and weeks at a time to volunteer. And my family was right by my side every step of the way, making the experience that much more rewarding.

I also learned that money plays too big a role in politics and it is going to be a long fight to take on the special interests that dominate our government. I was a strong believer in campaign finance reform before becoming a candidate myself; I'm an even stronger believer now. It is the reason I decided not to take any money from special interest PACs or lobbyists, so that if I got elected, I would have the credibility to help lead a movement for campaign finance reform. The fact that so many candidates and sitting elected officials have to spend so many hours on the phone asking people for money, is simply a crazy system. It is one reason why the PACs and lobbyists have so much power in Washington, because they make it easier for candidates to raise the millions of dollars needed to get elected. This is terrible for our democracy. We desperately need to reform the system.

And I learned that grassroots politics is powerful and that new people will participate if you invite them in. People are looking for honest talk and thoughtful solutions to the major issues confronting our country. But, it takes time to build a strong grassroots organization.

After my experience, I believe even more strongly that more people from the service and social entrepreneurship movements and the not-for-profit sector need to get involved in politics and serve in our government at every level. They bring an important perspective and experience of how to get things done while also being able to unite people from all sectors and backgrounds.

I am determined to continue to fight for a new vision of American politics and a new set of policies grounded in what is working. I was continually inspired that, despite the extraordinarily challenging economic times we live in, many people have an undaunted spirit. Finally, I believe a new era of Big Citizenship and Common Purpose is not only the best antidote to the challenging times we live in, it lies within our grasp.

9

THE LONG CAMPAIGN FOR BIG CITIZENSHIP AND COMMON PURPOSE

From co-founding and leading City Year as an action tank into a national non-profit, to traveling the world, to building coalitions and engaging citizens in saving AmeriCorps and helping enact the Kennedy Serve America Act, to my brief foray into electoral politics—I have become convinced of an overall view. We need a fundamentally new approach to how we meet the challenges and seize the opportunities of our times. This requires moving beyond the stale debate of big government versus no government to embrace a new public philosophy of Big Citizenship and Common Purpose.

Globalization has made the world smaller and more interdependent while producing a new cast of winners and losers. Hundreds of millions of people have moved out of poverty, but one billion remained trapped living on less than a dollar a day. The information technology revolution has empowered all of us with access to information. It has opened up a host of new possibilities in education and economic development. New citizen movements are possible as are, unfortunately, new terrorist organizations. The march of democracy from sixty-nine democracies in the world when the Berlin Wall came down to 119 today is a source of great hope; the displacement of communities as jobs are relocated or lost can be a source of great despair. Many of the challenges of our times are interrelated and cannot be addressed in silos. Climate change is not only an environmental issue, but also an economic issue, an energy issue, a national security issue, and an issue that requires global diplomacy and international agreement to successfully confront it. It also provides the opportunity to embrace a clean energy revolution that could provide millions of new jobs.

During what is the worst economic situation since the Great Depression, there was such rapid change in so many areas, that no one quite had a handle on it. It is, by definition, unsettling.

But, we need to have faith in our history: when we have boldly confronted our challenges in a unified way, we have not only prevailed, we have emerged stronger. That is our task today. Lincoln reminded us emphatically, "as our case is new, we must think anew and act anew." We need a new framework for how we address our problems and we need to change how we act in confronting them.

Over the past seventy-five years, America has swung between two very different public philosophies. Franklin Roosevelt, responding to the massive systemic threats of the Depression and the Second World War, made the federal government the centerpiece of addressing our problems and the center of new ideas, solutions and delivery mechanisms. His philosophy prevailed under Democratic and Republican presidents—under Eisenhower, the Interstate Highway system and the National Defense Education Act were established; under Nixon, the EPA was set up and a universal Health Care plan and a plan to guarantee a minimum income for all Americans was proposed.

Ronald Reagan tried to flip FDR's governing philosophy completely on its head by stating in his inaugural address, that government wasn't the solution, it was the problem. During his presidency, Reagan ushered in a philosophy of limited, even anti-government. Bill Clinton, a New Democrat, who had to govern for most of his eight years as President with a conservative, Republican-led Congress, famously stated in his 1996 State of the Union Address: "The Era of Big Government is Over." I believe the Hurricane Katrina disaster in 2006 marked the beginning of the end of Reaganism. Then, Newt Gingrich, among others, noted government had failed at every level—federal, state, and local . In many ways, that should not come as a surprise. After a quarter century of an anti-government philosophy, the country ends up with ineffective government.

The final blow to the Reagan "government is the problem" philosophy, came with the economic meltdown in September 2008, when almost all economists, from Martin Feldstein on the right to Paul Krugman on the left, called for much greater government action in response. Even the paragon of the unfettered free market, Alan Greenspan, acknowledged that perhaps he might have been wrong in assuming unregulated markets in the age of the global economy could work on their own, stating he had "found a flaw…in the model that I perceived is the critical functioning structure that defines how the world works."

Democrats are not innocent. In the face of attacks on government by Reaganite Republicans and clear evidence that government has become too bureaucratic, inflexible, and dominated by special interests, some Democrats too often find themselves defending the broken status quo. Members of both parties need to think critically and re-imagine a new role for government and a new way to solve problems in the twenty-first century. Often, political debate descends into an argument over how much money the Federal government is going to spend—Democrats often push for more and Republicans for less—rather than focusing on the real issue: what is the most effective way to address our social challenges and the best way to leverage limited government resources? Neither traditional Democrats nor traditional Republicans have articulated a new public philosophy for the dramatically different times of the early twenty-first century.

Arthur Schlesinger, Jr., argued American history moves in cycles between "public purpose" and "private interest," a cycle that begins anew approximately every thirty years.[19] At one end of the cycle, social change is initiated based in a shared sense of disappointment and dissatisfaction with the status quo

It was thirty years from the Proposition 13 California Tax revolt of 1978, which launched the Reagan revolution, to the election of Barack Obama in 2008. And yet, this time Washington remains stalemated.

▼▲▼

Big Citizenship and Common Purpose are a way of saying, first of all, we are all in this together and we all need to do our part. That starts with having an economy that works for everyone and reclaims America's historic place as an opportunity society. We cannot afford to waste the talents or contributions of any single person. Furthermore, a new philosophy of Big Citizenship and Common Purpose should be centered on several key tenets.

I. RELYING ON WE THE PEOPLE

Our Constitution does not begin with the words: "I, a member of the United States, in order to get more for me…" It begins, "We the People of the United States, in order to form a more perfect union…" America's greatest natural resource has always been its people, ourselves. The first question we should ask ourselves in confronting any problem is: "What role can the American people play to address this challenge?" Big Citizenship calls on each and every one of us to do what we can to contribute to America's ongoing journey towards a more perfect union. We can do this in multiple ways. At a minimum, we all need to vote. In addition, we can choose to volunteer on campaigns, advocate for causes we believe, and run for office ourselves, whether it is school committee, city council, State Representative, or Congress. America's robust democracy has more than 500,000 elected positions. Our founders did not envision a system of entrenched career politicians. Rather, they thought people should move from private life into a period of public service and then back into private life, so that our representative government would regularly be infused with new blood, energy and life experience. These are just a few of the many ways to become involved in politics.

Second, we need to use our talents to make a direct difference through national and community service. We need to continue to develop our nation's service system so that there are meaningful opportunities for service at every key life stage—beginning with service learning in elementary school through high school and college, the workplace, and continuing through the retired years. At the center of this system should be a year of voluntary full-time national service as a rite of passage between ages eighteen to twenty-eight in either civilian or military service. We should reward full-time service with life-changing benefits—a post-service award that could be used for college or graduate education, a down payment on a home, to start a business or non-profit, or begin savings for retirement. We should do this either by developing a civilian GI Bill, such that for each year of service the post service benefit would equal one year's tuition, books, and fees at a state university. Or we could establish a "service baby bond" in which every baby born in America would have a

529 type account set up through the government providing up to $5000 in tax credits. This investment could grow tax-free. The child would earn this bond (which, by age 19, would equal 18,000 dollars) once he or she had completed a year of service, in either a civilian or military service program.[20]

The GI Bill was one of the most successful government programs enacted in our history. For every $1 invested by the government, the return was almost $8. Millions of people were able to go to college, buy their own home or start a small business, and thereby enter the middle class. Through a new GI bill for civilian service, we should set a goal of at least one million Americans in full-time civilian national service every year. And those one million people in national service should help to leverage one hundred million Americans who volunteer every year.

The impact of this new citizen service force would be significant. For example, in 2008, 75,000 AmeriCorps members mobilized and managed 2.2 million community volunteers. This demonstrates the powerful force multiplier effect of AmeriCorps—helping nonprofits expand their reach and impact by recruiting and supervising volunteers. In 2009, 600 AmeriCorps members serving with Habitat for Humanity mobilized approximately 200,000 community volunteers to build 1,700 homes, while also generating more than $7 million in donations and gift-in-kind resources.

The voluntary contributions from Americans are already substantial and valuable. Recognizing that makes the prospect of doubling or trebling that contribution hugely attractive. As the Corporation for National and Community Service reported in the Highlights to their 2009 Volunteering in America study:

> • In 2008, 61.8 million Americans or 26.4 percent of the adult population contributed 8 billion hours of volunteer service worth $162 billion, using Independent Sector's 2008 estimate of the dollar value of a volunteer hour ($20.25).

- Despite the challenges of a tough economic situation, the volunteering rate held steady between 2007 and 2008, while the number of volunteers slightly increased by about one million.

- Over 441,000 more young adults (age 16-24) volunteered in 2008 than 2007, representing an increase from about 7.8 million to more than 8.2 million.

- Neighborhood engagement levels have risen sharply since 2007: the number of people who worked with their neighbors to fix a community problem increased by 31 percent, and the number of people who attended community meetings increased by 17 percent.

- As the economy slows and non-profit organizations struggle to provide services on smaller budgets, volunteers become even more vital to the health of our nation's communities. Between September 2008 and March 2009, more than a third (37 percent) of non-profit organizations have used more volunteers, and almost half (48 percent) foresee increasing their usage of volunteers in the coming year. Almost no non-profit organizations are using fewer volunteers.

- Volunteers were much more likely than non-volunteers to donate to a charitable cause in 2008, with 78.2 percent contributing $25 or more compared to 38.5 percent of non-volunteers.[21]

And the demand for people to serve continues to grow. In 2010, Teach for America, for example, had more than 46,000 applicants for just 4,500 positions in their national teacher corps. This is the third straight year that applications have grown by more than 30 percent. AmeriCorps experienced a 170 percent increase in on-line applications from 91,399 in 2008 to 246,842 in 2009. And these numbers do not reflect all applications to AmeriCorps because it is a de-centralized program in which grantees recruit and select their own participants. Not all grantees use the online application system, so well over 250,000 people applied to AmeriCorps in 2009. And it isn't just millennials, who want to serve. AmeriCorps is open to people of all ages. Many baby boomers are embracing "encore careers" to dedicate their experience and energy to making a difference through service.[22]

A new service system could focus on tapping citizen energy, citizen ingenuity, and citizen engagement to tackle our most pressing challenges in education, the environment, to fight poverty, preserve public health, respond to disasters, and to reinforce the ethic that at the end of the day we are all in this together. Shirley Sagawa's book, *The American Way to Change*, powerfully documents how national and community service at scale could make a tremendous difference in addressing our social problems.[23]

It is entirely possible to create an America in which one of the most commonly asked questions of people when they meet each other becomes "where do you serve?" A new commitment to Big Citizenship and Common Purpose can bring it about.

In addition to enabling and empowering our citizens to serve en masse to address our major problems, we also need our people to join together in movements for change. American history has been driven by a combination of citizen movements and visionary political leadership. From the citizen soldiers of our revolution to the civil rights activists, citizen movements have been essential to making progress. Today, we need active citizen movements to press our political and governmental leaders to take action on a myriad of issues from climate change to campaign finance reform and so much more. Mass citizen movements are essential to break the stalemate, logjam, and special interests that dominate politics in Washington.

II. FOSTERING INNOVATION
AND ENTREPRENEURSHIP

In order to both address the challenges and seize the opportunities of this century, a new public philosophy must maximize the potential and promise of innovation and entrepreneurship to develop the new ideas, new approaches, and new organizations in the private and public sector. Entrepreneurship is in America's DNA. Our founding fathers and mothers left the comfort of their native lands to create a new nation unlike any before. Each generation of immigrants renews that entrepreneurial spirit by their very act of leaving their own country and culture behind to start anew in America.

Looking to entrepreneurs and innovators has worked throughout our history. As Carl J. Schramm, President of the Kauffman Foundation, forcefully argues in his book, *The Entrepreneurial Imperative*, it is America's robust system of *entrepreneurial capitalism* that is our unique competitive advantage. Maintaining and strengthening that system is absolutely essential to reviving our economy and expanding the circle of opportunity. Similarly, Mayor Stephen Goldsmith in *The Power of Social Innovation*, argues for a stronger commitment to social innovation and civic entrepreneurship as absolutely essential to confronting our social challenges. This is not new. Civic entrepreneurs from the beginning of our country nurtured and sustained our civic life by inventing the public school, the public library, the settlement houses, and so much more.

It will be the clean energy entrepreneurs who will invent the new technologies that will finally free our dependence on foreign oil. Civic entrepreneurs behind organizations like Teach for America, New Leaders for New Schools, Mass 2020, The New Teacher Project and charter schools like KIPP Academy, are driving a revolution in education reform across our country.

The question becomes, how do we best draw on the great American tradition of entrepreneurship to address persistent societal challenges? The answer lies in developing a *civic entrepreneurial ecosystem*.

In the natural world, an ecosystem is an environment in which all of the living creatures and organisms, as well as the non-living physical features function in relation to one another and to the system as a whole. Each has a purpose; none is an alien outlier. A civic entrepreneurial ecosystem would contain different kinds of institutions and organizations filling different niches and functions but operating together as a system to maximize the potential for new social innovations to reach their optimal impact.

Government, philanthropy, the private sector, academia, and the media all have a role to play in developing a new ecosystem for civic entrepreneurship. One of the primary functions of government today should be to help facilitate a transition to this new system for civic entrepreneurship by encouraging more delivery of services through non-profits, while also providing matching resources and incentive funding to take proven and effective organizations, programs, and ideas to scale. Civic entrepreneurs will in turn lift some burdens from government. Bill Drayton, the visionary founder of Ashoka, has stated:

"There is nothing more powerful than an idea whose time has come when it is in the hands of a social entrepreneur."

When Vanessa and I were traveling the world, we realized America dominated the global economy because we have developed the most advanced and sophisticated system for private sector entrepreneurship in the world. That system incorporates several defining features, including:

- Very effective and functioning capital markets such that at any stage of business, capital is available to take it to the next level. Entrepreneurs draw on personal savings, angel investors, and venture capital to start a business; mezzanine and investment bank capital to grow it; and, ultimately, the ability to go public which enables new, effective businesses to get to scale.

- A government that realizes its job is not to run the economy and businesses but rather to set the standards and establish the rules of the game, provide reasonable regulation and oversight, but to let the market fundamentally drive results.

- A culture that celebrates the entrepreneur whether it is our Horatio Alger myth, or how we lionize and admire the great entrepreneurs in history or today, whether it is the Carnegies and Rockefellers of 100 years ago, or the Steve Jobs, Bill Gates, Oprah, Jeff Bezos, or Google Guys, Larry Page and Sergei Brin, of today.

- A higher education system that allows for both breakthrough research and development that often leads to new businesses, and a set of business schools that provide training for people such that, as a company grows, there are numerous people ready for hire who have the education and skills needed to help that company reach its potential.

- A set of supporting institutions including law firms, consulting firms, accounting firms, technology firms, and more to provide critically needed services to support the growth and development of a business at each stage.

- A set of media institutions to help cover, celebrate, and review the entrepreneurs and the entire private sector.

- A country that encourages and welcomes people from all

over the world to come here, so folks like the Google Co-founder Sergei Brin; Sun Microsystems Co-founders Andreas von Bechtolsheim and Vinod Khosla; Yahoo! Co-founder Jerry Yang; and Liz Claiborne Founder, Liz Claiborne,[24] just to name a few, come here to study and stay because this is the land of the American Dream and the entrepreneur. If you have a great new idea, you have the best chance in the world of making it happen here. Research at Duke University's School of Engineering found that one in four technology and engineering companies founded in the U.S. between 1995 and 2005 had at least one founder who was foreign-born.[25]

While maintaining and strengthening our private sector entrepreneurial ecosystem to drive economic growth and opportunity, we also need to develop a similar ecosystem for civic entrepreneurship. In pockets, the outlines of this new eco-system are beginning to take shape. It has the potential to revolutionize the way we address social problems and challenges in America. In order for this system to meet its potential, however, we need to consciously develop and invest in it, in the same way we have invested in our system to support private sector entrepreneurs. Some of the aspects of this system in need of further investment and development include:

Much more effective capital markets for the non-profit sector. Organizations such as Ashoka and the Echoing Green Foundation provide fellowships and startup funding for people who want to be social entrepreneurs. But more than one thousand people apply to Echoing Green annually for only twenty fellowships. We need more startup funding for people of all ages who want to be social entrepreneurs. The Purpose Prize, created by Civic Ventures, to support social entrepreneurs in their encore careers powerfully demonstrates that it is never too late to become a social entrepreneur. Organizations such as the Acumen Fund, Edna Mc-Connell Clark foundation, New Profit, New Schools Venture Fund, Sea Change Capital, the Skoll Foundation, and Venture Philanthropy Partners, are pioneering a new "venture philanthropy" approach to help social entrepreneurs and social entrepreneurial organizations to scale their efforts. But they represent an extremely small percentage of overall philanthropy. In addition to more civic venture capital, we need civic investment banks to provide major "mezzanine" financing to more rapidly replicate successful organizations.

And we need a much more effective and strategic use of government resources to help take both the effective ideas and organizations of successful civic entrepreneurs to scale. The recently established "Invest in Innovation (I 3) fund" at the Department of Education, specifically designed to help grow innovative education solutions to scale, is an excellent example of this. In just its inaugural year it received more than 1600 applications from a wide range of innovative projects demonstrating the significant potential for this kind of government leverage. The Social Innovation fund at the Corporation for National Service, established as part of the Kennedy Serve America Act, is another excellent example of this approach. These kinds of funds should be established throughout the government and they should have enough resources to take effective organizations to scale through significant challenge grants that require matching funds from private philanthropy.

We also need more schools that are focused on degree programs in non-profit management that become as highly respected and valued as the top MBA's. Some business schools are beginning to develop sophisticated programs and centers to support research and teaching on social entrepreneurship. Duke's Fuqua School of Business has the Center for the Advancement of Social Entrepreneurship, which conducts studies and makes recommendations for best practices, how to support social entrepreneurs, and more. Duke students interested in learning to "use your business skills to create a better world" can join the Net Impact club, where they network, attend special talks and events, and take advantage of career counseling services. Harvard Business School's Social Enterprise Initiative and Stanford Graduate School of Business' Center for Social Innovation are similarly invested in developing research and teaching to strengthen the field of social entrepreneurship. These and other business schools also offer special scholarships and debt relief for students interested in becoming social entrepreneurs, or joining a social entrepreneurial organization.

We need media institutions to report on and celebrate civic entrepreneurial and civic enterprise breakthroughs, challenges, and successes, so we can all learn from the achievements and mistakes. Just as we have a business section in the paper, we should have a non-profit section or civic enterprise section or civil society/citizen sector section. And there should be a "C-Span 4" that focuses on covering the civic sector, an idea which Arianna Huffington has long proposed.

We need to radically address the second-class nature of the non-profit sector, which is a big problem not only in America, but all over the world. We need to encourage our best and brightest to go into the non-profit sector and provide them the means to do so through loan forgiveness programs, fellowships and scholarships. In general, compensation for not-for-profits should not be equal to the private sector but it should at least be competitive, and grow over time such that people can afford to make work in the civic sector as a career and not just something to do for a few years out of college or graduate school before getting a "real job." For some reason, not-for-profit people are expected to earn low salaries and work in poor conditions with few resources.

This bias makes it harder to attract the most talented people into the non-profit sector, and harder for these people to think of having an extended career in the non-profit sector rather than a brief deployment between better compensated alternatives.

The need to attract top talent to the non-profit sector is only going to grow. A 2006 Bridgespan study concluded that America will need 80,000 non-profit leaders and 640,000 senior managers in just the next ten years. By 2016, it predicted non-profits would need to attract nearly 80,000 new senior managers and leaders *per year*. Non-profit salaries do not need to rise to the level of private sector salaries. They won't and they shouldn't. But, people who work in the non-profit sector and commit to it as a career need to be compensated well enough so that they too can access the key elements of the American Dream which include owning a home, being able to send your kids to college, and being secure in your retirement.

Most of all, we need to fundamentally change the role of government so it fosters rather than stands in the way of a much more powerful "marketplace" for civic entrepreneurial and civic enterprise activity, and helps to unleash the creative citizen talent to address and solve our most pressing social problems.

Both President Bill Clinton, when he said, "Somewhere in America someone has come up with a new solution to address an old problem," and President George H.W. Bush's "a thousand points of light…all the community organizations that are spread like stars throughout the Nation, doing good" rightly celebrated American ingenuity and spirit. But government needs to provide more of the electricity and work with the private sector and non-profit sector so these points of light can become beacons and entire electric grids. Once we find a solution that is working in one part of America, we need to use both the bully pulpit and resource power of government, matched with private philanthropy, to enable that solution to go from that one place in America all across the country.

In general in the private sector, resources tend to follow good ideas, strong entrepreneurs backed by solid management teams and sound organizations that can implement and execute well. In the public sector, too often programs develop in response to a pool of government money being made available to address an urgent issue or problem. Or funding is based on political considerations, population levels through "formulas" or political connections that result in earmarks. Once funding is allocated, a special interest group often arises to protect that funding regardless of how effective the programs truly are. That is not entrepreneurial behavior. And it doesn't lead to most effectively solving our problems.

In addition to building a new ecosystem for civic entrepreneurship and innovation to flourish, we also need to do everything we can to maintain our strong private sector entrepreneurial culture and spirit of innovation. Government has a strong role to play here as well in terms of how burdensome or not its regulations are—especially for small businesses—and in how it uses tax credits, spending on research and development, and its own significant purchasing power.

III. A NEW ROLE FOR "CATALYTIC," TRANSPARENT, AND ACCOUNTABLE GOVERNMENT

The role of government must change. Rather than addressing our problems from a top-down, bureaucratic, often one-size-fits-all approach, or just relying on the market to solve our problems, government needs to become more catalytic, transparent, and accountable. While not relying exclusively on the private market to meet our needs, we do need to use time-tested market principles in constructing new solutions and approaches. Government should set aspirational goals, establish standards, encourage entrepreneurship and innovation in both the private and non-profit sectors, create competition, identify what works, reward results, and invest to help take the best innovations, organizations and ideas to scale, while also being willing to acknowledge failure and to stop funding things that aren't working or achieving the highest impact. We also need to recapture a spirit of experimentation and risk taking as a way to encourage innovation. Not every program or organization funded by government is going to achieve its objectives, especially those that attempt breakthrough, untried solutions. When things work, we need to learn from them and expand them. When they don't, we need to stop doing them and move on, not simply continue with failed efforts because some powerful interest is fighting for it.

We should also take advantage of technology to make government more transparent and responsive and thus accountable. Legislation should, for example, be posted on-line before final votes are taken, so that citizens can share their opinions with their representatives. And just as private sector organizations like eBay have feedback ratings, citizens should be able to post their own ratings on-line whenever they interact with the government.

The re-inventing government movement of the early 1990s was a good first step in the debate about how to modernize and re-imagine a new catalytic role. But it focused too much on how to make government more efficient and effective, rather than incorporating a larger discussion and approach centered on how to best solve problems utilizing all three sectors—public, private, and not-for-profit. We don't need to just re-invent government; we need to re-imagine our governing philosophy. We need to fully explore the implication of Lincoln's insight that the genius of America is that we have a government of the people, by the people, and for the people. As citizens, we cannot simply see government as a process to elect representatives who will then solve our problems for us. We must recognize that it is up to us to engage in problem solving ourselves, as well.

The private sector has undergone a radical transformation in our society over the past twenty-five years to both respond to and take advantage of new technologies and new conditions summed up by a global marketplace. It has moved from the top-down, hierarchical, centralized, largely bureaucratic, vertically integrated firms of the industrial age, to a new, much more entrepreneurial, de-centralized, non-hierarchical, network, partnership, and technology enabled approach to creating and leveraging value. Noted organizational expert, Rosabeth Moss Kanter, has called this shift in corporate culture "giants learning to dance." Her words of wisdom for large companies seeking to become more flexible in a network society ring true for government, as well: "Large organizations must tear down the confining vertical structures that shape bureauspace—skyscrapers, towers, silos, walls, and tunnel vision. They must behave like networks of smaller companies, liberating people to think like entrepreneurs but connecting them to share knowledge and to form a fluid array of project teams, within the company and with partners."[26]

Government and many of our public delivery systems including education, health care, and programs that fight poverty are still stuck in an industrial-age system, using an industrial-age approach. We need no more paper records for health care, no more school calendars driven by the needs of the agricultural harvest and planting seasons.

Every new administration promises to solve the problems of education. The Obama Administration is creatively using the federal government to incentivize change. In addition to establishing an "Invest in Innovation" fund to grow innovative organizations and models to scale, it has set up a "Race to the Top" fund to incentivize education reform. This fund of $4.3 billion is available on a competitive basis to states that are undergoing significant reform efforts and achieving measurable results. Interestingly, more than forty states applied and twenty-two states changed their laws and policies in advance of applying in order to have a more competitive application. So, even before giving out one dollar in grant money, the federal government has provided a strong incentive for change across the country. Race to the Top is dramatically accelerating a reform movement that already had some momentum, but by leveraging both the bully pulpit and significant resources of the federal government, it has supercharged the education reform community and agenda. It is not the federal government telling states what to do, or providing unfunded mandates. It is also not the federal government giving states a blank check or block grant with few requirements. Nor is it the federal government taking a totally hands-off approach in the face of a national crisis. Rather, it is an excellent example of what new catalytic government can do. Every single cabinet agency of government should establish its own Race to the Top fund for its area of focus and replicate this strategy across a variety of national challenges.

The Corporation for National and Community Service is another example of creative, catalytic government that has worked extremely well. It is a unique government agency in that it is governed by a Board of Directors nominated by the President and confirmed by the Senate. In addition, it acts more like a government foundation than a government program. It now funds more than 2,000 local, state, and national AmeriCorps programs across the country and eventually, thanks to the Kennedy Serve America Act, there will be 250,000 AmeriCorps members annually in service. AmeriCorps programs raise hundreds of millions of dollars in matching private funds to leverage the government investment. Through this unique model, AmeriCorps operates effectively and efficiently, and is scalable. It is already well over ten times the size of the Peace Corps.

IV. ENCOURAGING PUBLIC-PRIVATE PARTNERSHIPS

Rather than looking to the government alone to address our problems, or relying exclusively on the private marketplace to take care of things, we need new public-private partnerships among government, the private sector, and the non-profit sector, each doing what each does best to address our most pressing challenges.

There are leaders in all three sectors that are ready to step up to the plate. Since the time we started City Year, more than twenty years ago, there has been a growing corporate social responsibility movement both in America and around the world. Many twenty-first century business leaders increasingly recognize that doing well and doing good are inextricably linked. They realize that in addition to their shareholders, they need to keep in mind and run their businesses with their *stakeholders* in mind, including their customers, employees, and the communities where they maintain their offices and factories and where they do business. More and more companies are providing paid time off for their employees to engage in community service. Strategic philanthropy, whereby a company focuses its philanthropic dollars and efforts and tries to make a measurable and tangible difference, is a growing trend as well.

Indeed, the most widely known business leader on the planet, Bill Gates, has called for "creative capitalism," in which talented private sector leaders use their skills to help create products and services for low-income people around the world. As he said to the Wall Street Journal, "The idea that you encourage companies to take their innovative thinkers and think about the most needy—even beyond the market opportunities—that's something that appropriately ought to be done."[27]

Gates is absolutely right. The private sector is full of people with great talent and leadership and managerial ability. The younger generation in particular is committed to a new kind of capitalism and more robust role for the private sector in helping to solve our problems. Net Impact, an organization for students interested in the intersection between civic entrepreneurship and business, has witnessed exponential growth, from one hundred students in six chapters in 1993, to several thousand students in forty chapters in 1999, to more than 15,000 students in 256 chapters from 140 countries.

Interestingly, in just the past couple of years, a new MBA oath, modeled on the Hippocratic Oath, has been launched. It is a voluntary pledge for graduating MBAs and current MBAs to "create value responsibly and ethically." The mission behind the oath "is to facilitate a widespread movement of MBAs who aim to lead in the interests of the greater good and who have committed to living out the principles articulated in the oath."

The oath started with a group from the 2009 class of Harvard Business School. It has now spread to a broad coalition of MBA students, graduates, and advisors, representing over 250 schools from around the world. Along with Professor Rakesh Khurana from Harvard Business School, they are partnering with the Aspen Institute and the World Economic Forum to make this oath standard across the business profession.[28]

Big Citizenship calls on leaders in the private sector to do their part and what they can to make a difference on our social challenges, helping to provide opportunities for the most unfortunate among us and strengthening our community.

The non-profit sector is also ready to step up its efforts. It is difficult to definitively quantify the growth of the non-profit sector, since many non-profits are small and community-based and may not register officially with the IRS. It is clear, however, that this is a sector that has been growing exponentially over the past thirty years. In 1977, the number of non-profit organizations registered with the IRS was approximately 740,000. By 1995, this number had grown to 1.1 million, and in 2005, there were 1.4 million non-profits registered, a growth of nearly 30% in just one decade. From 1995 to 2005, the US GDP grew approximately 35%[29], while the revenue and assets reported by the non-profit sector increased by 54% over the same time period.[30]

The non-profit sector now represents almost ten percent of our economy with one of every twelve individuals working in the non-profit sector.[31] While non-profits benefit a great deal from volunteers, they also employ more than 12.9 million people, and contribute nearly $322 billion in wages to the economy. The non-profit workforce outnumbers the combined workforces of the utility, wholesale trade, and construction industries. And the non-profit sector is the fastest growing employer in the nation (2.5 percent), outpacing the rate of growth for both government (1.6 percent) and the private sector (1.8 percent).[32] The non-profit sector accounts for 5.2 percent of gross domestic product and 8.3 percent of wages and salaries paid in the United States.[33] 115 nonprofits launch every day; and the total number of non-profit organizations has doubled in the last twenty-five years.[34] When, including volunteer resources mobilized by the sector, non-profits engage one in two Americans as volunteers, two in three as donors, and account for more than five percent of our national income (over one trillion dollars).

Similar trends are at play in the growth of civil society organizations worldwide. Lester Salamon and his colleagues at Johns

Hopkins described the importance of this phenomenon: "The rise of the civil society sector may, in fact, prove to be as significant a development of the late twentieth and early twenty-first centuries as the rise of the nation-state was of the late nineteenth and early twentieth centuries."[35] According to Salamon's research on the growth of civil society in 35 countries, in the late 1990s, the sector was a $1.3 trillion industry, representing 5.1 percent of the combined GDP of these countries. These organizations had a workforce of 39.5 million FTE[36] workers, employing 4.4 percent of the population, or nearly one out of twenty active persons. The authors put these numbers in contrast by stating that if the civil society sector of these countries were its own national economy, its expenditures would make it the seventh largest economy in the world, ahead of Italy, Brazil, Russia, Spain, and Canada, and just behind France and the U.K.

This is the good news. The bad news is that most non-profits are extremely small. More than 94 percent of all non-profits have annual budgets under one million dollars. And in a study Bridgespan conducted, they found that of two hundred thousand non-profits started between 1970 to 2003 (excluding hospitals and universities), only 144 had achieved revenues greater than $50 million annually.[37] In the non-profit sector, we still largely have a universe that is dominated by "mom and pop" organizations. That is one significant reason why we are not making more progress against our social problems and why we need to build a system that can more rapidly and effectively scale up innovations and organizations that have breakthrough approaches and results.

A special report conducted by Cone-Roper confirms the importance of public-private partnerships and the increasing willingness of consumers to support companies that are socially responsible.

Nearly nine in ten Americans (89%) said it is important that business, government, and non-profits collaborate to solve pressing social and environmental issues.

Eighty-five percent say it is acceptable for a company to involve a cause in their marketing compared to 66% in 1993.

Seventy-nine percent say they would be more likely to switch from one brand to another brand, about the same in price and quality, if the other brand is associated with a good cause, compared to 66% in 1993. (For millennials, it is 88%.)

Thirty-eighty percent have bought a product associated with a cause in the last twelve months compared to 20% in 1993. (For millennials, it is 51%.)[38]

For every issue we confront, we need to ask first what is the role of citizens, what is the role of entrepreneurs, and what is the right role of the government, the private sector, and the non-profit sector?

Twenty-first century solutions and systems will need to engage all five of these in powerful ways and in powerful combinations, if we are going to invent the new approaches, new institutions, and new solutions to our challenges.

V. "ARE WE BETTER OFF?"

Finally, we should have one central touchstone for all of our policies and programs—do they promote the common good and the national interest or are they favoring narrow, special interests? There are more than 13,000 registered lobbyists in Washington—more than 130 for every single Senator. They spent more than $3 billion dollars advocating for their causes in 2009. It is out of control. On issue after issue, special and narrow interests either stymie progress, or game the system, and the country as a whole suffers. The soul of America is being tested. We need to reject a politics that says the central question should be "are you better off?" and adopt a mindset of "are we as a nation better off?." The times facing us require nothing less than collective effort, collective sacrifice, and collective commitment. As we have in other periods throughout our history, if we can find the will to come together and honestly and directly confront our problems, we will emerge from these challenges stronger.

On my very first day of campaigning for the Senate, I visited a wonderful not-for-profit located in Pittsfield, MA, called Soldier On. Its mission is to help homeless veterans get back on track. A number of the residents offered their thoughts on what to do about this problem. George's story was especially memorable. He had been in the Marine Corps. He still has the tough, grizzled look and ramrod straight fit physique that reflects those days. After his tour of service, he fell into addiction. He eventually lost everything—his job, his home, his friends, and family. He got so low, he finally ended up in prison. Soldier On reaches out to the veterans that need help the most, and they found George in prison and convinced him to come stay with them when he got out. Slowly, with determination and dedication and the support of his Soldier On community, George turned his life around to the point where he now leads the veterans in helping to run Soldier On, including organizing regular community service projects for the residents. That empowerment approach is a key part of their model and of their success. I asked George what he had learned from his experiences:

"Alan, I've learned that if you can get the support to believe in yourself again, that you can be someone important and not just take from others, but give back to them. You can make your big dreams real."

Through the community at Soldier On, George once again became a Big Citizen and rediscovered the spirit of service, sacrifice, and common purpose. It is a spirit each and every one of us can discover. It is tangible and powerful and always lies just beneath the surface waiting to be tapped and unleashed. When we unite in common purpose, we *can* make our big dreams real. There is nothing more powerful or uplifting.

It has always been citizens who have made big dreams real in America. It was the citizen soldiers who put down their pitchforks and picked up their muskets to defeat the greatest empire of the day and give birth to a new nation of liberty, equality, and justice for all.

It was the abolitionists and hundreds of thousands of dedicated Americans who gave their "last full measure of devotion" to end slavery and ensure that "government of the people, by the people and for the people, shall not perish from the earth."

It was the suffragists who inspired a nation to embrace the 19th Amendment and grant women equality through the right to vote.

It was the trade unionists who organized and insisted that work must have dignity.

It was the Greatest Generation that volunteered in droves to defeat Hitler and Fascism.

It was the civil rights activists who rode freedom rides, sat in at lunch counters, and marched on Washington, that inspired our people to embrace civil rights as the moral issue of our times.

And it is always the individuals who risk everything to become entrepreneurs and to start and run small businesses that create the most jobs and opportunities for Americans.

And now, once again, it is up to each of us.

Through my work in the service and social entrepreneurship movements, I've been blessed to experience this America over and over again. City Year would only have happened, Saving AmeriCorps and Service Nation would only have happened, so many other extraordinary organizations and efforts only happen because there is a spirit of community, public service, a willingness to give back and be part of causes larger than our own self interest, that is tangible and palpable and can be tapped into. It is a powerful force in our country and we need to all work together to unleash and grow it.

Even as we face extraordinary challenges now, we need to remind ourselves who we are. We have faced great challenges before and when we unite we always prevail. The spirit of Big Citizenship and Common Purpose can be part of all of our experience. We need to rise to Truman's challenge and all aspire to fully hold the most important office in the land—that of citizen. Each in our own way and to the best of our own abilities. If we do that, there is no doubt that we will leave our communities and our country better than we found them. And we will leave a legacy to our children and grandchildren that we can all be proud of.

We are the thirteenth generation of Americans to march on that journey to a more perfect union. We have the potential and it is in our power to advance the dream in ways our founders could only have imagined. Let us begin.

APPENDIX A

KEY ASPECTS OF ACTION-TANKING

I believe that any non-profit and any social entrepreneur that wants to have a wider impact beyond their direct programmatic work, should strongly consider having an "action tank" aspect to their strategy for change.

Over the years, we realized that successful action-tanking involved at least ten key aspects.

Turn on your justice nerve by identifying a need or injustice that is the motivation behind your work.

Develop a powerful "one day" vision statement that clearly communicates the world you are trying to achieve.

Become an expert in your field—both from a programmatic and policy perspective.

Propose an innovative solution based on an entrepreneurial insight.

Establish an Action Tanking organization and recruit people and resources to role model your solution.

Demonstrate, improve, and promote the solution as part of a larger vision.

Develop a comprehensive policy agenda for achieving the "one day" vision.

Leverage your organization for institutional development, policy advances, and movement building.

Change tactics, program design, and goals in response to the changing environment and as necessary to confront obstacles and leverage progress towards achieving the "one day" vision.

Seek a fundamental shift in the public policy arena—a tipping point—through large-scale demonstrations and bolder public policy proposals.

APPENDIX B

The first phase of ServiceNation demonstrated that the meta-action, tanking model can powerfully impact the system and affect the culture. If done correctly, it could not only lead to new policies, but also new movements and cultural change. The key elements of this "meta-action-tanking" strategy include:

> Identify an issue area that is stuck either because it isn't getting attention in the national dialogue, or there needs to be some new thinking, or the traditional approaches are not working.

> Bring together a coalition that is, first and foremost, grounded and driven by practioners in that issue area, social entrepreneurs, and reformers who have hands-on practical experience and strategies in getting tangible and impactful results. In addition, add in "natural allies"—organizations and people who share a commitment to that issue and to making a dramatic leap forward on it. Also, make sure you have some experienced policy people as part of your coalition who can help translate the practical

approaches of your practitioners into a policy agenda and who can also help you understand and navigate the policy process.

Work with that coalition to develop an overarching agenda that is non-partisan and draws on the best thinking and experience of the left, the right, and the middle, and that thus can generate strong bipartisan support. Have the coalition understand that no one is going to get everything they want, but that if people and organizations are willing to work together, the whole really can be greater than the sum of its parts and a quantum leap in that issue area can be advanced. Start by getting agreement on the broad overall policy and cultural goals, and then work on a more detailed agenda to accomplish those goals.

Develop a comprehensive strategy that engages both the "grass tops" and grassroots and that leverages the collective reach of the coalition. In addition, bring together leaders and citizens from a variety of sectors and disciplines that often don't work together including the private sector, the government, the non-profit sector, the faith-based community, the military, the entertainment world, and others.

Find bipartisan legislative champions to work with you and your coalition to develop new legislation that will incorporate the policy agenda that you develop with your coalition. Work hard to build broad non-partisan and bi-partisan support for your agenda.

Launch this new effort with a high-profile "national summit" of leaders from all sectors that are committed to advancing a major new effort in that issue area.

Follow that "grass tops" summit, with grassroots actions

that can engage citizens at the local level through tangible events, as well as the Internet.

Leverage key strategic relationships in the media both new and old to bring attention to your agenda and new effort around that issue area.

Have an explicit strategy to engage the President and Administration.

Set both an achievable short-term goal to be enacted within twelve to twenty-four months following your summit that makes a significant leap forward, but also put out a longer-term goal that will be transformative.

Have an explicit strategy for how to leverage this work into a movement for lasting cultural change.

It is the coalition, stupid. Leverage, leverage, leverage.

James Carville, famously declared about the 1992 campaign, "It's the economy, stupid." Well, when it comes to meta-action, tanking, it is all about the coalition. The ultimate success of your campaign will depend upon the degree you can build a strong and broad-based coalition and leverage the enormous collective assets of that coalition in terms of both grass tops and grassroots relationships, capacities, strategies, and tactics.

Presidential campaigns offer a unique opportunity to bring major new issues and agendas to the national consciousness and debate.

One of the wonderful things about America is that every four years we have a national debate about the future of our country through the Presidential campaign. And because of the Iowa Caucuses and New Hampshire primary, as well as the nominating process as a whole, this is a debate that involves grassroots citizens. It is a virtual guarantee that the President of the

United States, no matter who he or she is, will have to share their vision and agenda with small groups of citizens in their living rooms, club meeting halls, and at town meetings. This is a tremendous opportunity to put new ideas and issues on the agenda if the right coalition and grass tops and grassroots strategy can be developed.

APPENDIX C

THE SAVE AMERICORPS TIMELINE[39]

June 6

AmeriCorps network received word that the Corporation had delayed their FY03 grant announcements until June 16, but deep cuts were expected.

June 14

Boston Globe publishes an editorial titled "National Disservice." This eventually builds to 100 editorials from newspapers around the country in support of AmeriCorps.

June 16

The Corporation for National Service officially makes first round of grant announcements, which embody an 80% cut.

June 17

Forty-nine Senators sign a letter calling for $200 million in emergency funds for AmeriCorps in fiscal year 2003. Eight Republican Senators sign the letter.

June 18

New York Times editorial comes out: "The Spirit of Service Betrayed"

June 18

Led by Senators Christopher Bond (R-MO) and Barbara Mikulski (D-MD), the Senate passes the Strengthen AmeriCorps Program Act, legislation to resolve a longstanding question about accounting practices at the Corporation for National and Community Service.

June 19

The House passes the Strengthen AmeriCorps Program Act, and, in thirty-six hours, resolves an issue that had been under discussion for almost six months. AmeriCorps member cuts are reduced from more than eighty percent to fifty-five percent.

June 20

The first Save AmeriCorps events are held in Rhode Island and Seattle.

June 25

One hundred sixty-five House members release letter in support of emergency funds for Americorps; effort led by Congressmen Harold Ford, Jr. (D-TN), and Tom Osborne (R-NE).

June 26

Full-page ad runs in the *New York Times* with 250 business and philanthropic leaders signing on.

June 26

National Press Club event held featuring voices from the field of national service, moderated by *U.S. News & World Report* editor David Gergen. At this event, a statement signed by 1,180 organizations which calls on President Bush and leaders of Congress to supply 200 million dollars in emergency funding for AmeriCorps, is released.

June 30

Newsweek column by Jonathan Alter comes out titled: "Lip Service vs. National Service."

July 1

Full page ad from 250 business and philanthropic leaders runs in the *Financial Times*.

July 3

President Bush signs the Strengthen AmeriCorps Program Act, saying this is an "important first step" for AmeriCorps.

July 7

President Bush submits his FY03 emergency supplemental appropriations request to Congress for 1.9 billion dollars without including any funds to restore the AmeriCorps program cuts. The Save AmeriCorps coalition realizes we need to get the Senate to include the funds as the first key step.

July 9

The Save AmeriCorps Coalition organizes Capitol Hill Day, when AmeriCorps programs, alumni, corporate champions, and state commission representatives visit key congressional offices. That same day the Senate Appropriations Committee, led by Senators Stevens, Byrd, Bond, and Mikulski, with unanimous bipartisan support, adds one hundred million dollars in emergency funding for AmeriCorps to Pres. Bush's FY03 supplemental request.

July 9

Save AmeriCorps ad runs in Capitol Hill publication, *Roll Call*.

July 10

One hundred forty-seven mayors, led by Mayors Tom Menino of Boston and Tom Murphy of San Diego, release a letter to President Bush and Congressional leaders calling for supplemental funds.

July 11

By a vote of seventy-one to twenty-one, the full Senate approves one hundred million dollars for AmeriCorps. The vote would have been seventy-nine to twenty-one, but eight Senators, who had previously announced their support for supplemental funding, are out of town.

July 14

US News and World Report publishes column by David Gergen titled: "A Flame That Must Not Die."

July 15

Fifty-five after-school program leaders release a letter in support of AmeriCorps.

July 18

Congressmen Ford and Osborne re-open their letter calling for emergency funding for AmeriCorps; a total of 228 representatives sign this letter—a clear majority.

July 21

Forty-four governors release a letter calling on the President and Congress to support up to $200 million in emergency funds. The letter is led by Massachusetts Gov. Mitt Romney and Pennsylvania Gov. Ed Rendell.

July 21

One hundred ninety college presidents release a letter supporting emergency funds.

July 22

The House Appropriations Committee defeats an amendment to add $100 million for AmeriCorps to the FY03 Supplemental Appropriations bill, but adds $136 million for other items. Remarks by Committee Chairman Young of Florida signaled a compromise on AmeriCorps funding may be within reach.

July 24

The House leadership refuses to appoint negotiators for a conference on the Supplemental Appropriations bill.

July 21

House Appropriations Committee reports out an FY04 VA/HUD Appropriations bill that recommends $345 million for AmeriCorps. This is the first time, since 1994, that the House appropriators include AmeriCorps funding in their committee mark. The full House passes the FY04 VA/HUD Appropriations bill on July 25.

July 25

House passes an FY03 Supplemental that only includes half of the funding President Bush requested for the Federal Emergency Management Agency (FEMA), nothing more. Money is left out of the bill for AmeriCorps, fire fighting, and NASA.

July 30

Wall Street Journal publishes an editorial titled: "AmeriCorps Follies" opposing supplemental funds for AmeriCorps.

July 31

Senate votes on House version of FY03 Supplemental. AmeriCorps and other emergency funding deferred until September.

Sept. 2-6

The Save AmeriCorps Coalition kicks off "Voices for AmeriCorps: 100 Hours of National Service Testimony." This five-day event was designed to move the focus of the debate from the mistakes of a federal agency to the impact of AmeriCorps at the grassroots level. More than 700 Americans—from Alaska to Mississippi, from CEOs to AmeriCorps alumni, and from senator to citizen—came to the nation's capital to testify in this unprecedented 'people's hearing' for national service. Fifty-one Members of Congress participated in the event, calling on the President and their congressional colleagues to save AmeriCorps, and include $100 million in emergency funding for FY03 in the final Supplemental bill.

Sept. 4

Senate Appropriations Committee reports out an FY04 VA/HUD Appropriations bill that recommends $340 million for AmeriCorps grants and educational awards, nearly $100 million below the President's request. The Committee Report also contains prescriptive language with regard to sustainability and suggests that the private sector match requirement be significantly increased and that federal funding for some programs be dramatically decreased or eliminated entirely.

Sept. 12

Late Friday evening, prior to the Corporation's Annual Grantee Meeting on September 16–18 in Washington, DC, CNCS releases to the field by email draft application, guidelines for the upcoming program year. The guidelines offer a new vision for AmeriCorps, proposing to redesign the program by shifting programmatic focus, establishing new criteria for sustainability, and systematically reducing the Federal share of program costs. The guidelines are the focus at the grantee meeting, titled "Moving Forward Together." As Hurricane Isabel bears down on the East Coast, many program representatives depart early from the conference.

Sept. 19

Another Friday night email is sent from the Corporation informing grantees that the Corporation Board will meet on these significant changes to AmeriCorps on Monday, September 22. Opportunity to provide limited written comment was requested over the weekend—with the Corporation asking programs to participate in a straw poll and rank the issues by importance. The Save AmeriCorps Coalition opposes the breakneck, closed-door process for drafting and implementing new grant application guidelines, and scrambles to draft a memorandum to the Board objecting to the process and substance of the proposed changes. The Coalition urges the Board to maintain the 2003 guidelines until the Corporation develops a process that allows key stakeholders—including grantees and Congress—to play a meaningful role in drafting substantive guidelines.

Sept. 23

The Corporation Board unanimously votes to continue using the 2003 guidelines until further notice. Several members suggest the 2004 draft guidelines represent a change in the vision for AmeriCorps. The Board passes a resolution postponing the implementation of 2004 grant application guidelines until issues like sustainability and the limitation of the federal share of program costs can be formally discussed with all key stakeholders. The resolution instructs the Corporation to use a formal federal rule-making process, and to consider adopting permanent guidelines.

Sept. 24

Both the House and Senate pass the remaining pieces of the FY03 Supplemental package. Despite overwhelming support in the Senate, emergency funds for AmeriCorps are not included in the compromise package.

Nov. 12

The Senate brings the FY04 VA/HUD Appropriations bill to the floor. While the bill provides an increase in funding for AmeriCorps, the appropriation remains nearly $100 million below the President's budget request. Senator Rick Santorum (R-PA) introduces an amendment to increase funding for AmeriCorps grants and educational awards by $93 million to the President's level. Although the amendment is withdrawn, Chairman Kit Bond (R-MO) agrees to work with Senator Santorum in conference to fully fund the President's request for AmeriCorps.

Nov. 12

Two amendments to the bill are unanimously accepted, helping to enhance national service opportunities in America. S.AMDT.2173, co-sponsored by Senators Kit Bond (R-MO) and Barbara Mikulski (D-MD), requires notice and comment rule-making, and prohibits disclosure of selection information, by the Corporation for National and Community Service. In summary, the amendment aims to protect the integrity of the grant-making process, by preventing Corporation officials from disclosing sensitive grant information and by insisting that the public has an opportunity to comment on any rule changes which would impact National Service programs. S.AMDT.2184, sponsored by Senator Hillary Clinton (D-NY) provides VISTA volunteers the option of receiving a National Service Educational award. In November 2002, VISTA volunteers were denied a choice and were provided with cash stipends regardless of their preference. The Clinton Amendment ensures that all eligible volunteers are again provided the option of receiving an education award instead of a cash stipend, consistent with the law and current practice.

Nov. 12

The White House issued a Statement of Administration Policy (SAP) in response to the Senate's FY04 VA/HUD Appropriations bill. While the Administration supports the passage of the Senate bill, the SAP expresses concerns with a number of provisions. On AmeriCorps, the White House repeats their support for the President's full budget request, $433 million for AmeriCorps grants, national and state grants, and education awards. Regarding the prescriptive language included in the Senate bill, the SAP states that the Administration opposes "harmful reductions to program costs that could not be sustained by AmeriCorps grantees, such as the increased [private sector] match...Further, while the Corporation and its grantees are implementing new management procedures to increase accountability, the Committee reduced funding for program administration and evaluation...The Administration strongly urges the Senate to fully fund this Presidential priority to ensure that the [Corporation for National and Community Service] can fulfill its mission of engaging more Americans in service to help strengthen communities."

Nov. 18

The FY04 VA/HUD Appropriations bill is unanimously passed by the Senate. A conference committee is assigned to reconcile the differences between the Senate bill and the House funding bill, which passed on July 25th.

Nov. 25

As the end of the legislative session draws near, eleven of the thirteen appropriations bills remain unfinished. Congress agrees to bundle the bills into one large funding package, commonly referred to as the Omnibus Appropriations bill. Negotiators in both the House and Senate agree on a $328 billion year-end spending bill which includes the largest allocation for AmeriCorps in the history of the program. The Omnibus package provides $444 million to AmeriCorps for fiscal year 2004, $100 million more than was originally included in either the House or Senate Appropriations bills and $11 million more than the President requested.

Dec. 8

The House of Representatives passes the Omnibus Appropriations bill by a vote of 242-176.

Dec. 9

This same day, the Save AmeriCorps Coalition holds a meeting in Washington D.C. for all D.C.- based members. Issues are discussed such as lessons learned from the previous year, and more importantly, the Coalition's vision for the future of AmeriCorps and how it plans to attain them.

Dec. 10

The Senate adjourns for the year without completing the FY04 Omnibus Appropriations bill. Congress will reconvene on January 20, 2004, at which time the Senate is scheduled to resume consideration of the funding package. Before adjourning on the 9th, the Senate confirms David Eisner as the new Chief Executive Officer of the Corporation for National and Community Service.

Jan. 22

Similar to the meeting held on Dec. 8, the Save AmeriCorps Coalition holds a meeting in Boston to discuss issues pertaining to the future of AmeriCorps.

Jan. 23

The U.S. Senate clears the $373 billion fiscal 2004 omnibus spending package, voting 65-28 to send the measure to President Bush for his signature. The bill, which provides funding for eleven federal departments, dozens of agencies, and a broad array of programs and projects, includes $444 million for AmeriCorps. The funding—with a proposed split of $314 million for AmeriCorps programs and $130 million for the National Service Trust Fund—represents the largest appropriation for AmeriCorps since the program's inception in 1993.

Jan. 23

President Bush signs the Omnibus Appropriations bill into law. In addition to the AmeriCorps Grants and Trust funding, he also approves $93.7 million for AmeriCorps*VISTA and $24.9 million for AmeriCorps*NCCC. Altogether, the Corporation for National and Community Service's 2004 appropriation for all programs amounts to $935 million—an increase of nearly twenty percent over last year.

NOTES

INTRODUCTION

page 4

1. Stephen Goldsmith, in his new book, *The Power of Social Innovation: How Civic Entrepreneurs Ignite Community Networks for Good* (Jossey-Bass, 2010), provides a detailed discussion of Civic Entrepreneurs and how they work to create change.

1. STARTING CLOSE TO HOME

page 28

2. The Prime Directive stated that no one should interfere with the internal affairs of other civilizations.

page 31

3. Leon Panetta became Bill Clinton's Director of the Office of Management and Budget and Chief of Staff and was appointed by Barack Obama to head the CIA.

page 33

4. Steven Waldman, *The Bill, How the Adventures of Clinton's National Service Bill Reveal What is Corrupt, Comic, Cynical—and Noble—About Washington* (New York, Penguin Books, 1995), Chapter 2.

page 37

5. Jeanne Shaheen was the first woman elected governor of New Hampshire and is currently the junior senator for New Hampshire.

page 40

6. Coro trains individuals from a range of backgrounds in leadership and civic participation through a nine-month, hands-on, community-based fellowship program.

2. BE PREPARED TO GIVE UP YOUR SHIRT

page 58

7. Robert Kennedy, Day of Affirmation Speech, University of Cape Town, South Africa, June 6, 1966.

3. BOOTS ON THE GROUND

page 85

8. *Good to Great*, Jim Collins, Harper Collins, 2001.

page 106

9. Today, City Year has evolved to where our predominant focus as an organization is on school partnership programs working to address the high school dropout crisis through a "Whole School, Whole Child" approach. As part of this partnership, City Year seeks a third of the funding from local school districts. This makes for a much more sustainable and scaleable organization as the resource base then becomes one-third funding from private philanthropy, one-third from the local school district, and one-third from the federal government's Americorps program.

4. AN "ACTION TANK"

page 117

10. Shirley Sagawa has been rightly called a "godmother" of the national service movement because of her leadership in crafting both the National and Community Service Trust Act, the legislation that created Americorps, and the Kennedy Serve America Act. Her new book, *The American Way to Change, How National Service &Volunteers Are Transforming America* (Jossey Bass, 2010), provides an excellent history of the modern national service movement and a powerful argument for the impact service can have in addressing a myriad of our nation's challenges.

5. SOCIAL ENTREPRENEURS AROUND THE WORLD

page 125

11. quoted in J. Gregory Dees, "The Meaning of 'Social Entrepreneurship,'" reformatted and revised, May 30, 2001. www.fuqua.duke.edu/centers/case/documents/dees_SE.pdf

12. The Entrepreneurial Imperative, Carl J. Schramm, 2006, p. 4.

page 126

13. J. Gregory Dees, "The Meaning of 'Social Entrepreneurship,'" reformatted and revised, May 30, 2001. www.fuqua.duke.edu/centers/case/documents/dees_SE.pdf

page 127

14. www.ashoka.org

page 132

15. It was during our world tour that I realized we had made a fundamental error in not charging at least something for our service work at City Year.

page 147

16. "Growing to scale" in the context of non-profits involves replicating or spreading an innovation that has been developed in one area across a country or region so that it has maximum impact and/or is available everywhere it's needed.

6. SAVING AMERICORPS

page 164

17. *Newsweek*, September 15, 2003.

7. SERVICE NATION

page 174

18. Michael Brown coined this term. The "social entrepreneur's trap" refers to the idea that most social entrepreneurs start an organization because they have a vision for much larger societal change and see their organization as a place to put that vision into action. Yet, once their organization starts to succeed and grow, they get "trapped" in having to spend almost all of their time managing, resourcing, and growing their organization and thus have very little time to devote to the larger movement for change.

9. THE LONG CAMPAIGN FOR BIG CITIZENSHIP AND COMMON PURPOSE

page 230

19. Arthur M. Schlesinger, Jr. 1999. *The Cycles of American History*.

page 231

20. For a thorough discussion of the service bond idea see "A Call to National Service," *American Interest Magazine*, vol. 3, number 3, January-February 2008.

page 233

21. http://volunteeringinamerica.gov

page 234

22. See *Encore, Finding Work That Matters In The Second Half of Life*, Mark Freedman, Public Affairs, 2007.

23. *The American Way To Change, How National Service and Volunteers Are Transforming America*, Shirley Sagawa (Josseybass.com, 2010).

page 238

24. "In Pictures: Famous Immigrant Entrepreneurs." *Forbes*. 5/21/2007. http://www.forbes.com/2007/05/21/outsourcing-en-trepreneurs-immigrants-oped-cx_mc_0522entrepreneurs.html

25. America's New Immigrant Entrepreneurs Part 1 January 4, 2007 *Duke Science, Technology & Innovation Paper No. 23*, Vivek Wadhwa, Annalee Saxenian, Ben Rissing, Gary Gerrefi.

page 244

26. Rosabeth Moss Kanter. 1996. "Can Giants Dance in Cyberspace?" *Forbes* 158(13): 247-248.

page 247

27. *Wall Street Journal*, January 24, 2008.

28. www.mbaoath.org, also see: *The MBA Oath: Setting a Higher Standard for Business Leaders*, Max Anderson and Peter Scher (Portfolio Hardcover, 2010).

page 248

29. Adjusted for inflation.

30. Facts and Figures from the Nonprofit Almanac 2008. Urban Institute. http://www.urban.org/url.cfm?ID=411664.

31. "Nonprofit Career Information, Facts, Resources, Cites," *YourCareerChoices.com*, http://www.yourcareerchoices.com,/WordPress/?_id=37.

32. "Nonprofit Almanac: Facts and Findings: Employment in the Nonprofit Sector," *Independent Sector*, http://www.independentsector.org/PDFs/npemployment.pdf, 2007.

33. "The Nonprofit Sector in Brief: Facts and Figures from the Nonprofit Almanac 2007," *The Urban Institute*, http://www.urban.org/url.cfm?ID=311373, August 2007.

34. "Nonprofit Career Information, Facts, Resources, Cites," *YourCareerChoices.com*, http://www.yourcareerchoices.com,/WordPress/?_id=37.

page 249

35. Lester Salamon, S. Wojciech Sokolowski, Regina List. 2003. "Global Civil Society: An Overview." Johns Hopkins Comparative Non-Profit Sector Project. Accessed online: http://www.jhu.edu/ccss/publications/books/index.html

36. Full-time equivalent.

37. "How Non-Profits Get Really Big," *Stanford Social Innovation Review*, Spring 2007, William Foster and Gail Perrault

page 250

38. "Past. Present. Future. 25th Anniversary of Cause Marketing." www.coneinc.com

APPENDIX C

page 261

39. This timeline is taken from the Voices for National Service website: http://www.voicesforservice.org/action/archives/sac_archive.htm

ACKNOWLEDGMENTS

As I put the finishing touches on this book, I have an overwhelming feeling of gratitude. There is a wonderful African saying: It takes a village to raise a child. Well, I've learned it also takes a village to make a difference in the world and I've been blessed to be surrounded by an incredible village of people, who have made the journey described in this book possible, meaningful, and more rewarding every step of the way.

There are literally thousands of people who have made the dreams and stories in this book happen. If I've learned anything, it is that no one person changes the world by themselves. I have been extraordinarily blessed to be part of a wonderful community of pragmatic idealists, change makers, and big citizens. I wish that in telling the story in this book I could have named every single person along the way that has made a big difference for me, but my editor wisely convinced me that would not make for a very readable book! So first a general thank you to all of the extraordinary friends and colleagues I am blessed to have in my life.

At the center of my village is my family.

Vanessa Kirsch, my wonderful wife, has inspired me since the moment I met her. Many of the ideas presented in this book—especially those having to do with social entrepreneurship and social innovation—have been developed through an ongoing eighteen year conversation with Vanessa that keeps getting better and better. She and her colleagues at New Profit are leading a movement for social innovation that is changing the country and is amazing to see unfold. I marvel at how Vanessa juggles multiple roles so beautifully: Mother, visionary, social entrepreneur, movement leader, friend, organization leader, and extraordinarily supportive and loving Wife. We are wonderfully blessed to be the parents of Mirabelle and Reece. They make us laugh every day, remind us what is most important and give us unyielding hope for the future. Thank you so much VB not only for inspiring me to write and finish this book, but for each and every day.

As I write in the book, my Mom and Dad, two great Big Citizens, are a major reason behind why I've chosen the path of service. Their example and love have motivated me to pursue my dreams from my earliest days and to follow them in trying to make a difference. Thank you so much, Mom and Dad, for everything.

And I'm fortunate to have three wonderful siblings. My sisters, Darla and Mia, have supported me in everything I've done since our days as kids, including writing this book. Thank you. My brother Lance has been integral to my getting this book done. He spent vacation time helping me develop the outline, reviewed multiple drafts, suggested numerous improvements, and helpfully distracted me when things got stuck with conversations about the Red Sox, Patriots, and Celtics. And when I decided to run for the Senate, Lance put his own career on hold, moved to Boston, and slept on our couch for three months to help with the campaign. Lance makes everything more fun, interesting and much better. Thank you so much, Lancer. You are the best.

I am also grateful to Vanessa's parents, Jay and Tina Kirsch. They are wonderfully supportive grandparents and parents. They took Vanessa and the kids to Vermont on several occasions to give me time alone to write and they make an extraordinary difference in our lives through their love and daily acts of kindness.

Michael Brown is not my family by blood, but he is like a brother to me. Since Saturday September 8, 1979, when we were assigned to be freshman year roommates, Michael has been an inspiration, thought partner, fellow idealist, and so much more. The story of City Year and pursuing the dream of national service is first a story of a great friendship and partnership. And no one ever had a better friend. Michael continues to inspire me with his commitment to America and our democracy and how he is leading City Year to greater and greater heights. I have learned so much from Michael and been fortunate for more than thirty years now to have his love and support. As I write in the book, Michael came up with so many of the creative names and phrases we use at City Year. He not only coined the term Big Citizenship, but has influenced and improved so much of my thinking and ideas over the years. Thank you.

At the risk of mistakenly leaving someone out, I do want to add some other specific thank you's.

First, to all of you who have made and continue to make City Year possible. As I write in the book, two others joined Michael and me in co-founding City Year: Jennifer Eplett-Reilly and Neil Silverston. Thank you Jennie and Neil for being the first to believe and step forward, and for your ongoing friendship. Without you, City Year would not have happened.

And to the hundreds of others who have joined City Year as tremendously dedicated staff people, thank you all. I'd like to mention just some of those I've had the chance to work the most closely with and learn from including: Abbie Allanach, Alexandra Allen, Jon Amsterdam, Kristen Atwood, Alyson Augustin, Penny Bailer, Jim Balfanz, Evelyn Barnes, Lourdes Barroso de Padilla, Neil Batiancila, Kaitlyn Beck, Bill Bernard, Spencer Blasdale, Belle Brett, Kevin Broughton, Edith Buhs, Sandra Lopez Burke, Lisa Morrison Butler, Carolyn Casey, Frank Campagna, Toby Chalberg, Selvin Chambers, Tyler Chapman, Emily Cherniack, Lisa Chick, Jennifer Cogswell, AnnMaura Connolly, Michael Diggs, Itai Dinour, Ernest Dulin, Lauren Dutton, Elliot Epps, Saskia Epstein, Marsha Feinberg, Wyneshia Foxworth, Alison Franklin, Pam Gerber, John Giesser, Rob Gordon, Alison Graff-Wiesner,

Jenny Gray, Ken Grouf, Darrell Hammond, Sean Holleran, Heidi Johnson, Cindy Laba, Judith Kidd, Robert Lewis Jr., Janet Mauceri, Seth Marbin, Julie Marcus, Ted Marquis, Jonathan Mayo, Dan McCallister, Jim McCorkell, Jennifer Mendelsohn, Andy Munoz, Chris Murphy, Jyothi Nagraj, Allyce Najimy, Jennifer Ney, Pawn Nitichan, Steve Noltemy, Chad Olcott, Gary Orren, Jeff Paquette, Laura Pochop, Mithra Irani Ramaley, Marie Louise Ramsdale, Anton Reese, Anna Reilly, Greg Ricks, Charlie Rose, Nancy Routh, John Sarvey, Peter Scanlon, Lisa Schorr, Eric Schwarz, Rachel Solotaroff, Stephen Spaloss, David Stolow, Gordon Strause, Kim Syman, Deb Taft, Lonni Tanner, Kadi Tieney, Andre Thomas, Liz Thompson, Priscilla Tyson, Priscilla Tuan, Lisa Ulrich, Mark Vasu, James Willie, Meredith Wienik, Karyn Wilson, Karen Wong, and Stephanie Wu.

City Year has also been blessed to have exemplary Big Citizens serve on our Board of Trustees and all of our Site Boards. Thank you all so much for your dedicated service and belief. Ed Cohen, Matina Horner, Ilene Jacobs, Eli Segal, Jeff Swartz, and Steve Woodsum, have served as Chair of the Board of Trustees and provided City Year with outstanding leadership and guidance. I've learned so much from each of you and deeply appreciate your friendship and mentorship.

And City Year would not be City Year but for our dedicated corporate partners, foundation and individual supporters. Everything about City Year is more important than money, and it all costs money. Thank you so much for your willingness to support us, not only with your financial resources, but often with your personal time and energy as well. And our work would not be possible without the numerous service partners who have helped to empower our young leaders to make a difference. You all are role models for the kind of Big Citizens we hope our corps members become. Thank you all.

Finally, I'm also continually inspired and energized by the more than 13,000 young people who have dedicated a City Year to making a difference. Without your willingness to serve and put your energy and idealism to work—there would be no City Year.

I am grateful to Sarah Beaulieu, Ross Cohen, Mark Edwards, Bill McClements, Greg Propper, Elizabeth Wilner and Michelynn Woodard, and all of my dedicated colleagues at Be the Change, Inc. who have done such a great job leading Service Nation and Opportunity Nation. And to Josh and Anita Bekenstein, Jonathan and Jeanne Lavine, Paul and Phyllis Fireman and Laurie Tisch, for your founding support, encouragement and belief. You all are great friends and I'm lucky to have you in my life.

While this book is part of my story, it is wrapped up in a much larger story of the service and social entrepreneurship movements in America over the past twenty-five years. It has been such a great privilege and blessing for me to be part of these movements. I have met amazing people who live their lives by their values, so many of whom have become dear friends and role models for me. The service movement is an ongoing collective effort by so many dedicated leaders and citizens across our country that are committed to having service become a common expectation and common experience for all Americans. It is because of them that we have reached this critical moment. Among the Service Movement leaders and friends I'd like to thank are: Karen Baker, Kelita Bak, Bill Basl, Elizabeth Blake, Tom Branen, John Bridgeland, Nelda Brown, Robert Burkhardt, Iris Chen, James Cleveland, Patrick Corvington, Steve Culbertson, Maureen Curley, Lorraine Driscoll, Don Eberly, Tom Ehrlich, David Eisner, Maria Hernandez Ferrier, Marty Friedman, Al From, Cal George, Stephen Goldsmith, John Gomperts, Nicky Goren, Darrell Hammond, Bill Hoogterp, Kevin Huffman, Maggie Jones, Deb Jospin, Sister Johnice, Jim Kielsmeier, Marguerite Kondracke, Wendy Kopp,

Roger Landrum, Mark Lazzara, Joanna Lennon, Jack Lew, Eric Liu, Adam Lounsbury, Joe Madison, David Mallery, Aaron Marquez, Will Marshall, Rosie Mauk, Zach Maurin, Kristin McSwain, Marsha Meeks Kelly, Wayne Meisel, Catherine Milton, Tom Nelson, Michelle Nunn, Jason Patnosh, David Paine, Dale Penny, Gregg Petersmeyer, Sally Prouty, Barb Quaintence, Bob Giannino Racine, Josh Randle, Jonathon Reckford, Bruce Reed, Shirley Sagawa, Paul Schmitz, Sandy Scott, David Smith, Gene Sofer, Wendy Spencer, Frank Slobig, Roxanne Spillett, Dorothy Stoneman, Lester Strong, Frank Trinity, Amity Tripp, Silda Wall, Steve Waldman, Rob Waldron, James Weinberg, Marty Weinstein, Jay Winuk, Mark Yonkman, and Karen Young.

The social entrepreneurship movement is one of the most exciting things happening in America today, as so many cutting edge innovators are inventing new ways to address pressing problems. I have been blessed to be part of this movement and have learned from and befriended so many amazing people including: Chris Myers Asch, Rick Aubry, Molly Baldwin, Steve Barr, Richard Barth, Charles Best, Jeff Bradach, Geoffrey Canada, Dan Cardinelli, Gerald Chertavian, Tiffany Cooper Gueye, Louise Davis, Eric Dawson, Greg Dees, Cheryl Dorsey, Bill Drayton, Jonah Edelman, Maya Enista, Mark Freedman, Martin Fisher, Michael Goldstein, Margaret Hall, Chuck Harris, David Harris, Sarah Horowitz, , Aaron Hurst, Brett Jencks, Matt Klein, Johann Koss, Aaron Lieberman, Kirsten Lodal, Michael Lomax, Lynn Margherio, Steve Marriotti, Bill Milliken, Ted Mitchell, Rebecca Onie, Earl Phalen, Jon Rice, Linda Rottenberg, Jon Schnur, JB Schramm, Debbie Shore, Andrea Silbert, Ed Skloot, Kim Smith, Max Stier, Lester Strong, Daisha Toll, Jill Vialet, Raj Vinnakota, James Weinberg, Joe Williams, and Andrew Wolk.

When you run for office, especially as a dark horse candidate, you really find out who your friends are. Vanessa and I discovered that we have a simply unbelievable group of friends across Massachusetts and the country. They made our improbable ride of a campaign possible, worthwhile, meaningful and fun. So many people went way above and beyond the call of friendship giving tremendously of their time, energy, financial resources, love and support. I am so deeply grateful. It is impossible to thank you all by name, but I would like to acknowledge the following people.

Teresa Vilmain and Kelly Ward for their dedicated leadership of the campaign. They both worked tirelessly and inspired everyone else to give their utmost while building a great sense of community and purpose within the campaign.

Jim and Kristen Atwood, David Belluck and Michael Alter, who made numerous trips from Chicago to Boston, for their terrific job leading our fundraising effort with a dedicated volunteer finance committee, under the strong guidance of Amalia Klein and our finance team. And special thanks to Sarah Newton and Rob Dickey and all my SPS friends; Geoff Gibbs, Tony Hollenberg, Alan Jones, Judy Levenfeld, Janet Nezhad, and all my Harvard Friends; and Deirdre Roney Cadarette, Dennis Kelleher, Jonathan Wiener, and all my HLS friends.

Craig Underwood, who worked around the clock as a volunteer, oversaw a fantastic policy team of Andrew Block, Carlos Monteguardo, and Charles Baakel. Supporting this team was an outstanding group of volunteer policy advisors including: Mark Barnett, George Bennett, Linda Bilmes, Barry Bluestone, Nick D'Arbeloff, John DeVillars, Martha Farmer, Jordan Meranus, Jon Orszag, Peter Rothstein, Shirley Sagawa, Jon Schnur, Eric Schnurer, Ron Walker, Haskell Werlin, Alan Woodard and many others.

Michael Meehan and Dave Jacobson for leading our dedicated communications team and I also greatly appreciated Josh Binswanger's and Martha Eddison Sinewicz's invaluable volunteer help. Fred Yang was wonderful to work with. Thanks also to Mark

Armour. And Lisa George, Mora Segal, Phyllis Segal and Karen Wong, were indispensable. And I greatly appreciated the support of outstanding public servants including: General Wesley Clark, Senators Hart, Nunn and Wofford, Mayor Michael Bloomberg, Max and Vicki Kennedy, Sheriff Andrea Cabral, Representative Smitty Pignatelli, Deb Kozikowski, Judy Myers, Susan Wolf Ditkoff and Paul Begala.

Our Field team under the leadership of Shaun Kelleher and Joe Dennison, with great volunteer assistance from Charlie Rose, Michael Ansara, Eric Schwarz and Chris Chafe, did a great job organizing our door to door and voter outreach effort. Special thanks also to Matt Baron, Ron Bell, Patti Bellinger and Dick Balzar, Jonathan Burkhardt, Gerald and Kate Chertavian, Sarah Compton, Adam Ellsworth, David Feinberg, Tim and Corinne Ferguson, Mollie Fox, Jessica Goldstein, Charles Hackman, Monica Hinojosa, Anne Holtzworth, John Isaacs, Liam Kerr, Larry Lessig and Bettina Neufield, Doug Maguire, Stephen Maher, Sibusisiwe Malaba, Brooke and Will Muggia, David and Marion Mussafer, Kathleen Norbut, Sam Novey, Mike Rice, Mike Sager, Cristina Sinclaire, Sam Teller, Kevin Tierney, Tim Stone, Graham Veysey, Susan Wadia Ellis, Samantha Waterman, John Werner, Harmony Wu, Travis Worl, and Mike Zuckerman. And I'd like to give a special shout out to all of our Citizen Co-Chairs and to Michelle Kydd Lee and all of my wonderful Wasatch friends.

I am also deeply grateful to a number of people who made invaluable contributions to this book.

Flip Brophy my agent, who Billy Shore introduced me to more than fifteen years ago and who kept encouraging me to write a book for years until I finally did so. Flip is not only a great agent, she is a terrific friend. Thank you for your unwavering belief and support. I also want to thank Davis Guggenheim for some essential feedback on how to develop the story for this book. And to Noor Johnson and Tim Zimmerman who provided invaluable assistance, especially in the early stages of the book, helping with the outline, reviewing drafts and offering tremendous encouragement, advice and improvements every step of the way. Charlie Sennott also gave excellent guidance on the outline for the book and helpful feedback on the draft. And thanks also to Swanee Hunt, Adria Goodson and the Prime Movers for your support and encouragement.

And Emily Cherniack, who I first met as a young idealistic City Year corps member who had a unique ability to walk in everyone's moccasins, has been essential as my Chief of Staff, not only in helping me with all aspects of getting this book done, but in juggling numerous other balls with aplomb and good humor. Thank you Emily for everything.

And to everyone at PublicAffairs, who have been simply a joy to work with. No author could have a more supportive team of people. Peter Osnos encouraged and believed in me and this book from the moment I spoke to him about it. Clive Priddle has improved this book in countless ways with his deft and skillful editing. He is a wonderful human being and a great new friend. And Marco Pavia did an excellent job on the copy edit. I've also greatly appreciated the support and advice of Susan Weinberg and of Jaime Leifer. Thank you all.

I also want to acknowledge some special mentors in my life. Eli Segal and Senator Ted Kennedy were both outstanding public servants and rugged idealists. Their leadership and commitment were absolutely essential to building the modern service movement. I was so blessed to have them both in my life and miss them greatly.

Ed Cohen, Hubie Jones, and Harris Wofford have believed in me and supported my dreams and aspirations from the very moment I met each of these extraordinary human beings. They have made a tremendous difference in my life as amazing friends, mentors and role models.

And finally to my dear friend Billy Shore, who has been an inspiration and wonderful friend from the first days I met him in the summer of 1983. In the spring of 1997 after I returned from travelling the world, Billy handed me a note in the middle of a City Year board meeting. It read: "Alan, you must write a book. You have an important message to share. You should leave this board meeting right now and start writing!" I smiled, and tucked the note away. It has taken me a while, but I finally followed Billy's advice. Thank you Billy, for your ongoing encouragement and invaluable help throughout the entire process of writing a book, and for your support in so many other aspects of my life.

INDEX

Louisiana, 169
  City Year Louisiana, 170–171
Love, Brett, 30
Loyalty, 28
Luray, Jenny, 163
Lyons, Jack, 60

Maguire, Tobey, 194, 198
Maldonado, Winda, 60
Malnutrition, positive deviance method
  vs., 132–133
Mandela, Nelson, 22–23, 58, 128, 139–
  141, 141, 178
Mantini, Angelo "Uncle Red," 20
Mantini, Anita, 18
Mantini, Augusto, 18
Mantini, "Bossa," 18–19
Marcos, Ferdinand, 22
Marquez, Aaron, 181
Martin, Carmel, 189
Mass Avenue Baptist church, Cambridge,
  103
Master of Business Administration
  (MBA), 248
Maurin, Zach, 181
MBA. See Master of Business
  Administration
McCain, Cindy, 199
McCain, John, 157, 164, 180–182, 190,
  194–196
McCarrick, Ed, 178–179, 190–191
McCloskey, Pete, 121
McCurdy, Dave, 56
McDonald's, 148
MCEC. See Military Child Education
  Coalition
McGrath, Katie, 219
McGuire, Mary Ellen, 179–18–
McKelvie public school, 21, 24
"Me" generation, 29, 59
Mead, Margaret, 58
"The Meaning of 'Social
  Entrepreneurship'", 275n11, 276n13
Mehta, Aditi, 145
Mehta, Ajay, 145
Melnick, Shep, 37
Menell, Rick, 140
Menino, Tom, 157, 264

Meta-action tanking strategy, 162, 257–
  259
Michelman, Frank, 41
Mikulski, Barbara, 157, 163, 262, 263
Military Child Education Coalition
  (MCEC), 8–13
Military service
  education benefits in exchange for, 164
  families, 7–12
  MCEC, 8–13
  as rite of passage, 25, 32–33, 143, 186,
  231
  universal voluntary national service, 25–
  26, 32–33, 143, 186, 231
  veterans, 1, 196, 202, 213, 252
Minimum income/wage
  guaranteed, 228
  less than, to corps members, 82, 118
Mission, 102
  Alexandra Youth Council's, 141–142
  clarity of and commitment to, 51–52, 91
  to create and sustain social value, 125–
  126
  -driven organization, 115–116
  first City Year service mission, 59–60
  to help poorest of poor, 130
  Israeli's sense of, 143
  of MBAs of Harvard Business School,
  248
  Mother Teresa's, 136–137
  of New Profit Inc., 148–149
  Rural ENT's, 134
  Soldier On, 252
  U. S., in Afghanistan, 215
Mogilnicki, Eric, 189
Mondale, Walter, 38
Monnett, Jean, 126
Montessori, Maria, 126
The Moral Equivalent of War (James), 26
Morobe, Murphy, 140
Mossadegh, Mohammad, 22
Mother Teresa, 136–137
The Moviegoer (Percy), 29
Mr. Smith Goes to Washington (movie), 158
Mt. Pleasant Street Tot Lot, 59, 75–77
MTV-like spin-off, 148
Muir, John, 126
Mullen, Mike, 194, 196

Until Everyone Speaks Once), 112

Not-for-profit organizations, 127, 205
  Bridgespan studies, 241, 250
  delivery mechanisms developed in, 4–5
  "growing to scale," 276n16
  "The Rise of the Non-Profit Sector," 128–129
  See also specific organization

Novelli, Bill, 191

Nunn, Michelle, 185

Nunn, Sam, 56, 117, 215, 222

Nunnelly, Mark, 73

Nyack, Debashish, 137–138

Oates, Jane, 163

Obama, Barack, 4, 181, 182–183, 190, 194–196, 273n3
  behind new service legislation, 201–202
  "Invest in Innovation," 245–246
  Serve America Act signed, 204–206

Obama, Michelle, 181, 199

Of Kennedys and Kings (Wofford), 71

Omidyar Network, 160

Omni Parker House hotel, Boston, 1, 223

Omnibus Appropriations bill, 158–165, 204–206, 262–271

Operation Desert Storm, 9

Opportunity society, 7, 230

Osborne, Tom, 264

Outward Bound, 94

PACs and lobbyists, 2, 3, 208–209, 225, 229, 234, 242, 251

Page, Larry, 237

Pagliuca, Steve, 220, 224

Pahlavi, Mohammad Rez (Shah of Iran), 22

Paine, David, 183

Pakistan, 215

Panetta, Leon, 31, 35, 70, 273n3
  commission for national service bill, 32

Parker, Richard, 41

Participatory democracy, 21, 27, 32, 118, 139–140, 150

Patagonia, 86

Patel, Ashraf, 138

Paterson, David, 198

"A Patriot's Handbook," 184

PD. *See* Positive deviance method

Peace Corps, 27, 40, 246
  alums of, 71, 73, 179, 199, 207
  Biden's support for, 181
  "citizen ambassadors" *vs.*, 33
  Dodd's proposal for growing, 180, 181, 183
  government funded, 114
  Kennedy, C., committed to, 184
  poverty *vs.*, 25, 32–33, 143, 186, 231
  stipends, 119
  urban, 76, 83
  youth of America responding to Kennedy, J., 107

Peat Marwick, 85–86

Percy, Walker, 29

Peters, Charlie, 37

Petersmeyer, Gregg, 118–120

Philanthropic leaders, 157, 190

Philippines, 22

Physical Training (PT) exercises, 94, 99, 107
  trust-building, 60

Picardi, Antina, 18

Picardi, John, 17–18

Pilot funds, for City Year, 64–65

Pinochet, Augusto, 22

Points of Light initiative, 164, 181, 185

Poland, 145

Polar bears, 176

Policy team, 2

Pollack, Stanley, 60

Poorest of poor, 130

Portman, Rob, 194

Positive deviance (PD) method, 132–133

Poverty
  America's, 13, 28
  best way to fight, 131–132
  Calcutta's, 136
  globalization's impact on, 227–228
  minimum income guarantee, 228
  Peace Corps *vs*, 25, 32–33, 143, 186, 231
  service system to fight, 173, 175, 177, 202–203, 234

Powell, Alma, 185, 191

The Power of Social Innovation: How Civic Entrepreneurs Ignite Community Networks for Good (Goldsmith), 235, 273n1

ABOUT THE AUTHOR

Alan Khazei is an award-winning social entrepreneur who has dedicated his life and work to strengthening American democracy through the engagement of citizens in service and public policy. He is the founder of Be the Change, Inc., which organizes national coalitions to craft, and advocate for, bold, post-partisan solutions to major national challenges. Prior to that, he was co-founder and CEO of City Year, a youth service corps that currently serves in twenty American cities, and helped inspire the creation of AmeriCorps. He lives with his wife, Vanessa Kirsch, and their family in Brookline, MA.

PublicAffairs is a publishing house founded in 1997. It is a tribute to the standards, values, and flair of three persons who have served as mentors to countless reporters, writers, editors, and book people of all kinds, including me.

I. F. STONE, proprietor of *I. F. Stone's Weekly*, combined a commitment to the First Amendment with entrepreneurial zeal and reporting skill and became one of the great independent journalists in American history. At the age of eighty, Izzy published *The Trial of Socrates*, which was a national bestseller. He wrote the book after he taught himself ancient Greek.

BENJAMIN C. BRADLEE was for nearly thirty years the charismatic editorial leader of *The Washington Post*. It was Ben who gave the *Post* the range and courage to pursue such historic issues as Watergate. He supported his reporters with a tenacity that made them fearless and it is no accident that so many became authors of influential, best-selling books.

ROBERT L. BERNSTEIN, the chief executive of Random House for more than a quarter century, guided one of the nation's premier publishing houses. Bob was personally responsible for many books of political dissent and argument that challenged tyranny around the globe. He is also the founder and longtime chair of Human Rights Watch, one of the most respected human rights organizations in the world.

•   •   •

For fifty years, the banner of Public Affairs Press was carried by its owner Morris B. Schnapper, who published Gandhi, Nasser, Toynbee, Truman, and about 1,500 other authors. In 1983, Schnapper was described by *The Washington Post* as "a redoubtable gadfly." His legacy will endure in the books to come.

Peter Osnos, *Founder and Editor-at-Large*